WHAT IS IT ABOUT TRIBES?

THE RESEARCH-BASED COMPONENTS OF THE
DEVELOPMENTAL PROCESS OF TRIBES LEARNING COMMUNITIES®

BONNIE BENARD
WESTED

CENTERSOURCE SYSTEMS, LLC WINDSOR, CALIFORNIA

Published in the United States of America by

CenterSource Systems, LLC
7975 Cameron Drive, Suite 500, Windsor, California 95492

This book was authored under a contract to WestEd.

Library of Congress Cataloging-in-Publication Data
Benard, Bonnie
What Is It About Tribes? The Research-Based Components of the
Developmental Process of Tribes Learning Communities®
Includes bibliographical references.

1. Cooperative learning. 2. Classroom environment. 3. Academic achievement.
4. Social learning. 5. School improvement. 6. Human development.

ISBN 0-932762-20-4

Library of Congress Cataloging-in-Publication Data on file with the publisher.

Book Design: Lynn Bell, Monroe Street Studios, Santa Rosa, California

PRINTED IN THE UNITED STATES OF AMERICA

10   9   8   7   6   5   4   3   2   1

Contents

Preface
BY JEANNE GIBBS

*F*irst of all, notice that the title chosen by Bonnie Benard for this book is not the usual casual query, "What is Tribes?" The title poses a delightful deeper question, "What Is It About Tribes?" And that is what I often ask myself!

What is it about this process that makes it work well throughout a wide diversity of school communities, countries and cultures? What is it that moves the process from teacher to teacher, principal to principal, parent to parent, school to school, and district to district without deliberate marketing? Most of all, what is it about Tribes that makes learning meaningful, longer lasting and enjoyable for students and teachers?

Throughout the years, we have emphasized that Tribes is not a curriculum, not a program—it is a "process." As many of you know, to describe "process" is always a considerable challenge. Today, that challenge is even greater in the United States due to the federally imposed "No Child Left Behind" law requiring high stakes standardized testing in reading and numeracy. Fortunately, educational leaders and policy makers in many other parts of the world seem more enlightened, and focus on development and learning for the whole child, well beyond one-size-fits-all adopted reading and math curriculum.

As you know, if you are interested in this book, the process-oriented approach of Tribes encompasses a myriad of factors that assure children's whole development, authentic learning, well-being and life success. That is why the process is based on a synthesis of a wealth of research on human development, social-emotional academic learning, resiliency, a caring culture, community building, professional development, authentic learning and assessment, reflective practices and systems change. Indeed, schools and learning for children and youth can and will be transformed—if and whenever well-trained dedicated teachers and administrators commit to daily use of practices based on research principles that support the developmental and learning needs of their student population. The process of Tribes enables educators to do just that. If we dismiss more than 40 years of research on learning and children's development, students will be the losers and hopes for school reform will fail.

Instead, we chose to take the higher road. Being proud of "What Is It About Tribes," we asked respected educator Bonnie Benard, Senior Program Associate with the Health and Human Development Program of WestEd in Oakland, California, to document the research-based studies and literature that are the foundation of the process of Tribes TLC. I know of no other person who could have accomplished the task as thoughtfully or as well as Bonnie has done.

Indeed, more than all, she has given me—the developer of Tribes TLC—a very significant gift…: verification of the efficacy of the underlying studies, literature and research as synthesized into a useable process. Also, now I realize why the process of Tribes really works and continues to spread to new networks of schools, districts and countries. It truly is not a curriculum, truly not a scripted program. It's a caring democratic people process—now very timely for our 21st Century Age of Learning.

It is our hope that *What Is It About Tribes?* will be a very important resource for thousands of current and potential Tribes Learning Community schools, school boards, administrators, grant writers, teachers and parents. Certified Tribes TLC Trainers are urged to have teachers use the book for study sessions, dialogue, and inquiry groups in order to clarify or intensify their knowledge of the components of Tribes. Parent workshops may be developed on cooperative learning, resiliency and other topics of interest.

May you use, may you learn and may you enjoy. In the words of the pelican, Reflection, "Trust the Process—even more!"

Introduction

School is a Model Home, a Complete Community, and an Embryonic Democracy.

$\mathcal{T}$he above words, written by Francis Parker (1894/1937, 2002), a colleague of John Dewey's in the early part of the twentieth century, arched over the stage of the school by the same name that my husband attended from 5th grade through high school. Francis Parker School lived up to these words, fostering a sense of home and belonging, building an inclusive cross-age learning community of preschoolers through high-schoolers, and educating for citizenship. Because of this school, my husband, labeled "mildly retarded" by teachers at his former school, thrived. This "mildly retarded" child was an honors student in college, received a masters, a doctorate, taught high school and was on the faculty of a major research university. So much for labels! And, so *much* for one's learning environment.

We all know stories like these, stories that reveal the transformational power of schools that focus on meeting students' developmental needs, that build caring cultures, that structure themselves as a community of learners, and that remain responsive to the ways students learn; schools, in other words, that are grounded in the very principles that comprise the Tribes developmental learning process. So who cares about research or the "research-based components" of Tribes when we know in our hearts—and maybe even in our school's data on attendance or office referrals—that Tribes "works?" Trusting our own insider knowledge, also called indigenous or craft knowledge by anthropologists, has served us well throughout our careers in education. This trust in our inner knowing, also referred to as self-efficacy by social scientists, has even been found by researchers of educational change (such as Michael Fullan and Peter Senge) to be a prerequisite for successful leadership and successful change efforts.

However, now in the United States, since the advent of a new educational mega-policy, the No Child Left Behind (NCLB) Act of 2001, the whole landscape has drastically altered. Both the U.S. Department of Education as well as our respective state departments of education implementing NCLB require districts to essentially choose an "evidence-based program" from an officially approved list. In fact, given the narrow and highly contested criteria for inclusion on the officially sanctioned federal lists (and for some states as well), it is extremely difficult for a respected educational process that is holistically developmental, environmental, process-oriented, and learner-centered—all the core attributes of Tribes—to satisfy the mechanistic federal criteria of experimental design, meta-analyses, and randomized control group trials.

So if all that the NCLB enforcers care about are "programs," why produce this document which is focused on providing Tribes Learning Community advocates with research support for the components or what I like to call the *principles* that comprise the Tribes process? It is the hope of Jeanne Gibbs and CenterSource Systems as well as myself that you will use the research supporting the efficacy of approaches that focus on the core principles of Tribes to not only further your appreciation for the rich research legacy of Tribes but, pragmatically, to assist your application for grants and other resources. According to Jeanne, "We want the school reformers to know that the process of Tribes is a synthesis of a wide range of theories and studies on human development, caring culture, resiliency, group process, community building, cooperative learning, teacher professional development and collegiality, etc., to promote students' development and meaningful learning" (2003). In making your case to "the school reformers," it is essential that you show your understanding and commitment to the Tribes progressive, principle-based theory of change that is developmental, environmental, process-based, and student-centered.

It is also my hope, as a person that has worked for over twenty years trying to move research-based principles into practice, that the current unilateral focus on narrowly defined "evidence-based programs" will pass, just as other adversities do; that this "'Big Science,' or official science [approach]," which according to anthropologist Laura Nader "is a social vehicle for silencing or subordinating other kinds of knowledge" (cited in Hamann, 2003, p. 439) will also pass; that commonsense, supported by the best of studies on human systems, will again prevail in federal and state policy. The wise words of the late educational researcher Alan Peshkin sum up this commonsense as follows: "No research paradigm has a monopoly on quality. None can deliver promising outcomes with certainty. None have the grounds for saying 'this is it' about their designs, procedures, and anticipated outcomes.... Reality, a slippery notion at best, does not become clarified by any one person's construction or approach to inquiry" (1993, p. 28).

I trust that principle-based approaches and processes, contextualized to the local school community, will again emerge, as they always do, as the most effective strategy to support research-based practice. We have a heritage of forty years of social science research that is longitudinal, developmental, and qualitative as well as evaluative, that has documented time and again the power of the Tribes core principles to effect positive change in development and learning. This document will share some of the highlights of this research.

However, it is imperative that we also, as advocates of the process called Tribes, not lose our deep practitioner wisdom and commonsense about what we know makes a difference. We must resist the message of NCLB and its political pundits—that we and our professional/craft knowledge do not matter. Several years ago a prevention researcher wrote me a letter that I will always remember. She mentioned how commonsensical resiliency theory was. She said that she had studied with another resiliency researcher, James Garbarino, who was fond of saying that ultimately *good* research will just tell you what your Grandmother always has.

Each and everyone one of us as human beings knows through our own lives and experiences that the process that is Tribes, in the end, satisfies our young people's deep longings, their intrinsic motivation for love and belonging, for respect, for power and competence, and for meaning. No matter what the latest educational mandate or fad, it is up to us to know that our deep wisdom is the definitive "standard" for which we remain accountable to our young people and ourselves.

CHAPTER ONE

Human Development and Learning

The primary focus of the Tribes school is not computer literacy, not a reading program or preparation for year-end tests... The focus is on the students. All policy, structures, decisions, curriculum and pedagogy [in a Tribes school] depend upon the response to one question: "How and to what extent will 'this' support the learning and developmental needs of these students?"

JEANNE GIBBS, 2003

*T*he Tribes TLC learning process is fundamentally grounded in and focused on human development. Tribes shares a heritage with other developmental psychological and holistic educational approaches emerging in the late 1960s–early 1970s whose foundations were in ecological systems and humanistic psychology and whose ancestors were progressive education (John Dewey) and dynamic psychology (Lois Murphy). According to Howard Gardner, the creator and leading thinker in multiple intelligence research and practice, it has only been since this time that "developmentalists and educators have begun to listen to one another and even to try to speak the same language" (1990, p. 25).

Responsive Education
Community of Learners
A Caring Culture
Human Development and Learning

During this time, investigators of human nature came to recognize that "growth reflects a complex interaction between genetic predispositions and environmental opportunities." They saw that, "Individuals do not develop merely by existing, or growing older, or becoming larger; they must undergo certain pivotal experiences that result in periodic reorganizations of their knowledge and their understanding" (Gardner, 1990, p. 3). However, it was Urie Bronfenbrenner who clearly articulated this "development-in context" (1979, p. 12) approach, defining human development as "the product of interaction between the growing human organism and its environment" (1979, p. 16). His book, *The Ecology of Human Development,* clearly articulates *how* family, school, and community systems interact with each other and with the developing child. For over two decades now Bronfenbrenner's work has offered researchers in the behavioral sciences a fresh theoretical perspective for research in human development, spawning the most exciting and informative body of research to date on human development.

Most importantly to Tribes practitioners, his work provides the ecological framework for the developmental process of Tribes that occurs not just at the individual/student system level, but operates in parallel processes at the school, family, and community levels as well. Chapters Two and Three of this document ("A Caring Culture" and "Community of Learners") will explore the characteristics of systems, also referred to as environments and settings, that promote healthy human development and learning, the very components of the Tribes Learning Community process.

The other taproot of Tribes lies in humanistic psychology, often referred to as human potential, drawing from brilliant thinkers like Abraham Maslow, Carl Rogers, Viktor Frankl, Fritz Perls, George Brown, and others who believed that every person had the innate capacity for healthy development and learning and that psychological and educational interventions were successful only to the degree that they tapped this human potential. It is the human potential theoretical roots of the Tribes TLC learning process, what the *person* part of the "person-in-the-environment" equation brings to Tribes TLC, that will be discussed in this chapter.

Embedded in the Tribes TLC process are the following research-based tenets of human development and learning that will frame our discussion in Chapter One:

- Human development is a *resilient* process, motivated by a self-righting, intrinsic, human drive and developmental wisdom.

- Human development is a life-long, wisdom-based process, occurring over time and in over-lapping *stages*.

- Being student-centered means focusing on the *whole child's* development: cognitive, social, emotional, physical, and spiritual.

- Cognitive development and *academic learning* are facilitated by focusing on the other aspects of development: social, emotional, physical, and spiritual.

- The concept of multiple *intelligences* provides a strengths-based schema for supporting holistic human development.

Resilience

The most powerful and informative studies in human development are those that are longitudinal, that follow individuals from infancy and childhood into adulthood and later adulthood. These prospective long-term human developmental studies serve as the final judge as to what really happens to people over their life course and what really makes a difference in terms of their inner well-being and external life success. Especially instructive into the process of human development and adaptation are the studies that follow what happens to children facing adversity and challenge in their families, schools, and communities. This line of research, now called resilience research, offers the most compelling evidence that *all* people have the capacity or "human potential" for healthy development and successful learning throughout their lives, even when faced with environmental risk. Furthermore, this body of research has identified the human strengths associated with healthy development and successful learning as well as the environmental supports and opportunities that facilitate the development of these strengths. The following discussion focuses on the human developmental process of resilience and the personal strengths associated with healthy human development. Chapters Two and Three will examine the protective factors, that is, the developmental supports and opportunities that must be provided by families, schools, and communities in order to engage a person's innate resilience.

■   Resilience as universal capacity for healthy human development

A consistent, yet amazing, finding over the last two decades of resilience research has been that most children and youth, even those from highly stressed families or resource-deprived communities do *somehow* manage to make it, that is, to develop the competencies and attitudes associated with life success. In fact, research has found that for just about any population of children who are at greater risk for later problems—children who experience divorce, step-parents, foster care, loss of a sibling, attention deficit disorder, developmental delays, delinquency, running away, religious cults, and so on—more children make it than don't (Rhodes and Brown, 1991). However, in most studies, the figure seems to average at least 70% to 75% for adults who as children were placed in foster care (Festinger, 1984), were members of gangs (Vigil, 1990), were born to teen mothers (Furstenberg, 1998), were sexually abused (Higgins, 1994; Wilkes, 2002; Zigler and Hall, 1989), had substance-abusing or mentally-ill family members (Beardslee, 1988; Chess, 1989; Watt, 1984; Werner, 1986; Werner & Smith, 2001), and grew up in poverty (Claussen, 1993; Schweinhart et al., 1993; Vaillant, 2002). In the worst case scenario, of multiple and persistent risks, the percentage of children overcoming adversity and achieving good developmental outcomes is around 50% (Rutter, 1987).

According to Werner and Smith, "Resilience studies provide us with a corrective lens—an awareness of the *self-righting tendencies* that move most children toward normal adult development under all but the most persistent adverse circumstances (1992, p. 202). Furthermore, this "self-righting tendency," which we call resilience, has been shown in study after study to apply to all people, not just those experiencing challenge and risk. According to Werner, "In most cases the factors that mitigated the negative effects of childhood adversity also benefited children who lived in stable and secure homes, but they appear to have particular importance when adversity levels are high" (2004, in press). It has been found to be a normative process of human adaptation, encoded in the human species and applicable to development in both favorable and unfavorable environments. According to another resilience researcher, Ann Masten, "What began as a quest to understand the extraordinary has revealed the power of the ordinary. Resilience does not come from rare and special qualities, but from the every-day magic of ordinary, normative human resources in the minds, brains, and bodies of children, in their families and relationships, and in their communities" (2001, p. 9).

Further reinforcing resilience research's message of innate self-righting are the last decade's studies documenting the plasticity of the human brain to recover and regenerate after trauma and throughout one's life. Recent neuroscience has challenged the prevailing assumption that the first three years of a child's life determine the rest of the child's development (Bruer, 1999; Diamond & Hopson, 1998; Eriksson et al., 1998; Kagan, 1998; Ornstein & Sobel, 1999; Ornstein & Swencionis, 1990). John Bruer, a leading thinker in cognition and neuroscience refers to this as the "myth of the first three years" (1999). Jerome Kagan, another prominent developmental psychologist, calls it "the seductive idea of infant determinism" (1998). According to Daniel Goleman's discussion of "the protean brain," the "finding that the brain and nervous system generate new cells as learning or repeated experiences dictate has put the theme of plasticity at the front and center of neuroscience" (2003, p. 334; Zull, 2002).

However, the message to policymakers and practitioners from looking only at the preponderance of positive individual outcomes in resilience studies as well as findings from neuroscience is not to do *nothing* since we are "self-righting" but to deliberately create the "resources" or practices in families, schools, and communities that tap into children and adults' innate resilience, practices that will be seen in Chapters Two and Three to form the process that is Tribes.

■ Resilience strengths associated with healthy human development

Besides documenting that resilience is innate to all human beings, resilience research also has identified the personal strengths associated with healthy human development. These individual assets do not cause resilience but are the positive developmental outcomes demonstrating that this innate capacity is engaged. These fall into four categories: social competence or relationship skills, cognitive competence or problem-solving skills, emotional competence such as autonomy and self-awareness, and spiritual beliefs such as sense of purpose, future, and meaning (Benard, 1991; 2004). While researchers and writers often use differing names for these personal strengths—the study of which has become a growing movement called "positive psychology"—this core set of competencies appear to transcend ethnicity, culture, gender, geography, and time (Masten & Coatsworth, 1998; Eccles & Gootman, 2002; Snyder & Lopez, 2002; Werner, 2004). In fact, the development of these strengths can be viewed as developmental tasks (Gibbs, 2001; Masten & Coatsworth, 1998). As will be shown later in this chapter, they also map well to the academic-social-emotional learning and multiple intelligences foundations underlying the Tribes TLC process.

While the study of human strengths is a relatively recent phenomenon in psychology, research suggests that human beings are biologically prepared to develop these strengths and to use them for survival (Watson & Ecken, 2003). What seems to be driving this process of human development, resilience, and adaptation is an internal force, an amazing developmental wisdom often referred to as intrinsic motivation (Maslow, 1954). Human beings are intrinsically motivated to meet basic psychological needs, including needs for belonging and affiliation, a sense of competence and mastery, feelings of autonomy, safety, and meaning (Baumeister & Leary, 1995; Deci, 1995; Hillman, 1996; Maslow, 1954; Richardson, 2002; Ryan & Deci, 2000; Sandler, 2001). How this connects to the development of human strengths is explained by Benard in her recent summary of resiliency theory and practice as follows:

> Because of our psychological need for belonging, we seek to relate to and connect with others, and thus develop our social competence strengths. Psychologists refer to this drive as our affiliation/belongingness adaptational system (Baumeister & Leary, 1995). Our psychological need to feel competent drives us to develop our cognitive problem-solving skills (Pearce, 1977/1992). This need to feel competent, combined with the psychological need to feel autonomous, leads us to seek people and opportunities that allow us to experience a sense of our own power and accomplishment. Psychologists refer to this as our mastery motivational system (Bandura, 1997). Our safety motivational system includes the need to avoid pain and maintain physical survival—which drives us to develop not only problem solving but also social competence, autonomy, and even purpose. Our need to find meaning in our lives motivates us to seek people, places, and transformational experiences that make us feel we have a sense of purpose, future, and inter-connectedness with life (Csikszentmihalyi, 1990; Nakamura & Csikszentmihalyi, 2002).

Psychologists refer to these innate needs as "fundamental protective human adaptational systems" (Masten & Reed, 2002, p. 82). Of course, how these needs are expressed and met varies not only within a person over time but from person to person and from culture to culture (Rogoff, 2002). The critical point is that all human beings are motivated by these needs. Whether they are allowed expression in prosocial, healthy ways depends to a great extent on the people, places, experiences, and opportunities they encounter in their families, schools, and communities.

What the concept of human resilience and the research behind it offers to Tribes TLC is, first of all, powerful research validation for a foundational tenet of Tribes: that human development is a *resilient* process, intrinsically motivated by a self-righting human drive and developmental wisdom. Operationalizing this belief means that Tribes focuses on creating the environmental supports and opportunities that invite and *draw forth* these internal assets. This strengths-based approach is in stark contrast to the many programs and approaches that operate from a deficit perspective focused instead on fixing the individual through behavior modification and other control-oriented approaches.

A second contribution of resilience research to Tribes TLC is that the personal strengths identified by resilience research as those associated with healthy and successful human development are precisely the personal strengths developed in the Tribes TLC process—social competence, problem solving, autonomy, and sense of purpose and future. Furthermore, these personal strengths are critical life success skills not only to children and youth but to teachers, school staff, administrators, parents, and other members of the school community. These strengths are tapped and nurtured in all members of the Tribes Learning Community through the very processes discussed in Chapters Two through Four of this document.

Stages of Child and Youth Development

■ Human development is a life-long wisdom-based process, occurring over time and in over-lapping stages

According to Howard Gardner, just "a generation ago, there was reasonable consensus that human cognitive development occurs in the same Piaget-described way across cultures and individuals" (1990, p. 5). The commonly accepted stages of development, grounded not only in the work of Piaget but also in the work of Erik Erikson, are nicely summarized in *Tribes: A New Way of Leaning and Being Together* (Gibbs, 2001b, pp. 41–42).

As Jeanne Gibbs writes, "These stages, however, do not tell the whole story" (2001b, p. 41). Gardner informs us that, "As a result of vigorous research in many settings during the past decades, a much more complex and less readily summarized perspective emerges" (Gardner, 1990, p. 5).

Just as neuroscientists in the last decade have documented that cognitive development is a far more flexible, dynamic, and plastic process than was earlier thought, researchers of human development are also finding that the stages of human development are also much more flexible, dynamic, and plastic than earlier thinkers like Erikson and Piaget had presumed. "Imposed upon whatever broad stages of intellectual development may exist are significant differences across individuals, groups, and cultures. Periods of learning and forms of mastery turn out to be more flexible than had been thought" (Gardner, 1990, p. 5). This newer research recognizes not only that development is a wisdom-based process but also recognizes the powerful influences of a child's immediate environment, that is, the family, school, community, and peer (referred to as micro- and macro-systems by Bronfenbrenner) as well as the larger cultural and institutional environment which Bronfenbrenner calls the meso- or exo-system.

Much of the newer thinking stems not only from cognitive scientists such as Howard Gardner but from developmental researchers expanding their study to younger and younger children, especially infants, and from cultural researchers following in the tradition of Margaret Mead , Beatrice and John Whiting (1975), Lev Vygotsky (1978), and Urie Bronfenbrenner (1979). In the case of the earlier and earlier study of child development, "Research [over the last 40 years] shows that infants enter the world with an innate capacity to learn about language, numbers, and nature" (Gardner, 9-7-2003). Jerome Kagan writes that, "The universal emergence of a moral sense at the end of the second year [not at age 4 to 7 as Piaget surmised or age 9 as Kohlberg assumed] is striking to those who study children" (1998, p. 10). In terms of the cultural influence on human development, researchers began to question "the assumption that the characteristics of both children and cultures were general… [and] became suspicious of the idea that children progress through monolithic, general stages of development. They noted that people's ways of think-ing and of relating to other people are in fact not broadly applied in varying cir-cumstances" (Rogoff, 2003, p. 41).

However, old habits die hard, especially when they are institutionalized in the process of schooling as is the case especially in the United States and Europe. "The focus on age as a way to divide the life stream is... widespread in the industrialized United States and Europe. It fits with other aspects of industrial society's developing priorities and practices, specifically the goal of efficient management of schools and other institutions, modeled on the newly developed factory system, with its division of labor and assembly" (Rogoff, 2003, p. 156). In fact, as Rogoff explains, Piaget's developmental theory did not find age the critical issue in the development of think-ing, rather it was the sequence of the stages in thinking that mattered. It was the Americanization of his theory that resulted in the age-stage approach and the conse-quent prescription of norms for achieving each of his developmental milestones. Not coincidental was the emergence of intelligence testing and age-graded classrooms!

Just as resilience research warns caregivers not to label young people based on their risks, developmental researchers ask us to not neatly "pigeonhole" the limita-tions and capacities of children and young people based on their age or supposed developmental stage. The perspective offered in Tribes, based on Bronfenbrenner's developmental ecology, is to see that, "Human development is an ongoing transac-tion between each of us and the surrounding systems. It is one's conception of an ever-widening world and one's interaction with it, as well as a growing capacity to discover, sustain, or change it" (Bronfenbrenner, 1979, p. 9). This means caregivers must support the developmental wisdom that is motivating children—and adults— to expand their connection with their world, with the people, places, interests, and possibilities that give their lives more social connection, more challenging problem-solving, more autonomy and identity, and more meaning and purpose.

The above said, a commonsense approach acknowledges, as do Rogoff and other cultural developmentalists, that, "There may well continue to be certain 'floors' in what can be learned at a specific age as well as certain species 'biases' in how materi-als are learned..." (p. 5). Josette And Sambhava Luvmour's field research (theoreti-cally guided by the early pioneering work of Maria Montessori, Rudolf Steiner, and Joseph Chilton Pearce) led them to their "natural learning rhythms" approach (1993,

1998, 2003), which offers caregivers an elegantly simple approach to developmental "floors" or broadly defined general life stages based on the philosophy of inherent developmental wisdom proposed in this document. Their developmental floors also match what responsive educator Chip Wood (1994/1997) refers to as "yardsticks." These yardsticks "can help us understand what our children are going through without limiting them or burdening them with unrealistic expectations. Although the patterns are universal, each child is unique—each child a gift, each child a surprise" (Wood, 1994/1997, p. 27).

Two "central tenets of Natural Learning Rhythms" (Luvmour , 2003) acknowledge that first of all, "Children grow in life stages" and that there is an "organizing principle," a deep motivation for health, or developmental wisdom, at the core of the life stage. Secondly, this approach recognizes that, "Children are whole and worthwhile as they are," that they are not incomplete because they are not yet adults. Each of the developmental wisdoms below are present throughout childhood and adolescence but become driving needs, motivations and organizing principles at certain stages of development, which fall into four primary life stages as follows:

- **BodyBeing** (*"I'm Alive"*): the *sensory* awareness of life that characterizes children from birth to around age 8½. In this stage learning occurs primarily through the body. "From conception until the age of 8½, the child has one primary job: to develop a working knowledge of her own body and the earth, the planetary body. Securing herself on the planet provides the foundation for all her future growth.... Body-Being's wise solution is egoism" (1993, p. 17).

- **FeelingBeing** (*"I and Others"*): the *feeling* awareness of life that characterizes children from approximately age 8½ through 12½. Learning is primarily though feelings. The child is "learning to decipher his own feelings and those of others. By doing so, he comes to recognize his own inter-relatedness with all life. Honesty, justice, and fairness—the beginnings of compassion itself—are the essence of Emotional-Being's wisdom" (1993, p. 37).

- **IdealBeing** (formerly WillBeing) (*"I Alone"*): the language of *inquiry* characterizes children from around 12½ to 17½. Learning takes place primarily "through the exploration of ideals in a variety of social environments" (2003). "The primary organizing principle of this stage is autonomy, which is self-governance that involves social ability and skill in relationships…. The secondary organizing principles are identity construction, freedom and personal power…. These powerful tools are in the service of the development of well-being and a healthy self" (2003). A solid sense of self that balances freedom and responsibility is the essence of IdealBeing wisdom.

- **ReasonableBeing** (*"Who Am I?"*): the language of *dialogue* characterizes young people from about sixteen to twenty-three. This is the fourth and last developmental stage of childhood (2003). Learning takes place primarily "through an ability to step into another's perspective and then re-organize in relationship to that. During ReasonableBeing "the child gains a deep knowledge of past and future, …of time and space. … [ReasonableBeing] creates meaning… and is built upon a balanced foundation of body wisdom, emotional wisdom, and ideal wisdom" (1993, pp., 83, 86). "Ultimately, the proper developmental diet yields self-knowledge that is interconnected with all aspects of the universe" (2003).

The above organizing principles "take the qualities, capacities and talents of the age and use them toward the well-being of the child" (2003). Furthermore, "Its nature changes in each successive stage of development" (2003).

Research is leading us to an understanding that human development is a wisdom-based process. These stage-specific wisdoms, which we could also see as innate resilience, exist in every person by virtue of being a member of the human species and guide the unfolding of every life. According to the Luvmours, "The aim of parenting and education is to allow the child direct conscious experience of her stage-specific wisdom" (p. xxii). Like resilience, the Luvmours explain, "Each kind of stage-specific wisdom [body, feeling, ideal, or reasoning] has a set of optimum conditions that, when met, best serve the full development of the child's consciousness" (1993, p. 10).

Success in working with children is dependent on caregivers "providing the conditions that made it possible for the stage-specific wisdoms to blossom…. When the inherent wisdoms read the world as safe, they deliver all the information the child needs to live a balanced healthy life—to fulfill his [or her] own destiny" (1993, pp. 10, 11). Thus, all caregivers of children and young people need to understand developmental needs and stages in order to provide the nurturing conditions that will allow them expression. When the nurturing conditions are not there, i.e., if developmental needs are not honored, "the child will bring attention to these needs," usually in the form of acting-out, anti-social behaviors. "Were the need satisfied, the acting out would disappear" (2003).

This is a message which, according to Alfie Kohn's research (1996), has eluded the way schools approach discipline. Typically, schools operate from a control or behavioral management paradigm. The developmental paradigm from which Tribes operates, on the other hand, works *with* development, understanding that behavior is motivated by developmental needs and requires only fertile soil from the environment in order to manifest in healthy, pro-social ways. When schools fail to understand and operate from a developmental perspective, the needs of their young people for connection, autonomy, challenge, and meaning are not allowed expression in healthy ways. A simple question Tribes practitioners can ask of their schools is, "Which will it be: gangs or Tribes?" Will we provide the nurturing, developmentally supportive conditions that comprise Tribes (which will be described in Chapters Two through Four of this document) and promote life success or do we let our students look elsewhere, possibly finding their connection, power, identity, autonomy, and meaning in ways that compromise their chances for a thriving life?

Whole Child Development

■ Being student-centered means focusing on the whole child's development: cognitive, social, emotional, physical, and spiritual

While the above belief seems commonsensical and a non-issue, it informs us as to how non-commonsensical our educational policies have become. If schools had the above statement as their mission and lived this mission, we would not only close the achievement gap, we would probably come close to solving problems like truancy and dropping-out and school violence, including bullying and harassment. Perhaps we would even reduce in a big way adolescent substance abuse and teen pregnancy.

The truth is educational policymakers define the mission of schools along only one aspect of development: cognitive. In fact, what is valued in terms of intellectual development is even being defined more narrowly, having moved from a focus on higher-order thinking skills such as critical thinking and problem-solving, to more rote memorization and test-taking. The underlying message to students is that their developmental needs are not important and that they as people do not matter.

If we were to succeed in this educational approach, we would be facing what educator and writer Haim Ginott warned against 30 years ago in his letter to educators:

Dear Teacher:

I am a survivor of a concentration camp. My eyes saw what no man should witness:

Gas chambers built by learned engineers.

Children poisoned by educated physicians.

Infants killed by trained nurses.

Women and babies shot and burned by high school and college graduates.

So I am suspicious of education. My request is: Help your students become human. Your efforts must never produce learned monsters, skilled psychopaths, educated Eichmanns. Reading, writing, and arithmetic are important only if they serve to make our children more humane (1972).

The good news is that good teachers and administrators know in their heart, from *their* developmental wisdom, that students are whole people. They know that when students' basic physical needs are met, when they are treated respectfully as individuals that matter and their strengths, interests, and goals are placed at the center of the curriculum, schools get results: students who learn and teachers who stay.

According to multicultural educator James Banks (1992), "Schools must become learner-centered to meet the needs of today's diverse students" (p. 3). One of the common characteristics of schools that have and are successfully closing the achievement gap is that they are student-centered, that is, they focus not only on cognitive development but on the social, emotional, physical, and spiritual (the latter defined as sense of meaning and purpose) development of their young people (Jerald, 2001; Noguera, 2001; Scribner & Scribner, 2001; Wimberly, 2002). This means they see meeting young people's developmental needs for social connection, for intellectual challenge, for physical safety and bodily movement, for power, and responsibility, and for meaningful engagement as critical to students' academic and life success. They also understand that, as the recent National Research Council and Institute of Medicine study, *Engaging Schools*, found, "Students who come to school hungry, tired, chronically ill, depressed, or preoccupied by family problems cannot engage fully in the academic curriculum" (2004, p. 145). These schools do whatever is necessary in terms of meeting their students' developmental needs.

In fact, in recent years a whole movement has grown up around meeting students—and their families—unmet nonacademic needs, especially basic physical, mental, and emotional health needs. Often referred to as "full-service" schools, the more popular and apt term is "community" schools. The Coalition for Community Schools describes community schools "as a set of partnerships that together create a set of conditions linked to learning" (http://www.communityschools.org/). One of the five core principles is that the basic physical, mental, and emotional health needs of young people and their families are recognized and addressed. According to the National Research Council's study, the Coalition has 18 evaluations which have found that, "Participation in community school activities was associated with varying combinations of improved grades in school courses and/or scores in proficiency testing; improved attendance; reduced behavioral or discipline problems and/or suspensions; greater classroom cooperation, completion of homework and assignments, and adherence to school rules and positive attitude; and increased access to physical and mental health services and preventive care" (National Research Council and Institute of Medicine, 2004).

For nearly a decade, a multidisciplinary task force of the American Psychological Association has reviewed research across many fields in terms of how schools should be redesigned and reformed to support student learning. Their "learner-centered psychological principles... are consistent with more than a century of research on teaching and learning" (American Psychological Association, 1997, p. 2). The bottom-line assumption of this effort is that schools must be learner-centered. "Education practice will be most likely to improve when the educational system is redesigned with the primary focus on the learner" (2004, p. 2).

Much research exists documenting the power of a student-centered/whole child approach to schooling. In fact, Sergiovanni (2000) summarizes much research on "good" schools, concluding that, "Good schools can be generally described as being student-centered" (p. 95). The research in this area consists primarily of evaluations of whole-child school reform models such as the Comer process schools (also known as the School Development Program) and the Child Development Program schools of the Developmental Studies Center as well as case studies of individual "turn-around" schools, the most well-known of the latter being Deborah Meier's Central Park East in Harlem.

The Yale Child Study Center's School Development Program (SDP) was developed by James Comer in the late Sixties and has been working with schools ever since. Dr. Comer sees healthy child development as the keystone to academic achievement and life success (Comer, J. et al., 1999). According to Comer, "We will be able to create a successful system of education nationwide only when we gage everything we do on what is known about how children and youth develop and learn" (2001).

Comer's model sees development as occurring in six developmental pathways: physical, psychological, social, cognitive, ethical, and language. "Overemphasis on one pathway to the detriment of the others promotes uneven development…. Balanced development [on the other hand] is characterized by strong linkages among all of the developmental pathways" (Comer et al., 1996, pp. 17–18). According to Comer, "The well-functioning SDP school is a social system in which the developmental needs of students can be addressed in the school's curriculum, pedagogy, and social activities" (Comer et al., 1996, p. 19). The School Development Program is thus designed to create a school environment where children, their parents, and their teachers—feel comfortable, valued, and secure. Improvement in Comer schools thus focuses on building supportive relationships among children, parents, and school staff to promote a positive school climate.

The *Educators Guide to School Reform* published in 1999 identified twelve evaluation studies published from 1987 through 1997 finding positive student achievement outcomes from this developmental approach (American Institutes of Research, p. B-12). The Institute for Policy Research evaluation (randomized control group study) of 10 inner-city Chicago elementary schools, involving more than 10,000 students over four years (1999), headed by Thomas Cook, found that the Comer School Development Program outperformed other K–8 schools in three crucial areas: improving school climate, raising students' academic performance, and reducing negative social behaviors. A long-term evaluation of the Comer School Development Program in twelve San Diego schools that began in 1993 also supports a direct relationship between supporting students' holistic development and their academic achievement (Borton et al., 1996).

The Child Development Project (CDP) of the Developmental Studies Center in Oakland, California is also incredibly well-researched. The CDP is a school-based program, begun in 1981, which focuses on children's holistic development, especially their social, ethical, and intellectual development. According to the developers, "The project is guided by an explanatory model which assumes that students have basic needs for autonomy, competence, and belonging, and are motivated to adopt and internalize the norms and values of a community that fulfills these needs" (Solomon et al., 1993, p. 2).

Over the last 16 years, there have been three separate quasi-experimental studies of CDP in diverse settings and with diverse student populations (17 program and 17 matched comparison schools) (National Clearinghouse for Comprehensive School Reform, 1998). These studies have consistently found both pro-social *and* academic outcomes from their "caring community of learners" approach. For example, researchers have documented significant increases in students' sense of their school as a community and in their school-related attitudes, motivation, and behavior; significant increases in a variety of social and ethical outcomes; and significant decreases in students' involvement in alcohol and marijuana use (Battistich et al., 1998; Developmental Studies Center, 2003; Solomon, et al., 1993; Watson et al., 1997). Especially critical is that in a longitudinal evaluation that followed elementary CDP children into middle school, there continued to be widespread, significant effects favoring CDP students well into the middle schools years in spite of no further intervention (Battistich, 2001).

Besides these positive effects on school-related attitudes, motivation, and behavior, academic effects, while not as powerful as other outcomes, have also been documented on reading comprehension and math scores, as well as standardized state tests. CDP is on most federal government lists of "science-based" or "evidence-based" programs (such as the Center for Substance Abuse Prevention and Safe and Drug-Free Schools & Communities), including as a comprehensive school reform model by the National Clearinghouse on Comprehensive School Reform (NCCSR) at Northwest Regional Educational Laboratory (2004).

This project is closely aligned with Tribes TLC both philosophically, with its focus on developing the whole child, and strategically, as we will see in the next chapter, on creating a caring learning community. Therefore, the CDP research can be applied to Tribes as further support for a developmental approach. We can also expect that the ongoing evaluation of Tribes TLC will find very similar positive developmental and academic outcomes.

Besides the above examples of research-based whole-child school reform models, the case studies and anecdotal stories of "turnaround" schools, also document the power of schools that are student-centered and focus on developing the whole-child. Examples of these include the well-known Deborah Meier's Central Park East, which was found to have raised the college-going rate from 15% to 85% in three years (Bensman, 1994). The bottom-line in this school was respect for *each* child as a whole person (Meir, 1995). According to a parent from Central Park East, "The teachers talked to the children like they were people, not just pupils that had to sit down and follow rules and regulations, and not really express themselves because there wasn't enough time with 40 children in a class. It wasn't like that. They took time with those children. They treated them as people" (Bensman, 1994, p. 57). Robert Bullough concludes his study of 34 elementary schoolchildren and how their personal lives impact their learning with the plea for schools and classrooms structured around the needs of children (2001).

Judith Deiro's qualitative study (1996, 2004) of teachers who made healthy connections with students found that one belief shared by this very diverse group of teachers was that they all put a focus on their students holistic—social, emotional, and moral as well as cognitive—development. They believed that "student growth is the most important goal of education" (1996, p. 68), ranking it higher than "basic academic skills." A similar finding was found by McLaughlin and Talbert (1990) in their earlier study of nurturing teachers (1990). The focus on holistic development is also discussed in book after book telling the stories of schools that are succeeding with students that others have given up on (Ancess, 1995; Benard, 2003; Delpit, 1995; Haberman, 1995; Swadener & Lubeck, 1995; Watson & Ecken, 2003). It is also proposed as the model for a culturally responsive education (Corbiere, 2000; Delpit, 1996).

These case study findings support the many, many stories of turnaround classrooms and schools that we read about in the newspapers (albeit not enough) and educational publications and listservs: the school staff care about their students as whole people, not just as test-takers. In fact, when asked in focus groups how they know their teachers care about them, hundreds of students have stated to the author that, "They get to know me as a whole person, not just a student."

One last, but certainly not least, body of research that makes a compelling argument for focusing on holistic developmental outcomes in schools are three powerful evaluation studies of *community-based* child- and youth-development programs that found that young people eventually did better in school as a result of having participated in a non-school program focused on holistic developmental outcomes. These studies are the longitudinal studies of the High/Scope Educational Research Foundation's Perry Preschool Program, Public/Private Venture's evaluation of Big Brothers/Big Sisters mentoring programs, and Hattie and colleagues' meta-analysis of adventure programs such as Outward Bound.

The High/Scope Educational Research Foundation's Perry Preschool Program is one of only a handful of long-term follow-up evaluations of prevention interventions. (Most longitudinal studies have simply followed students, without introducing and observing the effects of a specific health strategy.) It began in Ypsilanti, Michigan, in 1962 as a longitudinal study, and continues today. This part of the study has followed 123 children from poor African-American families; 58 were in the experimental group and 65 in the control group. Two important selection criteria were low parental socioeconomic status and a child's IQ, which at project entry was in the range of 70–85 (Schweinhart and Wiekart, 1980, p. 17). These children clearly had the odds against them. The youngsters attended a preschool program at ages 3 and 4 for either one or two years. The Perry Preschool Program focused on holistic development—cognitive, language, social, and behavioral.

The impact of the Perry Preschool Program has been profound. A 1984 study titled *Changed Lives* (Berrueta-Clement et al.) reported how children who participated in the Perry Preschool Program showed the following outcomes at age 19 compared with a matched control group:

- Increased cognitive gains

- Improved scholastic achievement during school years

- Decreased crime/delinquency

- Decreased teen pregnancy

- Increased post-secondary enrollment

- Increased high school graduation rate

- Increased employment rate.

The follow-up study of this Perry Preschool population was published in 1993 in *Significant Benefits: The High/Scope Perry Preschool Study Through Age 27* (Schweinhart et al.). This later study found project participants have made the transition to adulthood much more successfully than have adults from similar backgrounds. Among other findings: As adults, those who attended Perry Preschool have committed far fewer crimes, have higher earnings, and possess a greater commitment to marriage. All of these outcomes essentially resulted from experiencing a whole-child, developmentally-oriented preschool program.

The Big Brothers/Big Sisters mentoring evaluation (Tierney et al., 1995; Morrow and Styles, 1995) is another pivotal study supporting developmental approaches. Not only did it establish that caring relationships could be intentionally created, but it found that a *developmentally*-oriented relationship—in contrast to an adult-controlled relationship—could have positive social, emotional, spiritual, and cognitive outcomes. This classical experimental research study using a randomized control group found positive outcomes for mentees matched with an adult in the community in terms of decreased alcohol and drug use, decreased violence (hitting someone), improved family and peer relationships, and, most importantly for schools, improved academic outcomes in terms of grades, scholastic competence, skipping class or school (Tierney et al., 1995). This was only true for the developmental mentors!

The developmental relationships were grounded in the mentor's belief that he or she was there to meet the developmental needs of the youth—to provide supports and opportunities the youth did not have. According to the researchers, "While most developmental volunteers ultimately hoped to help their youth improve in school and be more responsible, they centered their involvement and expectations on developing a reliable, trusting relationship, and expanded the scope of their efforts only as the relationship strengthened" (Morrow and Styles, 1995, p. ii).

The significant finding for all youth-serving fields, especially for prevention and education, is best summed up in the words of the P/PV researchers: "Participation in a Big Brothers/Big Sisters program reduced illegal drug and alcohol use, began to improve academic performance, behavior, and attitudes, and improved peer and family relationships. *Yet the Big Brothers/Big Sisters approach does not target those aspects of life, nor directly address them.* It simply provides a caring, adult friend" (Tierney et al., 1995, p. 1). In fact, as this study so eloquently demonstrates, an exclusive focus on risk reduction and academic outcomes may push adults into trying to "fix" and control youth. In Big Brothers/Big Sisters programs, a "prescriptive" viewpoint on the part of the mentor (we can substitute "teacher" here) was associated with the youngster not making these gains, and often with the failure of the relationship as well. This is a message that No Child Left Behind and other prevention policies have yet to heed.

John Hattie and his colleagues' (1997) meta-analysis of about a hundred adventure program evaluations found that not only do these out-of-school experiential programs promote holistic developmental outcomes in young people, that is provide them ways to grow healthier emotionally, socially, physically, and spiritually, they documented that these experiences are associated with higher achievement in school as well. They found gains on 40 personal outcomes (which map well to the resilience strengths discussed earlier in this chapter), including gains in math, reading, core subject GPA, and problem-solving. In fact, according to the researchers, "A program effect of .34 and a follow-up of an additional .17, leading to a combined pre-follow-up effect of .51, are unique in the education literature" (Hattie et al., 1997, p. 70).

What is especially fascinating is that these gains actually *increased* over time, sometimes months after participants completed programs. And they increased over time even greater in the "high-risk" youth. This contrasts sharply with most educational and prevention interventions, in which effects do not last beyond the program. This adventure program meta-analysis provides another important message for educational policymakers: Supporting holistic child/youth development approaches can actually change an educational trajectory or course for a child, especially for a child considered at risk for educational failure.[1]

Just as the research on resilience is as applicable to adults as to children and young people, research validates that successful outcomes in any population—be they youth or adult—depend on the program, intervention, or system being "client"-centered. For example, programs and schools that successfully engage parents and families are found to be family-centered; that is, they meet the social, emotional, physical, and spiritual needs of the family members—as well as provide job training, literacy development, or whatever their specific programmatic focus (Blank et al., 2003; Dryfoos & Maguire, 2002; Schorr, 1988; Schorr, 1997). Similarly, successful schools are schools that are not only student- and family-centered but are staff-centered as well (Goleman, 2000; Lambert, 1998; Murphy & Louis, 1994; Perez, et al., 1999; Sergiovanni 1996, 2000; Waters et al., 2003).

Effective school leaders know that, "If you don't feed the teachers, they'll eat the students!" This means that meeting the social, emotional, physical, and spiritual needs of the teachers is understood as central to the mission of the school. As Philip Schlechty writes, "There are four basic values toward which educational reform efforts must be oriented if they are to gain the support of teachers and administrators:…(1) the need for positive recognition and affirmation; (2) the need for variety, both intellectual and professional; (3) the need to feel that what one does makes a difference;… and (4) the need for affiliation and collegial support and interaction (1990, p. 88). Perhaps a simple way to state this point is that successful systems—no matter what their specific focus—are first and foremost, people-centered. This systems understanding is why Tribes TLC is not just for students but for family members and school staff as well. Tribes is, indeed, a people-centered process.

Before we delve into the research from the perspective of how successful programs and schools support the holistic development of young people and their caregivers, of what they actually do to enable healthy social, emotional, physical, cognitive, and spiritual outcomes, we have two remaining and overlapping components of Tribes to make the case for: Academic, Social, and Emotional Learning and Multiple Intelligences. As we'll see, both of these fields of research add even more fuel to the argument for a core focus on human development and learning.

Academic, Social, and Emotional Learning

■ Cognitive development and academic learning are facilitated by focusing on the other aspects of development: social, emotional, physical, and spiritual

The following discussion of this research-based component of Tribes TLC, while overlapping with the above discussion of whole child development, will really focus on the wonderful work of the Collaborative for Academic, Social, and Emotional Learning (CASEL) housed at the University of Illinois-Chicago and headed up by a seminal researcher of social skills, Roger Weissberg (www.CASEL.org). "CASEL provides international leadership for researchers, educators, and policy makers to advance the science and practice of school-based social and emotional learning (SEL). CASEL's mission is to establish effective social and emotional learning as an essential part of education from preschool through high school" (CASEL, 2003, title page).

Social-emotional learning is the process of developing fundamental social and emotional competencies or skills in children and creating a caring and supportive school climate. "Social-emotional skills, or 'emotional intelligence,' is the name given to the set of abilities that allows students to work with others, learn effectively, and serve essential roles in their families, communities, and places of work" (Elias, 2003, p. 3). More specifically, "Social and emotional competence refers to the capacity to recognize and manage emotions, solve problems effectively, and establish and maintain positive relationships with others" (Ragozzino et al., 2003, p. 169). While many lists of SEL skills exist, the one below is offered by Jonathon Cohen, the Director of the Center for Social and Emotional Education in New York City and the major writer in the Series on Social Emotional Learning from Teachers College Press (1999):

■ Active listening

■ Recognizing how we—and others—feel

■ Being able to name emotional states and talk about them

■ Learning how to recognize and understand our relative strengths and weaknesses

■ Adaptively managing our emotional reactions

■ Solving problems flexibly and creatively

- Being able to articulate our goals and decision-making

- Cooperating in pairs and small groups

- Empathizing

- Recognizing conflicts and learning to solve them in creative and nonviolent ways

- Being able to say "no"

- Being able to ask for help

- Communicating directly and clearly

- Recognizing and appreciating differences and diversity

- Being a leader/follower and working effectively in groups

- Helping others (p. 199).

These specific skills are categorized by CASEL into five categories: self-awareness, social awareness, self-management, relationship skills, and responsible decision-making (CASEL, 2003). These categories map fairly well to the categories of resilience strengths discussed earlier—social competence, autonomy, and problem-solving. What is missing from SEL skills is actually not a "skill" per se but the "spiritual" developmental outcome of sense of purpose/meaning/future. As with resilience strengths, the above SEL skills are precisely the skills that young people—and old!—develop in a Tribes Learning Community.

Daniel Goleman's book, *Emotional Intellligence* (1995), did much to stimulate the popular consciousness around the importance of social-emotional skills and the heart-mind connection. In fact, his collaboration with long-standing social skills researchers/advocates Roger Weissberg and Maurice Elias catalyzed the creation of CASEL in 1997. Currently, the focus of most of CASEL's work is bringing research to bear on the case that academic performance is enhanced by social and emotional competence "and the learning environments that support their development" (Ragozzino et al., 2003, p. 169). Needless to say, this body of research is precisely what supports Tribes TLC.

An abundance of research exists making the SEL-academic success connection, including the studies cited in the Whole Child section of this chapter. Perhaps the most compelling case for SEL comes from the neuroscience research on the effects of emotion, especially stress, on one's ability to learn (Caine & Caine, 1991; Diamond & Hopson, 1998; HeartMath Research Center, 1997; Pert, 1997; Sylwester, 1995). If a child is not feeling safe in school, according to Renate Caine, she "downshifts" her brain into a "fight or flight" survival (limbic) mode (Pool, 1997). In this state, she cannot engage in higher-order thinking and learning. On the other hand, when a young person feels socially-emotionally supported at school, that is, loved and respected, this enables his neocortex to engage in higher-order thinking and creativity.

What neuroscience is essentially finding is the mind-body-heart connection. The body—the origin of emotions—is in constant communication with the brain. As Antonio Damasio, head of the Department of Neurology at the University of Iowa wrote in his best-selling book, *Descarte's Error* (1994), "The brain and the body are indissociably integrated by mutually targeted biochemical and neural circuits" (p. 87). Said more simply in a wonderful book on using emotion in the classroom, Sylwester writes that, "Our brain, endocrine, and immune systems, long viewed as separate entities, are now seen as an integrated biochemical system. Our emotional system is located principally in our brain, immune, and endocrine systems, but it also affects such organs as our heart, lungs, stomach, and skin" (1995, p. 75). Researchers at the Institute of HeartMath in Santa Cruz, California even make a strong case for the heart itself having intelligence. They write, "Our research and others' indicate that the heart is far more than a simple pump. The heart is, in fact, a highly complex, self-organized sensory organ with its own functional 'little brain' that communicates with and influences the brain via the nervous system, hormonal system and other pathways. These influences profoundly affect brain function and most of the body's major organs" (HeartMath Research Center, 1997, p. 3).

According to Candace Pert, a biochemist researching the chemistry of emotions, peptide molecules, the physical representation of our emotions, are found throughout our bodies. "Emotions are at the nexus between matter and mind, going back and forth between the two and influencing both" (1997, p. 189). It is essentially our emotions that organize our learning experiences, giving them meaning and relevance. "We know emotion is very important to the educative process," writes Sylwester, "because it drives attention, which drives learning and memory" (p. 74). He asks us to, "Think of our emotions as the glue that bonds the body/brain integration—and peptide molecules and emotion mechanisms as the physical manifestation of the bonding process.

Neuroscience is continuing to document the interconnectedness of each human life. "What does this unity of mind, body, and emotion, mean for educators?" Laura Ellison asks in her book on social and emotional learning (2001). "It means we are always dealing with all three. We may be focusing on the 'content' of a subject, but the state of each child's emotions is ever present" (p. 41). Tribes builds on this interconnectedness, acknowledging that each child is a whole being and creating a process of learning that first and foremost is social and emotional.

Another answer to Ellison's above question is that it also means it is folly to create educational programs and approaches that ignore the social and emotional nature of learning. Like resilience research, neuroscience research alone offers powerful evidence for education of the whole child and SEL. In a statement written before the advent of the 21st century and No Child Left Behind, Sylwester optimistically made the following statement: "John Dewey began this century with an eloquent plea for the education of the whole child. It would be good for us to get around to it by the end of the century—and emotion research may well be the catalyst we need" (1995, p. 77). Unfortunately, the "evidence-based program" mentality that is currently driving educational policy is not satisfied with longitudinal and neuroscientific research. Fortunately, we also have strong program evaluation research support in the form of research reviews and meta-analyses that we'll now examine.

Another source of research support for SEL comes from several large research reviews and meta-analyses, a statistical process of comparing multiple studies, sometimes hundreds, and comparing them across components and outcomes. One of the most frequently cited meta-analyses of learning outcomes in all of the CASEL literature was that of Wang, Haertel, and Walberg (1997) which "analyzed the content of 179 handbook chapters and reviews and 91 research syntheses and surveyed 61 educational researchers in an effort to achieve some consensus regarding the most significant influences on learning" (Greenberg et al., 2003, p. 470). Of the top 11 of the 28 categories of influence, eight involved SEL influences: classroom management, parental support, student-teacher social interactions, social-behavioral variables, motivational-affective attributes, the peer group, school culture, and classroom climate. Wang et al. concluded that "direct intervention in the psychological determinants of learning promise the most effective avenues of reform" (p. 210).

In another meta-analysis cited by CASEL (Ragozzino et al., 2003), Wilson, Gottfredson, and Najaka (2001) examined the effectiveness of various school-based prevention activities. They found that social and emotional learning programs increased attendance and decreased the dropout rate, two factors associated with academic success. In a soon-to-be-published study by Zins et al., these researchers found that SEL programs improved student attitudes, behaviors, and academic performance (in press). In fact, according to Greenberg and his colleagues (2003), Zins et al. claimed that, "The research linking social, emotional, and academic factors are sufficiently strong to advance the new term *social, emotional, and academic learning* (SEAL)" (2003, p. 470).

A research review of positive youth development programs by the Social Development Research Group at the University of Washington (Catalano et al., 1998) also confirms the social-emotional-academic link. To qualify as a "positive youth development program" in this review, "a program had to have one or more of the following objectives: promotes bonding; fosters resilience; promotes social, emotional, cognitive, behavioral, and/or moral competence; fosters self-determination, spirituality, self-efficacy, clear and positive identity, and/or belief in the future; provides recognition for positive behavior and/or opportunities for prosocial involvement; and/or fosters prosocial norms (Chapter 2, p. 1). Among their findings was that all 25 of the programs deemed as "well-evaluated and effective" (out of an original database of 161) promoted children's competencies on social, cognitive, and behavioral dimensions.

CASEL's recently published guidebook, *Safe and Sound : An Education Leader's Guide to Evidence-Based Social and Emotional Learning (SEL) Programs* (2003) provides yet another validating research review in that it rates 80 school-based SEL programs according to 17 components, one of which is "documented behavioral impacts." Twenty of these programs (including Tribes TLC as well as several mentioned in the Whole Child section of this chapter) were foresighted enough to include academic as well as social and emotional outcomes and thus provide support for the social-emotional-academic connection.

Unfortunately, until recently "education" and "prevention" have been disciplinary silos, with educational interventions documenting academic outcomes and even school-based prevention interventions documenting the non-academic behavioral effects (drug use/abuse, teen pregnancy, violence, etc.) of SEL programs. It is becoming increasingly clear that not only is it imperative that program evaluations document cognitive, social, and emotional outcomes but also behavioral ones as well in terms of involvement in health-risk behaviors such as substance abuse, teen pregnancy, school failure, and violence. Given that funding usually is problem-oriented, we need to continue to document both behavioral (problem prevention) and academic, social, and emotional outcomes. However, we do not need to get caught up in whether academic success promotes social and emotional skills or vice versa or whether health-risk behavior avoidance promotes academic success or vice versa or any other combination. From a developmental perspective, we know that when human developmental needs (cognitive, social, emotional, spiritual, and physical) are met in their families, schools, and communities, people naturally develop their capacities for social, emotional, cognitive, physical, moral, and spiritual competence, capacities which encourage school and life success and discourage involvement in behaviors that threaten their health and success.

Especially good news for the Tribes TLC community is that Tribes TLC has been chosen by CASEL as one of their "Select SEL Programs" in the *Safe and Sound* guidebook. To earn this designation a program had to meet "CASEL's standard of excellence in the three areas that CASEL recommends as the most important starting points for program selection:" outstanding SEL instruction (in the five SEL skills), evidence of effectiveness, and outstanding professional development. Only 22 programs met these standards. Of note is that in the rating chart, Tribes is given the top score for "Strength" in promoting self-awareness, social awareness, self-management, relationship skills, and responsible decision-making as well as in professional development, classroom implementation tools, and schoolwide coordination.

As research consumers, practitioners need to know the research reviews and meta-analyses cited above give the impression that hundreds of programs and studies exist documenting the SEAL connection. However, when you look at the actual lists of programs in SAMHSA's Model Programs, Blueprints for Prevention and other "evidence-based" lists, as well as the meta-analyses and reviews cited above, you find for the most part the same ones in each review. It is probably safe to say that about 25 programs (as found by the Social Development Research Group) are high-quality with SEAL outcomes.

While this is actually good news and more than enough evidence to prove the SEAL connection, very few have the long-term follow-up data that confirms this relationship. "A little more than half of the well-evaluated programs measured outcomes only at the end of the program. ...Whether those programs will continue to show positive results is a question that remains unanswered... It is clearly most desirable—and presents the most compelling evidence—when programs can demonstrate positive long-term outcomes" (Catalano et al., 1998, Chapter 4, p. 6). This is where we need to look at resilience research as well as the studies that do have long-term outcomes, some of which are cited in the Whole Child section.

One other cautionary issue we need to consider is that other research has found that over time the positive short-term effects of most individually-targeted skills-based programs wear out. They do *not* show long-term outcomes (Kohn, 1997; Kreft & Brown, 1998; Pianta & Walsh, 1998). Part of this may be due to the deficit or control perspective (i.e., kids are broken and need to be fixed) that underlies some of these programs and consequently gets communicated to the students. What resilience research has found from studies that have lasted as long as fifty years is that it is ultimately *how* we do what we do that counts. The "how" that works emerges from a strengths-based, developmental perspective that underlies Tribes and other effective approaches. As Tribes practitioners know, skills are not successfully taught nor learned in a non-supportive environment, in the absence of a caring, positive expectation, and participatory culture.

The critical issue is that students have the opportunity to express in healthy prosocial ways their intrinsic drives for social connection and emotional expression; in schools this means by participating in relational and experiential learning experiences as we'll discuss in Chapter Two. To the extent that a SEL "program" provides this supportive environment, is the degree to which it will be successful in promoting not only social and emotional outcomes but academic outcomes as well.

Multiple Intelligences

■ The concept of multiple intelligences provides a strengths-based schema for supporting holistic human development

No discussion of human development and learning would be complete without an examination of Howard Gardner's pioneering work in multiple intelligences. His groundbreaking book, *Frames of Mind: The Theory of Multiple Intelligences,* was published in 1983, creating a growing movement among parents and teachers that shows no signs of abating.

In this book, Harvard professor of education and cognition, Gardner, challenged conventional psychological wisdom that intelligence was a unitary construct, a general ability that was measured by IQ tests. "Clearly, a comprehensive science of human development needs in some fashion to consider the full spectrum of capacities and talents exhibited by mature human beings in diverse cultures" (Gardner, 1990, p. 7). While there were precursors to Gardner's theory earlier in the twentieth century and Robert Sternberg's triarchic theory of intelligence was contemporary with Gardner's (Santrock, 2001), it is really the multiple intelligences construct that has caught the passion of educators and practitioners. Hundreds of schools are currently using MI philosophy in redesigning the way they teach children.

Gardner defines intelligence as the capacity to solve the problems one faces and to create products/services that are valued by the culture. He originally proposed that there were seven types of intelligence, each involving unique cognitive skills, each equally valid and necessary for a person to function in society, and that each shows up in unique ways in both the gifted and idiot savants. He also suggested that all these intelligences are unevenly distributed, coexist, and can change over time in a person. These intelligences consist of skills in the following areas: verbal, mathematical, spatial, bodily-kinesthetic, musical, interpersonal, and intrapersonal (the latter two also referred to as "social" and "emotional" intelligences). They match well to both the resilience strengths (especially the inter- and intra-personal) and are definitely intelligences of the "whole child"—intellectual, social, emotional, physical, and spiritual.

In recent years he added the "naturalist" intelligence and then "existential" intelligence, the latter referring to the concern with ultimate life, death, and meaning issues. [See the excellent chart on page 64 of *Tribes* (2001b]. In fact, Gardner himself writes the following elucidation:

> I am confident that if there are seven intelligences, there must be more; and I am sure… that each of these intelligences has subcomponents as well. My goal is to convince readers of the plurality of intelligence and to offer a reasonable list of what the several intelligences might be. Also, I should stress that, except in the rarest case, intelligences work in combination. All of us possess these intelligences and all of us can use them productively. Where we differ from one another is in our particular combinations of intelligences and in the ways in which we most comfortably deploy them (Lazear, 1991, p. vi).

Psychologists and educators, according to Gardner, measured only two intelligences: logical-mathematical and linguistic, thereby ignoring the many and varied ways children learn and their diverse gifts. Gardner believed that MI could be used by educators in three ways: 1) to cultivate desired capabilities and talents in students; 2) to approach a concept, subject matter, or discipline in a variety of ways; and 3) to personalize education as we take human differences seriously (Nicholson-Nelson, 1998).

What MI offered to progressive and developmentally-oriented educators, who believed in recognizing each child's individuality and potential for growth, was a way to capture as *strengths* the varied and many ways students can be successful. Gardner challenged educators to figure out how to capitalize on each child's intelligence in the classroom, suggesting that "they use one intellectual strength to bolster another and form a bridge for students to learn subject matter with less appeal for them" (Viadero, 2003, p. 1).

According to Mindy Kornhaber, a colleague of Gardner's for many years, who is researching why teachers embraced MI theory so quickly, "Besides validating what they saw in their own students, she says, the theory complemented beliefs and philosophies teachers already had, such as the idea that all children can learn. Teachers also already had practices in their repertoires that meshed with the theory— approaches like project-based and hands-on learning. Multiple intelligences gave them a way to sift through those 'teaching closets' and organize what they had" (in Viadero, 2003, p. 3). In other words, MI, like resilience and whole child development, validates what practitioners know in their heart and from their own experience works! Sternberg sums up this "practical" wisdom as follows:

> We need to recognize that people who are smart in their lives are people who figure out what it is they are good at, and what it is they are not good at, and then make the most of their strengths while compensating for or remediating for their weaknesses.... Being smart in the real world means making the most of what you have, not conforming to any preset stereotypical pattern of what others may consider smart" (cited in American Association of School Administrators, 1991, p. 22).

The disciples of MI are many, and they have provided educators with all kinds of tools and guidance for incorporating this perspective into their daily classroom and school lives. Especially notable are the writings of Bruce and Linda Campbell (1999), Thomas Armstrong (1994), David Lazear (1991), and Susan Kovalik (2001). Like all effective educational approaches—and contrary to the view espoused by policymakers, MI is not a set program; teachers take the basic concepts and adapt them to their teaching and learning. Gardner says, "I'm really much more interested in affecting the way people think about things than I am about telling them what to do" (Viadero, 2003, p. 5).

Spoken like a true developmentalist, Gardner understands that if MI theory can help shift the paradigm from one of deficits, control, one-size-fits-all, students-need-to-be-fixed, etc., to one that is developmental, strengths-based, and student-centered, that is where real shifts in practice—and consequently in students' lives—will happen. "If by 2013 [the 30th anniversary of the publication of Gardner's *Frames of Mind*] there is a wider acceptance of the notion that intelligence deserves to be pluralized, I will be pleased" (Santrock, 2001, p. 129).

MI theory is totally supported by resilience research (this will be explained in detail in Chapter Two) as well as research on whole child student-centered learning. It is also supported by neuroscience, where researchers are using newer brain-imaging technology to study the neural pathways that are activated in the brain when people undertake different kinds of activities. "Some of those studies suggest that language, musical abilities, the ability to use movement, and mathematical abilities may indeed operate through separate neural systems" (Viadero, 2003, p. 4). According to the popular neurology professor and writer, Antonio Damasio, "Everything should suggest that further investigations in experimental and clinical neuropsychology will yield more evidence supportive of multiple intelligences" (Viadero, 2003, p. 4).

While there are no rigorous experimental studies—that federal policymakers are now demanding—of MI interventions, since MI is not a canned program, besides the neuroscience findings mentioned above, there are some evaluations of schools using MI as a guiding approach.

The Campbells' book, *Multiple Intelligences and Student Achievement: Success Stories from Six Schools* (1999), is the first book to examine educational programs that have used MI for five or more years. "Although each school's program is distinct, the programs resemble one another in two significant ways: MI provides a philosophic and curricular framework in each site, and the students have made significant academic achievement gains as measured by respected standardized tests, state assessment tests, and anecdotal comments from informed educators" (Campbell & Campbell, p. vi). Interestingly, the following list of the 11 "fundamental principles of successful MI programs" maps totally well with the 20 "research-based components" of Tribes TLC:

1. Teachers believe students are intellectually competent in multifaceted ways.

2. The school's mission, culture, and curriculum promote intellectual diversity.

3. Teachers become astute observers of students and adjust their instruction accordingly.

4. Student learning is active, hands-on, and multimodal.

5. Student strengths are used to improve academic weaknesses.

6. Students have opportunities to personalize their education experiences while also acquiring basic skills.

7. Students develop autonomous learning skills through initiating and completing independent projects.

8. Students are mentored in their intelligence strengths by school or community experts.

9. Students study core disciplinary concepts in multi-age groupings or through interdisciplinary perspectives for an in-depth understanding.

10. Students apply classroom learning in real-world contexts.

11. Assessment is as varied as instruction and includes performance-based measures, traditional tests, feedback from numerous sources, and active student self-assessment (p. 93).

A visit to the Project Zero website at Harvard Graduate School of Education (www.pz.harvard.edu) reveals several different research strands involving what looks like hundreds of schools, after-school programs, businesses, and creativity and arts efforts focused on both children and adults. Of particular interest to Tribes TLC is Project SUMIT, the 3-year national investigation of schools using MI theory. The purpose of this project, according to the website, is "to identify, document, and promote effective implementations of MI. These are applications of the theory that teachers and principals associate with increases in student achievement, test scores, quality of student work, attendance, behavior, and/or parent participation." The researchers found that 49% of the 41 schools involved in this project reported that MI was associated with positive outcomes on standardized tests; 54% with improvements in student discipline; 60% with improved parent participation; and 78% with improvements in students with learning differences.

Another supportive body of research is the comprehensive school reform model based on MI theory, Different Ways of Knowing. The DWoK is a multi-year professional development program for teachers, administrators, and other stakeholders that aims to engage and strengthen the multiple intelligences of students in grades preK–8. As of 1999, according to the American Institutes of Research catalog, DWoK was in over 400 schools nationwide (p. 60). According to the Northwest Regional Educational Laboratory's online *Catalog of School Reform Models* (www.nwrel.org/scpd/catalog), DWoK has been studied by different independent research teams in three large-scale implementation trials (a fourth one is ongoing). Compared to non-DWoK schools, the findings include student-demonstrated gains in standardized test scores and assessments in all subjects; increases in student motivation; positive changes in teachers' beliefs, knowledge, and practice; and significant growth in reading for minority students, including English Language Learners (Catterall, 1995; Catterall et al., 1995; Peterson et al., 1998; Petrosko, 1997).

In recent years the prolific writing of the popular best-selling physician, Mel Levine, has popularized the concept of "all kinds of minds," an approach very similar to Multiple Intelligences. His institute by the same name (All Kinds of Minds) is dedicated to the understanding of differences in learning. He writes, "I'm a pediatrician with a mission. I'm obsessed with helping children find success"—especially those children labeled with alphabets like ADD or LD or just plain "special ed" (2002, p. 13). His best-selling books explain to parents, community members, other physicians, and teachers eight "neurodevelopmental systems" that make up a child's "learning health:" attention control, memory, language, spatial ordering, sequential ordering, motor, higher thinking, and social thinking. He explains his approach as follows:

> As we watch our kids grow and develop over their school years, we need to focus on the progress of the eight systems. At any point, the strength of functions within each system directly influences performance in and out of school. Systems change in their capacities. The functions can grow in their effectiveness. They can level off. They can deteriorate. Therefore, it is important that caring adults keep an eye on the progress ion each system, promptly detecting and dealing with any important impairments or signs of delayed development (2002, pp. 30–31).

Looking at school environments, Dr. Levine especially makes the case for developmental settings that are "safe zones in which kids feel free to assume some intellectual risks" (2002, p. 318). Instead of looking at structural practices he really targets specific, harmful academic practices such as grade retention, punishing students for their weaknesses by banishing the use of their strengths (i.e., being kicked off a sports team for poor grades), being ridiculed for a wrong answer, and not giving students responsibilities. His long list of characteristics of schools for all kinds of minds is very much in sync with the characteristics of a Tribes school. His short description conveys the idea: "A school for all kinds of minds should be a microcosm in which students come to tolerate and respect one another, a young society in which the words 'weird' and 'cool' lose much of their meaningfulness. It should be a place where social conformity and peer pressure are dampened in favor of the celebration and encouragement of healthy differences" (2002, pp. 320–321).

Schools Attuned is a professional development and national service delivery program based on Dr. Levine's work. Based on the organization's own surveys and an older evaluation by the Dodge Foundation, the data indicate that Schools Attuned has a positive impact on the school culture, on parents, economically on the Special Education system, and improves the academic and personal outcomes of students who are struggling in school (www.allkindsofminds.org/ResearchEvaluation). Currently, All Kinds of Minds has launched three large-scale evaluation efforts by nationally recognized evaluation teams (WestEd, WESTAT, and Center for Educational Assessment at the University of Massachusetts) that will explore the impact of Schools Attuned on special education and regular student outcomes, on teacher practices, and on schools, as well as a variation of the model used in combination with mentoring.

The contribution of multiple intelligences and multiple ways of knowing and learning is enormous to the strengths-based paradigm of human development and learning that forms the core of the developmental process of Tribes. Central to this core is the belief in human potential and developmental wisdom. As we have seen, a long heritage of research and theory supports this belief, as does longitudinal research into human development and resilience. This belief acknowledges that human development is a unique unfolding of our whole selves—our physical, cognitive, social, emotional, and spiritual natures and that our work as caregivers is to support—and not thwart—this life force within our children and each other. As we will see in Chapter Two, creating a culture that supports human development and learning is precisely what the developmental process of Tribes TLC is about.

■   Endnotes for Chapter One

[1] To read research summaries by Bonnie Benard of the Perry Preschool, Big Brothers/Big Sisters, and the adventure program evaluations, please go to the National Resilience Resource Center's website at http://www2.cce.umn.edu/nrrc/, click on "Resilience Research," and scroll down to Resilience Research for Prevention Programs where you will find these and three other summaries of seminal studies that will be mentioned in later chapters.

CHAPTER TWO

A Caring Culture

The primary reason that efforts toward school renewal fail is because the nature of the school's culture is dismissed as unimportant. It needs to be recognized as the primary resource to be renewed or altered for adolescents' [and children's] growth and learning.

JEANNE GIBBS, 2001A, P. 65

*A*s we've just discussed, healthy development and successful learning depend on caregivers' understanding of human development as a transactional process between a person and his/her environment. This means that individuals and the systems in which they work must have a core philosophy and mission focused not only on child development, on meeting young people's holistic developmental needs, but on staff development, on meeting the holistic developmental needs of staff as well. At a deeper level, this understanding must translate to individual caregivers and systems of caregivers believing in the innate resilience and developmental wisdom that all human beings possess and then creating practices that engage and draw forth people's innate resilience and intrinsic motivation. We have discussed how this foundational belief, or paradigm, is prerequisite to caregivers being able to provide children the developmental supports and opportunities that foster healthy development and successful learning. Seymour Sarason (1990) even asks us to accept that, "The overarching aim of schooling should be to recognize, capitalize on, and exploit the obvious fact that children come to school already possessed of the major psychological attributes crucial to productive learning. They are thinkers and doers before they come to school" (p. 162).

Our next task for this chapter is to examine the qualities of caregiving environments, or cultures, that meet children's developmental needs. As mentioned in Chapter One, the perspective of a growing number of researchers (and the perspective of Tribes) is that human development must be contexualized and seen as unfolding culturally. As Barbara Rogoff, the leading researcher in this area asserts, "[People's] development can be understood only in light of the cultural practices and circumstances of their communities" (2003, pp. 2–3). Furthermore, cultural psychologist Jerome Bruner, makes the case that learning itself, "all mental activity," is culturally situated, "that culture shapes mind, that it provides us with the toolkit by which we construct not only our worlds but our very conceptions of our selves and our powers" (1996, p. 98).

"Culture" is the word commonly used to describe the climate, ethos, or spirit of a place that is determined by the qualities of the environment. According to the leading expert on school climate, Jerome Freiberg, "School and classroom climate have been studied separately in four research traditions" (1999, p. 35), with *school* climate research growing out of organizational climate and school effects research and *classroom* climate research spawned by psychological and classroom effects research. While "climate" is sometimes differentiated from "culture," the differences are often specious (Freiberg, 1999; Hoy & Feldman, 1999). "Both climate and culture attempt to capture the feel of organizational life" (Hoy & Feldman, 1999, p. 84).

Every organization, including every school, has a culture. Organizational developers Roger Harrison and Herb Stokes write that, "*Culture* is to an organization what *personality* is to an individual. It is that distinctive constellation of beliefs, values, work styles, and relationships that distinguish one organization from another" (1992, p. 13). In other words, "A school culture influences the ways people think, feel, and act" (Peterson, 2002, p. 2). Moreover, a school culture can either be a risk factor, often referred to as a "toxic" culture, or a protective factor; it can either enhance or hinder learning—both for students and staff. Jerome Freiberg (not surprisingly a former collaborator with the reknown humanistic educator, Carl Rogers) writes eloquently to this concept (substituting "climate" for "culture"):

> School climate is the heart and soul of a school. It is about that essence of a school that leads a child, a teacher, an administrator, a staff member to love the school and to look forward to being there each school day. *School Climate* is about that quality of a school that helps each individual feel personal worth, dignity and importance, while simultaneously helping create a sense of belonging to something beyond ourselves [i.e., it is that quality of a school that meets our human needs]. The climate of a school can foster resilience or become a risk factor in the lives of people who work and learn in a place called school (1999, p. 11).

Tribes is founded on the understanding, promulgated by the leading scholars of school culture (Deal & Peterson, 2003; Freiberg, 1999; Fullan, 2001), that, "Being able to understand and shape the culture is key to a school's success in promoting staff and student learning (Peterson, 2002, p. 1). According to these leading thinkers of school culture, shaping a school culture requires taking a cultural "reading" of its beliefs, work styles, and relationships, assessing the culture for both its strengths and challenges, and finally working to transform negative aspects of the culture. "With a strong positive culture that supports professional development and student learning, schools can become places where every teacher makes a difference and every child learns" (Deal & Peterson, 2002, p. 7).

■ **Reculturing is the most essential aspect of school reform. It's how we do what we do that really counts!**

This statement is the first research-based tenet of Chapter Two, *A Caring Culture.* Just as personal belief in human capacity and resilience is the foundation of developmental practice at the individual level, at the systems level a parallel process is in place. Before we can put in place or restructure the specific practices, programs, and organization of our schools (Chapter Three), for example, we have to make sure that the culture of our schools will support the reform we are attempting. "Standards-based reform efforts attempt to align content, teaching, and assessment. But without a culture that supports and values these structural changes, these reforms can fail" (Peterson, 2002, p. 7).

Most clearly articulated by the preeminent scholar of school reform, Michael Fullan says simply that reculturing precedes restructuring: "It is only by reculturing a school beforehand or along with any restructuring effort that meaningful improvement can be made" (1994 as quoted by Gibbs, 2003, p. 65). Fullan finds that reculturing a school is about changing the personal beliefs, relationships, and access to power of the staff within the school, a process fostered by the practices we'll discuss in this chapter and next. In other words, growing a developmental culture, just as supporting the growth of a healthy and successful student, is a transactional process between people and their environments. "Systems change when enough kindred spirits coalesce in the same change direction. This is why top-down structural change does not work. You can't mandate what matters because there are no shortcuts to changes in systems' cultures" (1993, p. 143). Evaluations of the implementation of two federal efforts in school reform, the High Performing Learning Communites Project (2000) and the Comprehensive School Reform Demonstration (2000) both found that "readiness for change" involved creating a supportive school culture.

We will begin more generally with what research has found across cultures and systems—be they family, school, or community—to describe the qualities of caregiving environments that meet people's developmental needs and produce positive developmental outcomes. Then we will look specifically at what research says about qualities of school environments that are associated with students' healthy development and successful learning as well as school personnel's job satisfaction and personal well-being.

The following are research-based tenets that frame our discussion of the role and qualities of the culture or caregiving environment in Chapter Two:

- Reculturing is the most essential aspect of school reform. It's how we do what we do that really counts!

- Environment or culture is more powerful than individual biology or family influence in determining healthy development and successful learning.

- Developmental supports and opportunities apply across human systems.

- Democratic classrooms invite the active participation of *all* students, school staff, and families.

Protective Factors

- **Environment or culture is more powerful than individual biology and even family influence in determining healthy development and successful learning**

One of the major findings of the resilience research described in Chapter One is that no matter what the biological or perinatal risk a person has (for example, for alcoholism, schizophrenia), environmental protective factors—the supports and opportunities that buffer risk and allow for healthy human development to unfold—are more powerful. In fact, Werner and Smith state that except in the cases of severe central nervous system damage, environmental protective factors outweigh the effects of biological risk. They write, "The developmental outcome of virtually every biological risk condition was dependent on the quality of the rearing environment" (1992, p. 191). Their research parallels findings from biological geneticists, perhaps the most well-known being Robert Plomin, whose research for nearly twenty years has consistently found that for any biological marker, environmental influence is the determining factor in whether it is expressed (Dunn & Plomin, 1990). In other words, "Social contexts can alter genetic expression" (Commission on Children At Risk, 2003, p. 19). Citing the research of another biological geneticist, David Moore (2002), this Commission explains that, "A social environment can change the relationship between a specific gene and the behavior associated with that gene. Changes in social environment can thus change the transcription of our genetic material at the most basic cellular level" (2003, p. 19).

Similarly, Judith Rich Harris' book, *The Nurture Assumption: Why Children Turn Out the Way They Do* (1998), rocked the world of research when it was published for she provided hundreds of studies—and a logical thesis—that found that environmental influences outside the family were the determining influences in individual outcomes. The issue here is not to argue "nature versus nurture," which indeed is no longer a valid dichotomy (Moore, 2002) but rather to make the case that no matter what a child's biological risk or even family environment, other caregiving or affiliative groups and settings, such as peer groups, community-based organizations, and classrooms and schools, can over-ride the biological and family risk.

Cognitive psychologist Frank Smith sums up this commonsensical finding simply as, "You learn from the company you keep" (1998, p. 9). Expressed in more research-ese, Werner and Smith write that, "Our findings and those by other American and European investigators with a life-span perspective suggest that these buffers [i.e., protective factors] make a more profound impact on the life course of children who grow up under adverse conditions than do specific risk factors or stressful life events. They [also] appear to transcend ethnic, social class, geographical, and historical boundaries. Most of all, they offer us a more optimistic outlook than the perspective that can be gleaned from the literature on the negative consequences of perinatal trauma, caregiving deficits, and chronic poverty." (1992, p. 202).

The National Research Council and Institute of Medicine's research summary of "engaging schools" that foster students' innate motivation to learn states, "There is considerable evidence for the power of the educational context, even as late as high school.... School contexts make a difference and can diminish, if not eliminate, negative effects of poverty on student engagement" (2004, p. 33). The theoretical model proposed from their extensive research review is a direct match to that under-girding resilience research and Tribes: The educational context engages students' human needs for competence and control (i.e., problem-solving and autonomy), values and goals (i.e., respect and sense of purpose/future) and social connectedness (i.e., social competence) which in turn promotes their academic engagement. A major component of educational context, according to the committee of researchers, is the culture or climate of the school, which they define as the "values, norms, beliefs, and sentiments associated with routine practices and social interactions in schools" (p. 97).

■ Developmental supports and opportunities apply across human systems

So, the burning question, now is, "Just exactly what are these protective factors that are so powerful in our lives?" Long-term studies of individual lives and human resilience in the face of stress, adversity, and challenge provide a research-based answer to this question. *Caring relationships, positive expectation messages and beliefs,* and *opportunities for participation and contribution* are the three critical developmental supports and opportunities consistently found in this body of research to promote the holistic developmental outcomes we know are associated with personal well-being and life success: social competence, problem solving skills, autonomy, and sense of future and purpose (Benard, 1991, 2004). The logical reason for their prevalence is that it is precisely through these developmental supports and opportunities that people, young and old, meet their developmental needs for love and belonging, respect, challenge, mastery, power, and meaning.

These three environmental "protective factors" were first conceptualized in Benard's 1991 paper, *Fostering Resiliency in Kids: Protective Factors in the Family, School, and Community*. Not only have they held up under scrutiny of research, they have formed the guiding principles of many prevention and education efforts over the last 10 years. They map well to the Search Institute's (Benson, 1997) categories of "external assets" and basically describe what the youth development field refers to as "supports and opportunities." They are also commonly referred to as "social capital," the interpersonal resources necessary for healthy development and life success (Putnam, 2000). Most importantly to Tribes practitioners, "The culture in Tribes school communities is based on these three well-proven principles that foster human resilience" (Gibbs, 2003, p. 22).

Keep in mind that while we discuss each of these as if it were a separate entity, they each are one aspect or component of a dynamic protective *process* in which they work synergistically together to weave a culture of caring. Caring relationships without high expectations or opportunities for meaningful participation fosters dependency and co-dependency—not positive youth development. High expectations that are not child-centered or that are not offered in the context of caring relationships and support to help youth meet them is a cruel "shape-up or ship-out" approach associated with negative outcomes. And one more example: caring relationships with high expectation messages but no opportunities for a child's active participation and contribution creates a frustrating situation that blocks the natural process of youth development (Benard, 2004).

Caring relationships convey loving support—the message of being there for a youth, of trust, of unconditional love. Resilient survivors talk about relationships characterized by "quiet availability," "fundamental positive regard," and "simple sustained kindness"—a touch on the shoulder, a smile, a greeting (Higgins, 1994, pp. 324-25). In Higgins' follow-back study of adults who had been sexually abused as children, they "strongly recommended that those of you who touch the life of a child constructively, even briefly, should *never* underestimate your possible corrective impact on that child" (p. 325). Even respect, having a person "acknowledge us, see us for who we are—as their equal in value and importance" figures high in turnaround relationships and places (Meier, 1995, p. 120).

These caregivers also convey a sense of compassion—nonjudgmental love that looks beneath a youths' negative behavior and sees the pain and suffering. They do not take the youth's behavior personally. They understand that no matter how negative a young person's behavior, she is doing the best she can given how she *sees* the world.

Finally, being interested in, actively listening to, and getting to know the gifts of their young people conveys the message, "You are important in this world; you matter." Alice Miller's account of resilient survivors of childhood sexual abuse and trauma validates the healing power of youth being able to tell their story to someone who believes them: "It turns out in every case [of successful adaptation] that a sympathetic and helpful witness confirmed the child's perceptions, thus making it possible for him to recognize that he had been wronged" (1990, pp. 50–51).

According to a research compilation from the National Research Council and the Institute of Medicine, "Supportive relationships are critical 'mediums' of development. They provide an environment of reinforcement, good modeling, and constructive feedback for physical, intellectual, psychological, and social growth." Furthermore, "The attentive, caring, and wise voice of a supportive adult gets internalized and becomes part of the youth's own voice" (Eccles & Gootman, 2002, p. 96).

A common finding in resilience research is the power of a teacher—often unbeknownst to him or her—to tip the scale from risk to resilience. Werner and Smith (1989) found that, "Among the most frequently encountered positive role model in the lives of the children... outside of the family circle, was a favorite teacher. For the resilient youngster a special teacher was not just an instructor for academic skills, but also a confidante and positive model for personal identification" (p. 162). The approaches, or "strategies," used by caring teachers and described above provide a set of best practices or benchmarks to guide our work in classrooms and schools.

At the core of caring relationships are *clear and positive youth-centered expectations*. Clear expectations refer to the guidance and regulatory function that caregivers must provide developing young people. This means creating a sense of structure and safety through rules and disciplinary approaches that are not only perceived as fair by young people but that include youth in their creation.

Positive youth-centered messages are those that communicate the adult's deep belief in the young person's innate resilience and self-righting capacities and challenge the youth to become all she can be. "She believed in me when I didn't believe in myself" is a common refrain echoed by adults reflecting on transformative messages in their lives in the author's workshops. An often-ignored subtlety of this now cliched term is that adult's high expectations must be child-/youth-centered. They must be based on the strengths, interests, hopes, and dreams of the youth—not what the adult wants the youth to do or be.

Moreover, effective caregivers of both children and youth are youth-centered: they use the young person's own strengths, interests, intelligences, goals, and dreams as the beginning point for learning and helping. Thus, they tap young people's intrinsic motivation, their existing, innate drive for learning and personal growth. John Seita, who grew up in multiple foster homes, tells the story of his turnaround social worker: "Mr. Lambert, who was a recent graduate of college when he first met me, had no training in bonding with relationship-resistant youth. Few of us do. But he reached me through the back door. He doggedly attempted to find a *special interest* of mine, namely my dreams of being a sports hero. Although I did not trust other adults, he connected with me through a special interest" (Seita, et al, 1996, p. 88).

"Turnaround" people assist youth, especially those who have been labeled or oppressed, in understanding their innate resilience, their personal power to reframe their life narratives from damaged victim to resilient survivor (Wolin & Wolin, 1993). They help youth see the power they have to think differently about and construct alternative stories of their lives. They help them (1) to not take *personally* the adversity in their lives ("You aren't the cause of, nor can you control, your father's drinking /your friend's racist remarks"); (2) to not see adversity as *permanent* ("This too shall pass"); and (3) to not see setbacks as *pervasive* ("You can rise above this;" "This is only one part of your life experience") (adapted from Seligman, 1992/1998).

Creating the opportunities for participation and contribution is a natural out-growth of relationships based on caring and high expectations. This category consists of providing youth the chance to participate in engaging, challenging, and interest-ing activities or "flow" experiences (Csikszentmihalyi, 1990). Werner and Smith found that while their resilient survivors weren't unusually talented, "They took great pleasure in interests and hobbies that brought them solace when things fell apart in their home lives (1992, p. 205).

This category also refers to providing opportunities to youth to participate in activities that allow them to belong, "to be a part of a cooperative enterprise, such as being a cheerleader for the home team or raising an animal for the 4-H Club [as well as] active involvement in a church or religious community"—activities that ful-filled their need to belong, that connected them to a group that became a surrogate family (1992). As we will see later in this chapter, cooperative learning research con-sistently documents the power of this "cooperative enterprise" to protect healthy development and successful learning.

Having the opportunities for reflection and dialog in a small group around issues meaningful to youth—as adolescents especially those related to sexuality, drug use, and family communication—is continually identified by youth as what they want to do in their families, schools, and communities (Brown & D'Emidio-Caston, 1995). When youth are given the opportunity—especially in a small group context—to give voice to their realities—to discuss their experiences, beliefs, attitudes, and feelings—and are encouraged to critically question societal messages—those from the media and their own conditioned thinking around these issues—we are empowering them to be critical thinkers and decision-makers around the important issues in their lives. Through this critical pedagogical practice of reflection and dialog we are also preparing them to be engaged citizens, without whom our nation will not remain a democracy.

Opportunities for participation also include having chances to problem-solve and make decisions, to have some freedom and self-determination, i.e., control over one's self direction. In this way, youth develop autonomy (Deci, 1995; Ryan & Deci, 2000). Real decision-making and leadership responsibilities are often the character-istics distinguishing successful from unsuccessful youth programs and settings (Gambone and Arbreton, 1997; Werner and Smith, 1992; McLaughlin et al, 1994; Tierney et al., 1995).

Opportunities for contribution, to do things that matter, that are meaningful to one's self, family, school, and community are also key components of this category of protective factors. When youth have the opportunities to "give back" their gifts to their families, schools, and communities, they see themselves as no longer just recipients of what we adults have to offer—even if it is the good stuff of caring and positive beliefs—but as active contributors to the settings in which they live. Giving back is a powerful "hook" for all youth, especially for those not used to thinking of themselves as successful. It helps them reframe their self-perceptions from being a problem and *receiver* of services to being a resource and *provider* of services. This is evident in the positive holistic outcomes for students who participate in high-quality service-learning in their schools and communities (Melchior, 1996; 1998).

It is through having the opportunities to be heard, to voice one's opinion, to make choices, to have responsibilities, to engage in active problem-solving, to express one's imagination, to work with and help others, and to give one's gift back to the community that youth develop the attitudes and competencies characteristic of healthy development and successful learning: social competence, problem-solving, and a sense of self and future. This is the final component of the protective human development process that connects youth to their families, schools, and communities. Acording to Barbara Rogoff, human development and learning *is* a process of "guided participation in cultural activities.... It is a process of taking on new roles and responsibilities" (2003, p. 283-284). It is a process that defines successful schools and classrooms; it is the process of Tribes TLC.

All of the successful approaches and programs discussed in Chapter One—from the Comer School Development Program, the Developmental Studies Center's Child Development Project, the High/Scope Perry Preschool Program to the Big Brothers/Big Sisters mentoring program, adventure programs, service-learning (discussed in more detail in Chapter Four), multiple intelligences-focused schools, and other successful school reform models such as Robert Slavin's *Success For All* and Hank Levin's *Accelerated Schools* (American Institute for Research, 1999), as well as case studies of successful schools and approaches (Ancess, 2000; Ayers & Ford, 1996; Day, 1994; Deiro, 1996; Delpit, 1995; Haberman, 1995; Meiers, 1995; Swadener & Lubeck, 1995; Watson & Ecken, 2003)—all are focused on promoting caring relationships, conveying positive and high student-centered expectations, and providing ongoing opportunities for participation and contribution. These successful approaches all either implicitly or explicitly recognize that engaging the intrinsic motivation of students, parents, and staff is necessary to creating a successful school. Thus, they operationalize these protective factors into the philosophy, mission, and practices of their respective programs.

Furthermore, CASEL's model for promoting academic, social, and emotional learning now clearly begins with creating a "learning environment that is safe, caring, well-managed, and participatory" (Collaborative for Academic, Social, and Emotional Learning, 203, p. 7). Maurice Elias' review of the research (2003) for the International Academy of Education names ten essentials for promoting social-emotional learning, with the first one being "Learning requires caring" (p. 8). He writes, "Lasting social-emotional learning, sound character and academic success are founded on classrooms and schools that are not threatening to students and challenge them to learn more, but do so in ways that do not discourage them. Also, these schools are places where students feel cared about, welcomed, valued and seen as more than just learners—they are seen as resources" (p. 8).

While the research support for these protective factors is virtually endless, a study that has brought much national public attention to the issue of "school connectedness," that sense of belonging and affiliation to school, is the National Longitudinal Study of Adolescent Health (Resnick et al., 1997). This federally-mandated research effort, involving several universities and research institutions, is really the first national survey to examine protective factors as well as risk factors in the individual, family, and school for adolescent health. Across all health-risk behaviors—emotional health, violence, substance use, and sexuality—these researchers found that family and/or school connectedness was protective against every health risk behavior (Resnick et al., 1997). According to these researchers, "It is clear that when demographic characteristics are controlled, social contexts count. Specifically, we find consistent evidence that perceived caring and connectedness to others is important in understanding the health of young people today" (Resnick et al., 1997, p. 830). In terms of the school environment, the researchers also stated that, "While much emphasis is placed on school policies governing adolescent behaviors, such policies appear… to have limited associations with the student behaviors under study." Rather, it is school connectedness, "influenced in good measure by perceived caring from teachers and high expectations for student performance," that makes the critical difference (Resnick et al., 1997, p. 831).

One last study receiving much research attention is that of the Chicago school reform effort over this last decade. Anthony Bryk and Barbara Schneider (2002) write that the missing ingredient of school reform is "relational trust" grounded in respect, competence, integrity, and personal regard for others. Without trusting relationships among teachers, principals, parents, and students, school reform efforts are doomed to fail. These researchers back up their statements with data from three years of field work in 12 Chicago elementary schools as well as teacher surveys and student performance data that correlate a school's trust levels with its students' academic improvement. Among their findings: Schools performing in the top quartile on standardized tests were more often schools with high levels of trust; Schools reporting strong trust links in 1994 were three times more likely to report eventual improvements in reading and math scores than those where trust levels were low. In a recent interview, Schneider concluded that, "This is about *not* forgetting the people" (Gewertz, 2002, p. 4). This is why Tribes TLC is founded on the belief that, "At the heart of the Tribes Learning Community process are the relationships among us."

Looking at research from the youth development field, these protective factors map well to the "Features of Developmental Settings" compiled by the National Research Council/Institute of Medicine in *Community Programs to Promote Youth Development* (Eccles & Gootman, 2002):

- Physical and psychological safety

- Support for efficacy and mattering

- Appropriate structure

- Opportunities for skill building

- Supportive relationships

- Integration of family, school, and community efforts

- Opportunities to belong

- Positive social norms

- Basic care and services.

Similarly, schools that are closing the achievement gap for those students most often left behind in education improvement efforts—Latino, African American, Native American, and low-income children—can be considered resilient schools for they are overcoming the odds and producing students that are succeeding both academically and socially-emotionally. The strengths in these "high-performing/high-poverty," "priority," or "high flying"schools match very well to the three protective factors (Baldwin, 2001; James et al, 2001; Jerald, 2001; Lewis & Paik, 2001; MacBeath et al., 1995; Rutter et al., 1979; Scribner & Scribner, 2001; Williams, 2003; Wilson & Corbett, 2001). Moreover, Michael Rutter and his colleagues' (1979) classic study of these schools found not only that they were characterized by an "ethos" or climate of caring relationships, high student-centered expectations, and many opportunities for participation and contribution, but that the longer students were in these nurturing schools, the more their problem behaviors declined (delinquency and dropping out).

The practices that constitute a caring culture are essentially those that comprise the Tribes TLC process and are discussed throughout this document, especially in the remaining part of this chapter and in Chapters Three and Four. Another in-depth summary of these practices can be found in Benard (2004, pp. 65-88).

Moreover, creating a culture based on the three protective factors is not just for students' well-being but for the well-being of school personnel and parents as well (Comer et al., 1996; Henderson & Mapp, 2002; Louis & Ingram, 2003). While the protective factors were described in terms of young people, they apply to all people, young and old (Benard, 2004). Creating a caring, respectful, collaborative culture does not happen at only the teacher-to-student level but at the teacher-to-parent, principal-to-teachers and student-to-student, teacher-to-teacher, and parent-to-parent levels as well. To really meet people's needs for connection and belonging as well as autonomy and power requires not just one-to-one relationships but membership in a group where one has a voice in decision making, such as in a Tribe (Bryk & Schneider, 2002; Eccles & Gootman, 2002; Harris, 1998; Werner & Smith, 1992).

Individuals begin to refer to these places as "like a family" or "my community." Educational policymakers and school reformers ignore this human element at their peril according to long-time advocates for humanistic and progressive school reform such as William Glasser (1990) and Alfie Kohn (1996, 1999). As the wise scholar of both educational, organizational, and personal change, Seymour Sarason, wrote over a decade ago in *The Predictable Failure of Educational Reform* (1990), elaborating many of the arguments he made over thirty years ago in *The Culture of the School and the Problem of Change* (1971): "When one has no stake in the way things are, when one's needs or opinions are provided no forum, when one sees oneself as the object of unilateral actions, it takes no particular wisdom to suggest that one would rather be elsewhere" (p. 83). Needless to say, this disconnection and alienation applies to parents and school staff as well as students.

The inter-connected nature of creating a caring culture is the major reason that the *community school* movement is gaining increasing momentum over the last several years. Research is finding that the schools that are successfully serving young people (success being measured by holistic outcomes, including academic achievement), especially those in under-resourced communities, are also the schools that are serving their families and other community members as well (Coalition for Community Schools, May 2003; Henderson & Mapp, 2002). In fact, "Evaluations of 20 community school initiatives across the United States found notable improvements in four areas: student learning,… family engagement,… school effectiveness [stronger parent-teacher relationships, increased teacher satisfaction, a more positive school environment and greater community support], and community vitality" (Coalition for Community Schools, May 2003, p. 1). An enormous volume of research supporting the student-school-family-community connection is synthesized by Anne Henderson and Karen Mapp of the National Center for Family and Community connections with Schools in *A New Wave of Evidence: The Impact of School, Family, and Community Connections on Student Achievement* (2002).

In sum, even when we look beyond the long-term studies of human development that comprise much of resilience research to examine the research on the characteristics of healthy families, schools, neighborhood-based organizations, and workplace organizations that are producing good outcomes in people and even to what we've learned from brain science and program evaluation research, we see the power of these three principles to promote positive outcomes [for an extensive discussion of protective factors, see Benard, 2004]. It is clear that successful development in any human system is dependent on the culture of that system—on the quality of relationships, the beliefs, and the opportunities for participation in that system. Protective factors, like human developmental needs, can be seen as "cultural regularities," patterns of human development that make sense of differences and similarities in communities' practices and traditions" (Rogoff, 2003, p. 3). Furthermore, as we will see in our examination of the characteristics and practices of ideal learning cultures in schools, of democratic classrooms, and of the many processes and structures that comprise a Tribes Learning Community, what becomes obvious is that each of these research-based components of Tribes is grounded in these three protective factors.

Ideal Learning Culture

The concept of the "ideal learning culture" was articulated by Jerome Bruner in his 1996 book, *The Culture of Education*. This book brings together nine essays on cultural psychology and its implications for education. "Cultural psychology deals with how individuals make sense of the world, how they engage with established systems of shared meaning, with the beliefs, values, and symbols of the culture at large" (London, 2004, p. 1). It focuses on how individuals construct their realities based on common cultural narratives and symbols and how reality is cultivated through social interaction. In other words, learning, like development cannot be de-contextualized and is determined to a great extent by the beliefs and expectations, often the implicit assumptions, that teachers have about children. He writes that, "Beliefs and assumptions about teaching whether in a school or in any other context, are a direct reflection of the beliefs and assumptions the teacher holds about the learner" (p. 47). For example, "Learning in its full complexity involves the creation and negotiation of meaning in a larger culture, and the teacher is the vicar of the culture at large. You cannot teacher-proof a curriculum any more than you can parent-proof a family" (p. 84).

Bruner is basically making the case for a paradigm shift in our human institutions, especially in schools, which means changing the culture, which, in turn, translates to changing the beliefs of school staff about children's capacities to learn. Bruner (1996) asserts that, "To a degree almost entirely overlooked by anti-subjective behaviorists in the past, our interactions with others are deeply affected by our everyday intuitive theories about how other minds work. These theories, rarely made explicit, are omnipresent but have only recently been subjected to intense study" (p. 45). He further states that, "The emerging thesis is that educational practices in a classroom are premised on a set of folk beliefs about learners' minds, some of which may have worked advertently toward or inadvertently against the child's own welfare." (pp. 49–50; Senge, 2000).

For example, if a teacher believes in the innate resilience of a child, that is, in the young person's inborn capacity for healthy development and successful learning, the teacher will more than likely be encouraging, reminding the child of her strengths, her interests, her power, and connecting this knowledge to opportunities to use her strengths, interests, and power. Furthermore, the teacher will use community-building and inclusive teaching strategies such as Tribes. Research has shown that when teachers have *high* expectations for a student, they will call on her more, wait longer for the student's answer, and attribute any failing on the part of the student to her not studying hard enough (Carta, 1991; Weinstein, 2003; Wheelock, 1992). On the other hand, if the teacher believes that some people are resilient and others are not, he very likely will arbitrarily assign some of his challenged students to the "non-resilient" category, perhaps even "track" these students in low-ability groupings, and communicate messages that, "This task may be too difficult for you" or "You're just like the rest of them" and so on. Furthermore, research has shown that when a teacher has *low* expectations for a student, he will call on the student less often, wait less time for the student's response, and if the student fails, attribute the failure to her lack of intelligence (Carta, 1991; Weinstein, 2003; Wheelock, 1992).

In other words, pedagogy and teaching practices flow from teachers' beliefs about their students as learners, and through these practices, the deep beliefs are communicated to students. Thus, he writes, "Pedagogy is never innocent. It is a medium that carries its own message" (p. 63). Unfortunately, all too often these deeply held cultural beliefs take the form of the hurtful "isms" of racism, sexism, classism, and ageism that can create the "hidden curriculum" of the school and classroom.

Bruner writes that there are four dominant "mental models" or beliefs about learners' minds that "have held sway in our times" with each emphasizing different educational goals and distinctly different pedagogies. These range from seeing the student as (1) learning from imitation or modeling, (2) learning from didactic exposure (the spawner of objective testing), (3) seeing the student as thinker who constructs meaning through discussion and collaboration with others (metacognition), and (4) seeing the student as knowledgeable, as able to test his socially constructed beliefs against historical and empirical evidence. He makes the case that while the tendency of educational theorists is to focus on only one of these models and debunk all the others, each of these models should be seen as part of an integrated whole. He writes that, "Older views of mind and how mind can be cultivated [#1 and #2] need to be shorn of their narrow exclusionism, and newer views [#3 and #4] need to be modulated to recognize that while skills and facts never exist *out* of context, they are no less important *in* context" (p. 65). This argument is reminiscent of the nature-nurture debate discussed in Chapter One, in which we concluded that development and learning are dynamic transactional processes between the person and the environment, with each system growing in the process.

Bruner's arguments around cultural beliefs provide yet another lens on learning and development that further supports the power of beliefs of the caregivers, in this case, the teachers, to determine students' success. When teachers hold the bottom-line beliefs that their students are thinkers creating their own knowledge (#3) and are knowledgeable and capable of testing their personal knowledge against historical and empirical evidence (#4), they will evolve pedagogy that looks very much like Tribes, that places the learning of skills and accumulation of knowledge into a context of student-centered learning that is constructivist, cooperative, reflective, active, and authentic. "Modern pedagogy is moving increasingly to the view that the child should be aware of her own thought processes [what we called 'self-awareness' in Chapter One], and that it is crucial for the pedagogical theorist and teacher alike to help her to become more metacognitive—to be as aware of how she goes about her learning and thinking as she is about the subject matter she is studying" (p. 64). Metacognition is a major aspect of self-awareness, that sense of self discussed in Chapter One as a critical resilience strength and the cornerstone of emotional intelligence. It is primarily developed through self- and group-reflection processes, one of the research-based components of the Tribes TLC process.

In his essay entitled, "The Complexity of Educational Aims," Bruner speaks to the critical importance of school culture and to the fact that most discussions of educational policy ignore this most basic element of successful school reform. He writes, "What is needed in America—as in most countries of the developed world—is not simply a renewal of the skills that make a country a better competitor in the world markets, but a renewal and reconsideration of what is called *school culture*. On the basis of what we have learned in recent years about human learning—it is best when it is *participatory, proactive, communal, collaborative and given over to constructive meanings* rather than receiving them. We do even better at teaching science, math, and languages in such schools than in more traditional ones" (p. 84). In what sounds like a reiteration of the protective factors, Bruner further explains that, "No education reform can get off the ground without an adult actively and honestly participating—a teacher willing and prepared to give and share aid, to comfort, and to scaffold" (1996, p. 84).

Jeanne Gibbs' *Discovering Gifts in Middle School* (2001a) and *Guiding Your School Community To Live A Culture of Caring and Learning* (1999) have charts that compare Bruner's components of the ideal learning culture to the Tribes process (pages 67 and 28 respectively). Needless to say, they also map to the three protective factors that characterize environments that nurture healthy human development and successful learning. We could also classify all of the successful whole-child approaches mentioned in Chapter One along these dimensions. Especially critical to meeting the needs of our diverse classrooms and schools, these components also map to the "five standards" that Roland Tharp and his colleagues at the Center for Research on Education, Diversity, and Excellence at University of California-Santa Cruz have found from 35 years of work that are critical to improving learning for students from diverse ethnic, cultural, linguistic, or economic backgrounds. These are *joint productive activity, language and literacy development, contextualization/making meaning, challenging activities, and instructional conversation* (Doherty et al., 2003). According to Tharp, "If you have several different languages and races in the same classroom, there is no recourse but to provide a common culture in the classroom" (Viadero, 2004, p. 3).

A major contribution Bruner makes to the "reculturing precedes restructuring" argument made by Fullan (1991, 1993), Gibbs (1999, 2000, 2001), Benard (2004), Benard and Marshall (1995), systems guru Peter Senge (1990; Senge et al. 2000), Deal and Peterson (2002) and many others, is that he gives us a place to begin the process. He says that the first step in creating a nurturing school culture is examining the cultural beliefs or mental models of school staff. This means making the implicit explicit through a process of self- and group reflection, a "consciousness-raising" process that parallels how we help students test their personal beliefs about the world against history and other sources of knowledge. So much "can be accomplished by getting teachers (and students) to think *explicitly* about their folk psychological assumptions, in order to bring them out of the shadows of tacit knowledge" (p. 47). Tribes TLC is grounded in just this process. This process also encompasses one of Peter Senge's (Senge et al., 2000) five disciplines essential to effective organizations, that of exploring our "mental models," that is, becoming more aware of the sources of our thinking. This self-awareness was identified earlier as an essential resilience strength (Benard, 2004) and major source of "emotional intelligence" (Goleman, 1995).

What is particularly challenging for the Tribes process, as well as other approaches grounded in the developmental paradigm, that is research-based and environmentally- or culturally-oriented is the current educational policy that is deficit-based and control-oriented. This latter cultural belief gets operationalized in approaches such as one-size-fits-all standards, in the concern only with scientific-logical thinking over narrative-artistic thinking, and in character education programs that try to directly teach children social and emotional competence in a de-contexualized curriculum. Several of Bruner's essays address this current educational establishment belief. He writes that, "All the standards in the world will not, like a helping hand, achieve the goal of making our multicultural, our threatened society come alive again, not alive just as a competitor in the world's markets, but as a nation worth living in and living for" (1996, p. 118). What we need, Bruner contends, is a school reform movement "with a better sense of where we are going, with deeper convictions about what kind of people we want to be" (1996, p. 118). What we need is the Tribes TLC process for renewing and reforming our schools.

Democratic Classroom

■ Democratic classrooms invite the active participation of ALL students, school staff, and families and are committed to social justice

The ideal learning culture or caring culture in a school translates at the classroom level to what is often called the democratic classroom. This concept is at the core of the progressive education tradition which goes back even further than John Dewey. However, Dewey's prolific work on democracy in almost all aspects of social life clearly earns him the title of "Giant" in this area. In his classic book, *Democracy and Education* (1916, 2003), Dewey outlined the purpose of schooling as a dual one: education for citizenship and for academic learning. While many progressive schools since have leaned in one or another of these directions, often described as the affective-cognitive dichotomy, Dewey himself maintained that schools must integrate these two purposes through active learning processes that meet both goals (Puckett, 1989). Carl Glickman, an educational researcher and reformer who writes on democracy in education, makes the following point, reminiscent of our earlier Haim Ginott letter to administrators:

> "What difference does it make if we graduate 100 percent of our students, or if SAT scores rise twenty points, or if our students beat other countries in achievement in science when they have not learned how to identify, analyze, and solve the problems that face their immediate and larger communities? Our country would be better served by schools that produce caring, intelligent, and wise citizens who willingly engage in the work of a democracy than by schools that produce graduates who do well on isolated subgoals" (1998, p. 9).

Once again, our commonsense, not our educational policy, tells us that while living in an increasingly multicultural world as we all do, it makes even more sense today that we see schooling for democracy as even perhaps a *more* important goal than schooling for academic competence. Unfortunately, as two of the prominent promulgators of this concept, James Beane and Michael Apple assert, "Despite the rhetoric of democracy in our society and the commonsense idea that the democratic way of life is learned through democratic experiences, schools have been remarkably undemocratic institutions" (Beane & Apple, 1995, p. 12). However, what has become even more true in 2004 than it was when they wrote in 1995 is that even "the *idea* of democratic schools has fallen on hard times" (Beane & Apple, p. 3). In fact, a visit to the First Amendment Center's Interactive First Amendment Schools survey (www.firstamendmentcenter.org) finds some disturbing trends. For example, only 49% of educators taking the survey said "Yes" to the statement, "Freedom of expression, including a due consideration for the rights of those holding dissenting or unpopular views, is protected" in their school. Moreover 47% said "No" to the statement, "All stakeholders have opportunities to participate in decisions that shape school rules and policies."

Fortunately, for Tribes' practitioners, the Tribes TLC process is not only resiliency in action but democracy in action as well and provides a benchmark of best practices for creating democratic classrooms that serve Dewey's two-fold goals of citizenship and academic learning. Given how dangerously willing many Americans and their policymakers have been to give up their democratic rights in the face of the fear of terrorism, this component of the Tribes process is especially critical not only to education but to the future of democracy in America. In this section, we will first define what we mean by the democratic classroom and school, examine the components, relate these to Tribes processes, and compare to the qualities of many of the effective approaches we have already examined, as well as others.

Dewey wrote that democratic schools and classrooms share the following qualities: shared interests, freedom in interaction, participation, and social relationships. Getting somewhat more specific, Beane and Apple (1995) find that the central concerns of democratic schools and classrooms consist of the following:

- open flow of ideas, regardless of their popularity

- faith in the individual and collective capacity of people to create possibilities for resolving problems

- use of critical reflection and analysis to evaluate ideas, problems, and policies

- concern for the welfare of others and "the common good"

- concern for the dignity and rights of individuals and minorities

- an understanding that democracy is a set of values that we must live and that must guide our life as a people, and

- organization of social institutions to promote and extend the democratic way of life (pp. 6–7).

According to writers and researchers of democracy in education (who we will refer to throughout this section), educators have the responsibility of creating both structures and processes as well as curriculum that give life to the above concerns. The structures and processes of democratic schools and classrooms include, first and foremost, *widespread participation in issues of governance and policy making* of all who are directly involved in the school: students, parents, teachers, and other school staff. Schoolwide structures for promoting participation include committees, site councils, and other forms of participatory governance. In classrooms, students and teachers engage in collaborative planning and problem-solving, reaching decisions that are responsive to the concerns, aspirations, and interests of both. "This kind of democratic planning, at both the school and the classroom levels, is not the 'engineering of consent' toward predetermined decisions that has too often created the illusion of democracy, but a genuine attempt to honor the right of people to participate in making decisions that affect their lives" (Beane & Apple, 1995, p. 9). Underlying this tenet (which, remember, is one of the three critical protective factors of a successful system, including a Tribes Learning Community) are years of community development as well as organization development research on the power of participation to create and maintain change efforts (Cutler & Edwards, 2002; Golarz & Golarz, 1995; Kretzman & McKnight, 1993; Little, 1993; McLaughlin & Talbert, 1990; McLaughlin et al., 1994). We even have an "old" adage: "People are committed to what they helped create."

Two researchers from the Claremont Graduate School's Institute for Education in Transformation, were troubled by the fact that none of the educational reforms being advocated in the late Eighties and early Nineties were based on "voices from the inside" of schools. Interestingly, as Mary Poplin and Joseph Weeres (1992) and their team of researchers began just listening to the concerns of students, parents, and teachers and other school staff, they made an astounding discovery. The climate of the classroom and school actually began to improve—just because these normally silenced voices were heard—and subsequently the engagement and achievement of the students! Unfortunately most school reform efforts in 2004, and especially NCLB, still continue to ignore the research findings on democratic participation in schools and classrooms, and consequently, will continue to fail.

Democratic structures and processes, according to Apple and Beane (1995) and others, must also be guided by *democratic values,* which is not always the case with local decision-making. This requires a bottom-line commitment to or mission based on protecting the rights of groups that are often disenfranchised and oppressed by local decision-making processes. This is why a Tribes TLC democratic classroom has non-negotiable community agreements based on maintaining the critical tension in a democracy between rights and responsibilities.

A fourth structural component of democratic schools and classrooms, that is certainly essential in creating a community of learners, is a sense of *shared purpose*. "The common good is a central feature of democracy. For this reason, the communities of learners in democratic schools are marked by an emphasis on cooperation and collaboration rather than competition" (Beane & Apple, 1995, p. 11). Hence, a major structural as well as cultural component of the Tribes TLC process is cooperative learning. The development of a shared purpose/mission/vision based on the common good is not only sine qua non in a democratic school and classroom but is also the absolute first step in building a shared and nurturing culture in a school (Senge, 1990, 2000; Fullan, 1993, 2002).

A fifth inter-related structural component of democratic schools and classrooms is *structural equity*. This translates to every student having not only equal access to educational opportunities but to the supports that will help them access these opportunities. This often means removing the institutional barriers, such as tracking, ability grouping, and biased testing, which have been shown to deny access on the basis of race, ethnicity, gender, and socioeconomic class (Kohn, 2000; Meier, 2000; Oakes, 1985; Ohanian, 1999; Sacks, 1999). Thus, the Tribes TLC process emphasizes not only cooperative learning but learning communities, peer leadership, multiple intelligences, authentic assessment, to name a few approaches shown to promote structural equity.

Another structural component of democratic schools and classrooms is the creation of an inclusive *community of learners*, which is the structure of Tribes and the focus of Chapter Three of this book. Communities are by nature diverse and in democratic classrooms, diversity is an asset, not a deficit. "Separating people of any age on the basis of their differences [in age, culture, ethnicity, gender, socioeconomic class, aspirations, and abilities] or using labels to stereotype them simply creates division and status systems that detract from the democratic nature of the community and the dignity of the individuals against whom such practices work so harshly"

(Beane & Apple, 1995, p. 10; Kretzmann & McKnight, 1993). Research has documented for over 20 years the negative effects, especially on marginalized groups, of sorting processes like tracking and standardized testing (Kohn, 2000; Meier, 2000; Oakes, 1985; Ohanian, 1999; Sacks, 1999). This is why a major structural component of Tribes TLC is creating a Community of Learners (which will be discussed in Chapter Three).

A last structural component of democratic schools and classrooms is their *connection to the community*, their understanding that democratic schools and classrooms don't occur in a vacuum but are inter-related with creating more democratic, socially just communities in which the school exists. According to Beane and Apple, "The educational landscape is littered with the remains of failed school reforms, many of which failed because of the social conditions surrounding the schools. Only those reforms that recognize these conditions and actively engage them are likely to make a lasting difference in the lives of the children, educators, and communities served by the schools" (1992, p. 11).

We have already documented the positive findings for students, their families, and their communities of the community school approach (Dryfoos, 1998, 2003; Coalition for Community Schools, May 2003; Henderson & Mapp, 2002; Schorr, 1997). Further research support lies in the positive student, school, and community outcomes from community service-learning initiatives which testify to the power of deepening the school-community connection, especially in giving students the opportunity to make a difference in their community and then to connect this experience to not only the school curriculum but to the students' own lives (Melchior, 1996, 1998). The highly successful, award-winning Kids As Planners model of community service-learning considers itself "apprentice citizenship" (KIDS Consortium, 2001). Community service-learning is considered a vital element of democratic classrooms and schools.

It is this last commitment to creating socially just school communities that really distinguishes democratic schools and classrooms from other progressive schools, such as those that are simply child-centered or humanistic. While democratic schools are both of these, "Their vision extends beyond purposes such as improving the school climate or enhancing students' self-esteem. Democratic educators seek not simply to lessen the harshness of social inequities in school, but to change the conditions that create them" (Beane & Apple, 1992, p. 11; Oakes et al., 2000). It is this commitment to social justice that especially informs the curricula of democratic schools and classrooms.

Beane and Apple refer to the above structures of democratic schools and classrooms as the "'hidden' curriculum by which people learn significant lessons about justice, power, dignity, and self-worth" (1992, p. 13). While democratizing these structures is essential to creating a democratic school and classroom, attention must also be paid to what they call the "overt" curriculum. "Educators in a democratic society have an obligation to help young people seek out a range of ideas and to voice their own" (p. 13). As we have seen in the past several years, the curriculum has been narrowing to what Apple refers to as "official or high status knowledge that is endorsed by the dominant culture" (Beane & Apple, p. 13). As research has consistently shown, this narrowing results in the silencing of more and more voices that lie outside the dominant culture, such as students of color, girls, and students with physical or mental challenges, resulting in the much touted "achievement gap" for these marginalized groups (Williams, 1996, 2003). As the curriculum narrows, the achievement gap grows.

However, the main curricular approaches that are found in democratic schools and classrooms include not only cooperative learning, the involvement of students in curriculum planning and in parent-teacher conferences, thematic curricula focused on the study of social problems, and community service-learning but have as a major focus, *multicultural education* and *critical pedagogy*, both of which are forms of responsive education. It is impossible to talk about democratic classrooms and schools without also discussing multicultural education (Perlstein, 1996). Similarly, one cannot discuss multicultural education without also discussing critical pedagogy. All three approaches overlap considerably and are incorporated in the Tribes TLC process. According to Geneva Gay (1995), a prominent scholar of multicultural education, this approach shares many similarities with other educational reform initiatives: intergroup education, progressive education, humanistic education, child-centered education, citizenship or democratic education), and critical pedagogy (a process of critical thinking, reflection, and action)—most of which we have discussed in this document since they are all part of Tribes TLC. Multicultural education and critical pedagogy, however, share the commitment to social justice that distinguishes democratic education.

What they add to the concept of democratic schooling is the assertion that democracy in education is not possible without attending to culture. "If educational equity and excellence are to be provided to all students, cultural pluralism must permeate every aspect of the schooling enterprise" (Gay, 1995, p. 159) through an intergroup process like Tribes. As we've discussed earlier in this chapter and in Chapter One, culture influences all dimensions of human behavior, including teaching and learning. Furthermore, as Bruner emphasized throughout *Culture and Education* (1996), all knowledge is socially constructed and is mediated by purveyors of knowledge, in this case, our teachers.

Sonia Nieto (1992, 1994, 2003), perhaps the most authoritative writer on multicultural education, makes the case that multicultural education should be considered "as comprehensive school reform and basic education for all students" (1992, p. 208). In other words, the lens through which she frames school reform is multicultural education, just as Tribes is the lens through which Tribes practitioners frame school reform. She then builds the case that multicultural education is all the following: antiracist education, basic education, important for all students, pervasive, education for social justice, a process, and critical pedagogy, all of which can also be said of Tribes TLC. She writes that multicultural education can positively impact four major barriers for creating a caring culture for ethnically diverse students: racism and discrimination, structural factors within schools, cultural differences, and language diversity. Once again, Tribes meets her criteria for what good multicultural education does.

Geneva Gay, however, defines multicultural education much more narrowly and makes a distinction between it and critical pedagogy, writing that, "While multicultural education gives priority to reforming curriculum content and classroom instruction, the centerpiece of critical pedagogy is how the institutional ideology and cultural ethos of schools reflect and perpetuate the oppressive practices of society" (1995, p. 162). Multicultural education, for example, would traditionally emphasize changing school curricula to include groups and experiences that traditionally have been excluded from the traditional Western lexicon. However, "Recognizing and providing ownership to multiple voices in the educational process requires changing the nature and quality of pedagogy as well as changing curriculum content" (Gay, 1995, p. 172; Cuban, 1973).

Critical pedagogy emerges from the work of the late Brazilian educator, Paulo Freire, whose success in the national adult literacy campaign in Brazil in the 1960s influenced literacy campaigns all over the world. Freire believed that literacy was one means to democracy and felt that literally being able to "read the word" was interconnected to being able to "read the world," that is "to analyze the political and social conditions that circumscribe people's lives, in order to envision how those conditions should be changed" (Senge et al., 2000, p. 208). Freire and his colleagues met in "culture circles" with poor and illiterate villagers and engaged them in dialogue about their lives, hopes, and dreams. Their stories became their "primers" for learning to read and in the process they learned not only literacy but became politically and socially educated as well. They learned that "silence"—the absence of words—contributed to their powerlessness and that "voicing" their concerns was a source of power. Tribes practitioners can see that Tribes TLC is essentially a culture circle and a critical pedagogical processs.

In the 1970s, after the publication of his book, *Pedagogy of the Oppressed* (1970), a network of educators influenced by the writing and teaching of Freire developed the term "critical pedagogy," and many progressive theorists now use it to mean a deliberate effort to educate for social responsibility. Progressive educators "believe that the main purpose of education is not to transmit knowledge and preserve social traditions but to *transform* society by helping students develop a perceptive and inquisitive consciousness of the conditions within our culture. They are concerned with changing cultural, economic, and political institutions and believe that a functioning democracy requires purposeful collective action, not simply personal choice" (Miller, 2004, p. 24). Maxine Greene (1998), one of the leading writers in this area, says teaching for social justice means helping young people deal critically with the world the way it is. It also means teaching students to imagine and experience the world that does not yet exist.

According to Peter Senge and his colleagues (2000), critical pedagogy is essentially "a pedagogy for the five disciplines and a language for transformation" (p. 205). In fact, it is often referred to as "transformative pedagogy" and has spawned a movement, "transformational learning" (Mezirow, 2000; Taylor, 1998). Critical pedagogy is a socially constructive process of inquiry, exploration, discovery, and reflection that parallels Tribes Discovery Learning process of the Five E's: engage, explore, explain, elaborate, and evaluate. However, just as the Tribes Discovery Learning process is not just for students but for teachers, administrators, and families, critical pedagogy is also at the heart of reculturing any organization. Senge and his colleagues (2000) write that, "Transformative pedagogy can help people create significant and enduring change in their organizations—especially schools—by developing fundamental shifts of attitudes and beliefs about the nature of schooling, the social construction of leaning, and how knowledge always forms the basis for social action—in any organization" (p. 207).

Multiculturalists and critical pedagogues are both driven by the idea (which is substantiated by earlier research findings, including those of Jerome Bruner) that the pedagogical process is the most significant determinant of the quality of the educational opportunities students actually receive in the classroom" (Gay, 1995, p. 172). What this means is that the instructional process, or pedagogy, like the curriculum content, must be informed by cultural pluralism. Perhaps the most poetic writer on critical pedagogy, Bell Hooks, writes, "When we, as educators, allow our pedagogy to be radically changed by our recognition of a multicultural world, we can give students the education they desire and deserve. We can teach in ways that transform consciousness, creating a climate of free expression that is the essence of a truly libratory liberal arts education" (1994, p. 44). To do this, according to Hooks, is a way of teaching that anyone can learn. "That learning process comes easiest to those of us who teach who also believe that there is an aspect of our vocation that is sacred; who believe that our work is not merely to share information but to share in the intellectual and spiritual growth of our students. To teach in a manner that respects and cares for the souls of our students is essential if we are to provide the necessary conditions where learning can most deeply and intimately begin" (1994, p. 13).

In essence, Hooks is describing a pedagogy that is grounded in the three protective factors undergirding the Tribes TLC process: caring for the whole student, positive child-centered and strengths-based expectations, and reciprocity in terms of sharing power and giving voice. It is a pedagogy in which "teachers are able to challenge their students to consider alternative life possibilities, to become critical thinkers, and to consider transformation of their current life situations and the life situations of others" (Ball, 2000, p. 1006). According to Nieto (1992), "In the final analysis, multicultural education is simply good pedagogy. That is, all good education takes students seriously, uses their experiences as a basis for further learning, and helps them develop into critical and empowered citizens" (p. 222).

This connecting pedagogy is essentially that of the school Jesse Goodman (1992) describes in his case study of Harmony School, *Elementary Schooling for Critical Democracy*. He, like Hooks, finds the element of the "sacred," writing that, "There existed within Harmony's elementary school a subtle, delicate, and loving spirituality" which he defines as "the life-affirming intellectual and emotional connection that existed among the teachers and students [that] gave substance to Harmony's democratic ideology and practices" (p. 178). He concludes that although the practices for democratic schooling can be named as we have above, "The key to what makes Harmony a meaningful democratic alternative was the spiritual nature of its enterprise" (p. 178).

As we look for additional evaluation research showing that democratic classrooms do indeed work, we must mention that virtually all of the effective approaches cited in Chapter One (for example, Comer's School Development Program, Developmental Studies Center's Child Development Project, the High/Scope Perry Preschool Program), also have an emphasis on democracy in both the school and classroom. Similarly, the case studies cited earlier of successful schools inevitably document a focus on democratic classrooms and schools. In fact, at the heart of Debra Meier's famous Central Park East high school was a critical inquiry process she refers to as five "intellectual habits"—"habits that should be internalized by every student, and used no matter what they are studying about, both in school and especially out of it!" (1995, p. 41). Paraphrasing her discussion, the habits consist of the following set of questions (p. 41):

HABITS	QUESTIONS
Evidence	"How do you know that?"
Viewpoint	"Who said it and why?"
Cause	"What led to it?"
Effect	"What else happened?"
Hypothesizing	"What if? Supposing that..."

In essense, this is a exactly a process of scientific inquiry our friend Bill Lofquist (2003) (see Conclusion) advocates we engage in if we really want to do "science-based" prevention or education. We can add that this is also a process of democratic inquiry and media literacy itself, and to remain a democracy, it is imperative that all citizens, young and old, engage in this type of critical thinking and discovery learning. Tribes TLC offers a process for doing just this.

One other supportive body of research needs to be mentioned: the plethora of research on small schools, most of which have a commitment to democratic education (Ayers et al., 2000). Perhaps no other movement testifies more strongly that the ideals of progressive education continue to hold a powerful attraction for educators and education scholars than the movement for small schools. It's position to traditional education parallels what dynamic humanistic psychology's position is to functionalist/behaviorialist psychology (Zimiles, 1987). For the most part, however, until the 1990s small progressive schools, many of them going back to the time of Dewey, have remained in the private sector and have served more well-off families committed to progressive ideals (Semel & Sadovnik, 1998).

The very good news is that in the 90s the "small schools" movement began gaining momentum, thanks to all the publicity Debra Meier's successful school in East Harlem received. In many ways, the *small schools movement* is carrying on the banner of progressive, i.e., democratic, education, especially in their mission and shared emphases of fairness, equity, and justice (Ayers et al., 2000). Researcher Michelle Fines sees that the goal of small schools is to produce "citizens with a soul and a conscience as well as literate young women and men" (2000, p. 169). To do this, democratically oriented small schools focus on the following:

- Social relations within and around the school that are characterized by an ethic of respect and reciprocity and the challenging of power inequities

- Curriculum and pedagogy for social justice

- Schoolwide dedication to high expectations for all and narrowing of achievement gaps

- Insistence upon systemwide education for justice (p. 170).

The National Research Council and Institute of Medicine report on engaging schools (2004) concluded that, "The research evidence on small schools suggests that reducing substantially the size of schools is a promising strategy for achieving the kind of personalized education that engages youth" (p. 113). They found three conclusions supported by research: (1) Smaller school size is associated with higher achievement under certain conditions (Fetler, 1989; Lee, 2000; Lee and Smith, 1997; Wasley et al., 2000); (2) Small schools improve achievement equity (Ancess, 2000; Fine, 1994; Lee and Smith, 1997; Wasley, 2000); and (3) Smaller schools may be especially important for disadvantaged students (Howley & Bickel, 2000). In terms of this last study, the National Research Council and Institute of Medicine state that research has even found that small school size reduced the impact of poverty on student achievement (2004, p. 115).

The National Longitudinal Study of Adolescent Health similarly has found a correlation between students feeling connected to school (as mentioned earlier, this is also protective against all health-risk behaviors) and smaller school size (McNeeley et al., 2002). An extensive literature review From Northwest Regional Educational Laboratory (Cotton, 2001) also comes to the above same conclusions but in addition provides research evidence documenting smaller school size effects on holistic child and youth development as well as family and staff engagement as well. Similarly, an *ERIC Digest* (Raywid, 1999) summarizing the current literature on small schools concluded that, "It is rare indeed to find empirical support or justification for the large high school" (p. 1). In fact, the research evidence seems to be so conclusive in support of small schools that scholars have moved on from quantitative studies making the case for small schools to qualitative studies examining how they are being implemented.

Besides the overlap between small schools and democratic schools/classrooms, we also need to superimpose community schools as they too tend to be small and devoted to the values and mission of democratic education. As we have seen, several evaluations have documented both social-emotional (citizenship) as well as academic outcomes for students attending community schools (Dryfoos, 1998, 2003; Coalition for Community Schools, May 2003; Henderson & Mapp, 2002; Schorr, 1997).

If small is truly beautiful as the wise E.F. Schumacher (1973, 1989) wrote over thirty years ago, spawning a movement that has not abated to this day, then one of the most exciting and hopeful happenings in education is the funding of small schools by the Bill and Melinda Gates Foundation. What is critical, however, to this movement's success is abiding by the values and goals that have served as the foundation for democratic education and the commitment to an ideal learning culture that is communal, participatory, proactive, collaborative, and constructivist (Bruner, 1996) and based on research identified protective factors—caring relationships, high expectations, and opportunities for participation (Benard, 1991, 2004).

While small school size is a different entity than a small group, this research does lend support to creating smaller groupings, be they schools, classrooms, or groups such as Tribes, in which these protective factors, or Bruner's qualities of ideal learning cultures can be facilitated. It supports the research identified earlier in this chapter on the power of small groups to influence behavior and learning, not to mention the enormous body of research on cooperative learning that we will examine in Chapter Four (Brown & D'Emidio-Caston, 1995; Eccles & Gootman, 2002; Harris, 1998; McLaughlin et al., 1994; Werner and Smith, 1992).

In summarizing Chapter Two, we find that attention to creating a caring culture is acknowledged by virtually all of the supporting research discussed in Chapter One to be essential to the success of their whole-child approaches that focus on human development and learning. Resilience research has found that it is through a caring culture that young people develop the holistic competencies and attitudes associated with life success: social competence, problem-solving, sense of self, and sense of purpose and future. Neuroscience tells us that students need to feel safe, nurtured, respected, and have opportunities for self-efficacy. Multiple Intelligence research asks us to create classrooms that honor, respect, and invite forth all the different intelligences and gifts students bring. Evaluation research of effective whole-child approaches such as Comer's School Development Program, High/Scope Educational Research Foundation's schools, and Developmental Studies Center's Child Development Project as well as case studies of turnaround schools like Debra Meiers' or turnaround teachers such as Judy Deiro's, not to mention effective practices such as mentoring, adventure/active learning, or cooperative learning, all recognize that creating a caring culture or context is essential to their success.

So, the Big Question is, "Where and how do we begin the process of reculturing?" Consulting the leading reculturing experts upon which the Tribes TLC process is founded—such as Michael Fullan (1993, 1999), Peter Senge (1990, Senge et al., 2000) , Jerome Bruner (1996), Philip Schlechty (1997), and Seymour Sarason (1971, 1990), as well as other community development experts like John Kretzmann and John McKnight (1993) at the Asset-Based Community Development Institute at Northwestern University—we find virtually total agreement on a process that focuses on developing a shared vision based on shared beliefs and on what we want our students to become, a tangible mission consisting of goals and principles to realize the vision, creating the school structures that support the vision and then rolling out strategies that operationalize the mission and are supported by the school structures and that, in a self-renewing cycle, feed back into a positive school culture.

These experts concur that the reculturing process begins in the hearts and minds of school staff, with their beliefs about the children they serve. For example, Jerome Bruner asserts that, "It is our ideas that need restructuring, before we can redesign our institutions" (1996). Multiple intelligence researchers, Linda and Bruce Campbell, concluded that the most "surprising finding from [their] study of MI schools is that restructuring is not necessarily achieved through external programs, resources, facilities, or district or state mandates. Indeed, meaningful restructuring first takes place within the minds of teachers and their beliefs about the nature and possibilities of their students. From there, all else follows" (1999, p. 97). Asa Hilliard, a scholar of multicultural education, provides a supportive example:

> To restructure we must first look deeply at the goals that we set for our children and the beliefs that we have about them. Once we are on the right track there, then we must turn our attention to the delivery systems.... Untracking is right. Mainstreaming is right. Decentralization is right. Cooperative learning is right. Technology access for all is right. Multiculturalism is right. But none of these approaches or strategies will mean anything if the fundamental belief does not fit with new structures that are being created (1991, p. 36).

To illustrate this successful change model with the Tribes TLC process, we look first at the graphic from *Discovering Gifts in Middle School* (Gibbs, 2001a, p. 64) which serves to structure this document. The vision and mission of a Tribes school is represented by the inner circle, Human Development and Learning. The vision is that all children will experience healthy human development and meaningful learning. The specific mission of Tribes is to assure the healthy development of every child so that each has the knowledge, competency, and resilience to be successful in a rapidly changing world" (2001a, p. 18). This vision and mission are based on several decades of research that support a focus on the whole child; on resilience as an intrinsically motivated wisdom; on developmental stage-specific wisdom; on academic, social, and emotional learning; and on multiple intelligences. To this end, Tribes has the inter-related goals of creating A Caring *Culture* (Chapter Two), based on proven protective factors, the ideal learning culture, and the democratic classroom and school, as well as a Community of Learners *structure* that manifest the protective factors and ideal learning culture discussed in Chapter Three. Moreover, from the Tribes culture and structure unfold the Responsive Education learning strategies (Chapter Four). These learner-centered strategies are tailored to human development and meaningful learning and further promote a caring culture, thus creating a self-renewing feedback loop to insure not only successful school change but the sustaining of it as well.

As we have discussed throughout Chapters One and Two, undergirding this entire process is the belief in human potential and innate resilience. Without this belief, the process becomes a house of cards, with no mortar to hold it together. This is why the first step in becoming a Tribes learning community involves professional development focused on flipping the traditional paradigm, which we have already described as a deep belief, of schooling from one focused on deficits and structured around *controlling* development and learning to one focused on strengths and structured around *supporting* development and learning. With this shifting of beliefs, the school's culture also starts to shift—to relationships that are caring, to communication that conveys positive and high expectations, and to the sharing of power by opening up opportunities for participation on the part of before silenced groups. At this point the school has indeed created a culture of readiness for change, a culture that can now support the structures through which these human development- and learning-supportive processes can flow and create a school that is self-renewing (Joyce et al., 1993).

The single structure that research has identified as supporting the vision of healthy development and learning in schools is that of the *learning community* held together by the mortar of shared beliefs culminating in a shared vision for their school. Peter Senge speaks eloquently to this: "A shared vision is not an idea. It is not even an important idea such as freedom. It is, rather, a force in people's hearts, a force of impressive power. It may be inspired by an idea, but once it goes further—if it is compelling enough to acquire the support of more than one person—then it is no longer an abstraction. It is palpable. People begin to see it as if it exists. Few, if any, forces in human affairs are as powerful as a shared vision" (1990, p. 206). Let's now look at just what we know about this powerful structure that is the Tribes Learning Community.

CHAPTER THREE

Community of Learners

We are convinced as are many educators that "restructuring schools" should be about restoring connections, creating a caring climate and community rather than switching roles, tinkering with policy, inviting in more experts or shuffling curriculum. Structuring supportive groups (tribes) throughout the system formalizes connections and re-cultures the school into a working community of trust and respect. Once connected to others within small groups, everyone gains a sense of belonging (inclusion), a sense of value (influence) and social support (community).

JEANNE GIBBS, 1999, P. 80

*C*reating learning communities is the essential work of Tribes TLC. It is also what school reform as well as professional development literature has advocated for over two decades [see the May 2004 issue of *Educational Leadership* for articles summarizing both lines of study]. Furthermore, the best of educational research has found this concept to be associated with successful schools that promote *student* development and learning and teacher empowerment and well-being—and retention.

Thomas Sergiovanni, one of the leading theorists of the school community concept writes that the defining characteristics of schools as communities is "the bonding together of people in special ways and the binding of them to shared values and ideas…. Communities are defined by their centers of values, sentiments, and beliefs that provide the needed conditions for creating a sense of 'we' from 'I'" (1994, p. 4). "Community" stands in stark contrast to "bureaucracy" in any chart on shifting paradigms. It flows directly from philosophies based on human potential and innate resilience. Community is precisely what develops when the three protective factors are in place in a classroom or when a classroom or school has an "ideal culture" for learning that Bruner described as participatory, proactive, communal, collaborative, and constructivist. "A community" is also how students who have overcome the odds describe the classrooms that were turnaround places for them (Benard, 2003). "Community building must become the heart of any school improvement effort. Whatever else is involved—improving teaching, developing sensible curriculum, creating new forms of governance, providing more authentic assessment, empowering teachers and parents, increasing professionalism—it must rest on a foundation of community building" (Sergiovanni, 1994, p. xi).

In this chapter we'll look first at classroom learning communities, at the research supporting this structure, and then at the research supporting components of the Tribes community-building process: cooperative learning, including peer leadership; the personal skills and attitudes associated with small group membership, community agreements, group processing/reflection, and the stages of group development. Systems thinking tells us—and research confirms—that creating and sustaining classroom learning communities is facilitated by first establishing learning communities for staff. This is precisely the process used in building a Tribes Learning Community. So in the last part of Chapter Three we will also highlight some of the abundant research on what is now referred to as "professional learning communities."

The themes that will guide our exploration of learning communities:

- Restructuring to promote healthy development and learning means learning communities, learning communities, learning communities!

- Honoring the community agreements is the sine qua non practice for creating a caring culture and a community of learners.

- Quality cooperative learning is democracy and resilience in action—and creates a community of learners.

- Group membership builds critical resilience skills and attitudes.

- Group processing/reflection is critical to successful groups/cooperative learning.

- An understanding of group development is essential in promoting quality cooperative learning.

- Creating a classroom community of learners is dependent on staff having a professional learning community.

Learning Communities

■ Restructuring to promote healthy development and learning means learning communities, learning communities, learning communities!

Alexander Mickeljohn is considered one of the "fathers" of the learning community movement during the 1920s for his emphasis on the importance of structure, curricular coherence, and community in higher education, with many colleges still structured around what we now call integrated thematic instruction or project-based learning. The other "father" is, once again, John Dewey, less for his emphasis on structure than on the process of student-centered and active learning. According to one resource on this concept, "Recent work in such diverse areas as the social construction of knowledge, collaborative learning, writing and critical thinking, feminist pedagogy, and cognitive and intellectual development supports and resonates with the learning community effort. They all stand on the common ground of learning as development, the value of building connections [i.e., relationships], and the power of shared inquiry" (Gabelnick et al., 1990, p. 17). Certainly, we could add that *all* of the Tribes components are based on this concept.

According to a recent review of the concept, "The term *learning community* has taken on a variety of meanings in the literature" (Roberts & Pruitt, 2003, p. 6). While the concept of learning communities is often used narrowly to refer to a distinctive type of learning community, such as the purposeful restructuring of the curriculum to link together courses or course work in higher education as conceived by Mickeljohn, we refer to the broader Deweyan definition which overlaps more this last decade with the work of Peter Senge (1990; Senge et al., 2000), who applied systems thinking to organizational development and did much, along with Michael Fullan, to bring the concept of "learning community" to the field of education.

The following are several leading thinkers' definitions of this concept. In *Improving Schools From Within,* Roland Barth (1990) describes a community of learners as "a place where students and adults alike are engaged as active learners in matters of special importance to them and where everyone is thereby encouraging everyone else's learning" (p. 9). In *Recreating Schools,* Myers and Simpson (1998) describe learning communities as "cultural settings in which everyone learns, in which every individual is an integral part, and in which every participant is responsible for both the learning and the overall well-being of everyone else" (p. 2). Marsha Speck (1999) defines a learning community as follows: "A school learning community is one that promotes and values learning as an ongoing, active collaborative process with dynamic dialogue by teachers, students, staff, principal, parents, and the school community to improve the quality of learning and life within the school" (p. 8). Cultural anthropologist Barbara Rogoff and her colleagues see a learning community as an approach in which "instruction builds on children's interests in a collaborative way, where learning activities are planned by children as well as adults, and where parents and teachers not only foster children's learning but also learn from their involvement with the children" (2001, p. 3). Lastly, Ernest Boyer (1995) writes that, "The school becomes a community for learning when it is a purposeful place; a communicative place, a just place, a disciplined place, a caring place, and a celebrative place" (pp. 17–18).

As you can see from the above definitions, a learning community is commonly defined in the literature by the presence of the following qualities: "respect, caring, inclusiveness, trust, empowerment, and commitment to its members and purpose" (Retallick, 1999, pp. 111–112). Dalton and Watson (1997) write that four keys exist for building a classroom learning community: fostering caring relationships, teaching humane values, honoring intrinsic motivation, and learning for understanding. Learning communities "try to establish conditions that promote coherence, community, and a sense of common purpose" (Gabelnick et al, 1990, p. 10). Alfie Kohn

(1996) explains the qualities of learning communities as follows: A learning community is "a place in which students feel cared about and are encouraged to care about each other. They experience a sense of being valued and respected; the children matter to one another and to the teacher. They have come to think in the plural; they feel connected to each other; they are part of an "us" (p. 101).

Thomas Sergiovanni (1994) shows that schools become productive learning communities as they become the following:

- **reflective communities** within which students (and teachers too) develop insight into their own strengths and weaknesses as learners, and use this information to call upon different strategies for learning;

- **developmental communities** within which it is acknowledged that students (and teachers too) develop at different rates, and at any given time are more ready to learn some things than others;

- **diverse communities** within which different talents and interests of students (and teachers too) are not only recognized, but acknowledged by decisions that are made about curriculum, teaching and assessment;

- **conversational communities** within which high priority is given to creating an active discourse that involves the exchange of values and ideas among students, among teachers, and between students and teachers as they learn together;

- **caring communities** within which students (and teachers too) learn not only to be kind to each other and to respect each other, but to help each other to grow as learners and as persons; and

- **responsible communities** within which students (and teachers too) come to view themselves as part of a social web of meanings and responsibilities which they feel a moral obligation to embody in their present behavior as students, and future behavior as citizens (1999, pp. 16–17).

As Tribes practitioners know and as we have and will discuss in this document, Tribes is a process that promotes reflection, development, diversity, conversation, caring, and responsibility—all in the context of community!

Research on effective schools and school reform finds that community is a vital component of successful schools and school change (Lieberman, 1992, 1994; McQuillan & Muncie, 1994; Newmann, Rutter, & Smith, 1989; Sizer, 1992; Newman & Wehlage, 1995). Several of the school reform models described in Chapter One, such as the Comer model and the Child Development Project of the Developmental Studies Center, have community-building at the heart of their approach (Battistich et al., 1998;). Furthermore, a cursory review of *An Educator's Guide to Schoolwide Reform* (American Institutes for Research, 1999) finds that creating community is a central component of the successful models. The case studies of successful schools cited in Chapter One (Ancess, 1995; Benard, 2003; Dalton & Watson, 1997; Day, 1994; Delpit, 1995; Diero, 1996, 2004; Haberman, 1995; Meier, 1995; Swadener & Lubeck, 1995; Watson, 2003) also have the creation of a learning community at the heart of their transformation. The Transforming Learning Communities Project, a statewide initiative of the Ohio Department of Education, found participating schools were able to create and sustain their reform efforts through a community-building process (Johnson et al., 2001). Jacqueline Ancess (2003) describes three public high schools that by becoming "communities of commitment" helped their students "beat the odds."

In *Among Friends: Classrooms Where Caring and Learning Prevail* (1997), Dalton and Watson argue that it is even more imperative in today's world that schools become learning communities:

> As other adults in children's lives have less time to spend with them and as neighborhoods operate less as communities where people know and help one another, we as teachers have begun to more deliberately provide children with the experience of membership in a community—their school and classroom community—and more focused in helping them acquire the skills for maintaining community (p. 5).

This call is echoed in most of the learning community literature, not to mention the research on social capital (Putnam, 2000). In her book on building "resilient community" in schools, Calderwood (2000) writes that, "The infusion of a sense of community is often suggested as a remedy when our institutions cannot effectively function as we desire. Resilient community is celebrated not only because it enhances our humanity but because many people believe that other worthy ends can be accomplished best in the presence of community. This longing for and celebration of community as a means to achieving important goals is pervasive in our schools" (p. 1). And rightly so, given not only the association with successful schools but also with positive student outcomes.

A body of research posits a strong positive relationship between student outcomes and their experience of community in the classroom and school (Ancess, 2000; Battistich et al., 1995; Blot & Calderwood, 1995; Bryk & Schneider, 2002; Bryk, Lee, & Holland, 1993; Coleman & Hoffer, 1987; Resnick et al., 1997; Sale & Springer, 2001). Especially notable here are the outcomes from the National Longitudinal Study of Adolescent Health mentioned earlier that found student connectedness to school (feeling cared about, respected, a sense of belonging and fairness, and feeling happy at school) was protective against every adolescent health risk behavior. Another validating large-scale evaluation was the Center for Substance Abuse Prevention's National Cross-Site Evaluation of High-Risk Youth Programs (Sale and Springer, 2001). This 5-year study of 48 sites found that, "Strong bonding with school and family show the greatest associations with reduced substance use for these youth at risk" (p. 7). Interestingly, school bonding or connectedness (youths' perceptions that school is a positive and rewarding environment in which they can succeed) was even more powerful a protective factor than family bonding. This bears testimony to yet another commonsensical pithy statement from Frank Smith (1998): "You learn in communities of people who do what you are expected to do" (p. 44).

Yet another study linking positive health and well-being *and* academic outcomes to the sense of community in the school environment is the Project on High Performing Learning Communities (Felner, 2000). This longitudinal study, involving more than 1,500 schools, 1 million students, and more than 60,000 teachers, builds on earlier work by Felner and colleagues (1988, 1993) that found that reorganizing high schools into small developmentally supportive communities (120 or less students) for all of their core academic subjects with a teacher-advisor resulted in declines of 40-50% or more in the school dropout rate (Felner and Adan, 1988).

The current Project expands on this work and has been concerned with answering the critical question: "How do we create educational contexts in which all children and youth are nurtured and challenged in ways that lead them to be highly effective learners, achieve and perform at high levels, and be healthy, responsible, and productive citizens in our democracy" (p. 283). Note this project, like Tribes TLC, focuses on the whole child, that is, on both human development and learning. Also, the comprehensive theoretical framework guiding this project very much matches the framework of Tribes. The main strategies used in this "developmentally-focused" school reform also parallel much of what is advocated in this document: small learning communities, a core academic program, high expectations for all students, empowering decision making for students, teachers, and administrators, professional development, fostering health and safety for all student and school community members, engaging families in the education of their students, and creating strong school-community and schoolwork linkages. The investigators so far have found that students who were in schools that had more fully implemented these strategies achieved at much higher levels than those in non-implemented schools and substantially better than those in partially implemented schools" (p. 291).

We can even make the case that a Tribes learning community actually constitutes an "authoritative community." This is a new public policy and social science term developed by the Commission on Children At Risk and promoted in a recent report, *Hardwired to Connect: The New Scientific Case for Authoritative Communities* (2003). This report makes the two-fold scientific case that humans are hardwired (1) to form close relationships with other people and (2) to search for meaning and purpose, the two major components of a community we discussed earlier. Meeting these needs for connection to people and purpose is the task of authoritative communities—"groups of people who are committed to one another over time and who model and pass on at least part of what it means to be a good person and live a good life" (2002, p. 14). The Commission claims, in a vein similar to most books on learning communities, that, "The weakening of authoritative communities in the U.S. is a principal reason—arguably the principal reason—why large and growing numbers of U.S. children are failing to flourish. As a result, strengthening these communities is likely to be our best strategy for improving the lives of our children, including those most at risk" (2003, p. 15). So let's now look at just what structures support classroom and school learning communities.

Community Circle/Community Agreements

The first step in creating a learning community, Tribes or another, is to use the structure of a *community circle* that meets on a regular basis, hopefully several times a day. The major task of the community circle is the creation of community norms or agreements that will govern the work of the larger learning community and later the work of the smaller Tribes learning communities. Both the Tribes community circle and the Tribes agreements have not only a long tradition but an ancient tradition in practice with a more recent research tradition documenting their effectiveness in promoting a positive school culture and positive student outcomes.

The circle is probably the most ancient symbol of the continuity of life. The sacred wheel of life and of the cycles of the seasons were all represented by the circle (Campbell et al., 1991). Circles have been part of human society for as long as we have existed. "The circle is an ancient and universal symbol for unity and wholeness. For many millennia human beings have met in tribal or village circles to tell stories, provide mutual support, and arrive at an understanding of the common good" (Garfield et al., 1998). In industrialized countries, the village circle often gave way to the kitchen table. Rachel Remen warns in her best-selling book, *Kitchen Table Wisdom* (1996), that even the kitchen table is giving way to forces of disconnection. She writes the following:

> The less time we spend together at the kitchen table, the more how-to books appear in the stores and on our bookshelves. But reading such books is a very different thing than listening to someone's lived experience. Because we have stopped listening to each other we may even have forgotten how to listen, stopped learning how to recognize meaning and fill ourselves from the ordinary events of our lives. We have become solitary; readers and watchers rather than sharers and participants (p. xxvi).

It, thus, comes as no surprise that, just as researchers have come to the conclusion that community is what we all need, that it truly does "take a village to raise a child," we are now witnessing a burgeoning of "circle" movements.

For example, we have informal "wisdom circles," that are being formed in communities all over the Western World that bring people "together in small groups that share the same goal: the creation of a compassionate community that values the wisdom and the welfare of all its members" (Garfield et al., 1998, p. 7). The Asset-Based Community Development Institute headed by John Kretzmann and John McKnight (1993) recently created a "Neighborhood Circle Project" with 17 demonstration sites in nine states. We have a Canadian community development effort formed around "community action circles," an informal collaborative way of developing strong networks that in turn develop strong communities and positive social action (www.nfhs-pg.org). We have *Utne Reader*'s "salons" that bring people together in neighborhood groups based on social issues. We also have community "study circles" organized around concerns such as racism (Mengual, 2003) and school improvement (Pan & Mutchler, 2000).

An exciting development over the decade has been the restorative justice movement that seeks to move the criminal justice system from a retributive to a healing paradigm. "Sentencing circles, " often referred to as "peace-making circles" use traditional circle ritual and structure to involve the victim, victim supporters, the offender, offender supporters, judge and court personnel, prosecutor, defense counsel, police, and all interested community members. "Within the circle, people can speak from the heart in a shared search for understanding of the event, and together identify the steps necessary to assist in healing all affected parties and prevent future crimes. (*Restorative Justice Fact Sheet,* www.ojp.usdoj.gov). Kay Pranis, one of the leading proponents of this circle process in the U.S., writes in her new book, *Peacemaking Circles: From Crime to Community* (Pranis et al., 2003) that the circle process builds an intentionally safe space where we can bring our best selves to some of our most difficult conversations. One study conducted in Canada (where this process has been used more extensively) found that fewer offenders who had gone through the circle recidivated than offenders who were processed by standard criminal justice practices (*Restorative Justice Fact Sheet,* www.ojp.usdoj.gov).

For the last ten years, the Study Circle Resource Center (www.studycircles.org) has worked to help individuals and communities across the United States use the model to create a "deliberative democracy" in this country (SCRC, 2000). Study circles, however, are over a hundred years old, emerging by that name in the late nineteenth century through the Chautauqua adult education movement which attracted thousands of Americans to participate in voluntary, participatory, small-group meetings in their neighbors' homes to learn about and discuss social, economic, and political issues. According to an evaluation of this process, community-wide study circles can result in changes that range from individual learning to small-group action, organizational change, community-wide initiative, and public policy change (Pan & Mutchler, 2000). The Southwest Educational Development Laboratory (SEDL), in collaboration with several universities and civic groups conducted a study of the use of study circles to bring policymakers and the public together around issues of public education, specifically around broadening input in decisionmaking, increasing support for public education, and promoting community and school partnerships (Pan & Mutchler, 2000).

The community circle structure was a key component of the High/Scope Educational Research Foundation's Perry Preschool Program (PPP) (Schweinhart & Weikart, 1997; Schweinhart et al., 1993). As we mentioned in Chapter One, this is one of the only *longitudinal* (participants are now approaching mid-life) evaluations of a preventive intervention. This study found positive personal, social, and economic outcomes not only for late adolescents but also for *adults* that had been part of a preschool program based on active participation and child-initiated learning and referred to as the "plan, do, review" process, a process bearing a strong resemblance to Tribes TLC. The PPP preschoolers began every morning with a community circle in which they planned their morning. They then went off in small groups to pursue the activity/ies they had planned. They then closed each morning with another community circle in which they reviewed or reflected on what they had planned for and done that day.

Clearly, there is an undeniable power in the structure and shape of a circle. It offers the hope of belonging and community in which each person is invited, known, and heard. It offers the possibility of meeting our basic human needs for safety, love/belonging, respect, challenge, autonomy, and meaning. It offers the promise of providing the critical protective factors of caring relationships, positive expectation messages, and meaningful participation and of creating the ideal culture for learning: communal, participatory, proactive, collaborative, and constructive. Turning hope, possibility, and promise into reality requires that the circle create shared expectations/norms for behavior.

■ **Honoring the community agreements is the sine qua non practice for creating a caring culture and a community of learners**

TRIBES AGREEMENTS

- **Attentive listening** To pay close attention to one another's expression of ideas, opinions and feelings; to check for understanding; and to let others know that they have been heard.

- **Appreciation/No put-downs** To treat others kindly; to state appreciation for unique qualities, gifts, skills and contributions; to avoid negative remarks, name-calling, hurtful gestures and behaviors.

- **Right to pass** To have the right to choose when and to what extent one will participate in a group activity; to observe quietly if not participating actively; and to choose whether to offer observations later to a group when invited to do so.

- **Mutual respect** To affirm the value and uniqueness of each person; to recognize and appreciate individual and cultural differences; and offer feedback that encourages growth (Gibbs, 2001b, p. 74).

The glue that holds the community circle together is a set of shared norms such as the Tribes Agreements. According to the gurus of group process, Richard and Patricia Schmuck (their book *Group Processes in the Classroom* is now in its eighth edition), "Norms are shared expectations for how the participants of a classroom should perceive, think, feel, and behave" (2001, p. 213). This is almost a direct match for how Jeanne Gibbs defines the Tribes agreements: "Tribes agreements are positive and relational, defining how people want to relate to and treat each other" (2001a, p. 119). "Agreeing to core values that describe ways of relating to others as a community of learners" is an essential community ritual, along with opening and closing of the circle (Collay et al., 1998, p. 9).

As we will see with the study of groups, the study of norms have a rich century-old heritage in the field of sociology beginning with the work of the early sociologist William Graham Summer in his classic study, *Folkways* (1906). William Whyte (1943) and Robert Angell (1958) conducted some of the classical studies of norms in the mid-twentieth century. More recently Seymour Sarason (1971, 1990) is credited by Schmuck and Schmuck (2001) with doing "the best normative analysis of schools" (p. 222). Sarason pioneered the study of school culture, seeing school primarily as a "social situation." He advocated the importance of identifying both the systemic *regularities* or norms and the *universe of alternatives* to the existing patterns.

While norms are usually "implicit group agreements that guide the psychological and behavioral processes of classmates," according to Schmuck and Schmuck, "teachers should attempt to establish *explicit* group agreements in the peer group that support individual diversity and uniqueness" (p. 196). They should strive for such supportive agreements not only because they have value in themselves, but also because individuals' learning of academic subject matter tends to progress with less anxiety when they feel supported by their peers" (2001, pp. 196, 198). "In general, classroom life, and in particular, academic learning, will tend to go better when the norms of the peer group support cooperation, helpfulness, supportiveness, and inter-personal empathy" (2001, p. 208). These can be restated as inclusion, influence, and community. In fact, Ginsberg and Wlodkowski (2000) have found that establishing classroom and/or schoolwide agreements is essential for creating culturally inclusive classrooms and schools. Moreover, Michael Rutter's (1979) now classic study of high-performing high-poverty schools found that shared school norms was a characteristic of the schools with high levels of student motivation and learning.

Because "class norms play a large role in determining whether students will work together effectively," Schmuck and Schmuck's research has found that, "The most important time for affecting classroom norms is during the first two weeks of school" (p. 205). Having mutually shared positive expectations and norms for behavior is one of the three protective factors we discussed in Chapter Two that meet students' needs for safety—both physical and social-emotional (Ridley & Walther, 1995). Without establishing safety early on, learning cannot take place. That is why creating the Agreements is the first task of a Tribes learning community.

The most important principle to remember in creating shared norms, is that, "Norms will truly change only after all students understand and are motivated to go along with the new norms" (p. 205). Not only the Schmucks' research but resilience research (Benard, 2004), research on successful change efforts (Fullan, 1993, 1999), and research on human motivation (Covington & Dray, 2002; Deci. 1995; Kohn, 1993a; McCombs & Pope, 1994; Ridley & Walther, 1995; Ryan & Deci, 2000; Stipek, 2002; Wigfield & Eccles, 2002) has found that, student *participation* is the way to achieve that condition," of intrinsic motivation (Schmuck & Schmuck, 2001, p. 206). "By helping a class to form its own group agreements, teachers are seeking the students' commitment to the agreements. Instead of mere compliance to rules, teachers hope that their students will internalize the group agreements" (p. 206).

Norms are made explicit through the participatory structure of a class meeting, preferably in a circle such as Tribes. "Since sharedness is the essence of normativeness, the teacher who wishes to modify behavioral norms must hold discussions with the entire class" (Schmuck & Schmuck, 2001, p. 202). According to these experts' summary of the research, "The most significant thing to be done about behavioral norms is to work toward establishing a norm of reciprocity supported by a dispersed friendship structure within the peer group. Each class should strive to avoid some students feeling like outcasts" (p. 202). This is exactly what the Tribes Agreements of listening, appreciation/ no put downs, right to pass, and mutual respect accomplish. The agreements set the stage for building the Tribes process of inclusion, influence, and community.

Other researchers have used different terms to refer to classroom agreements. For example, Seymour Sarason writes eloquently and passionately about the need for creating a "classroom constitution" *with* students, not for students. His research team studied elementary school classrooms with the purpose of finding out who "forged" the classroom constitution (1990). They asked, "What were the rules and regulations that governed the classroom and how were they arrived at?" (p. 82). He writes about what they found:

> The answer [to who wrote the constitution of the classroom]—to which there was no exception—was that the teachers wrote the constitution. They articulated the rules and regulations (frequently post hoc) but provided no rationale. There was absolutely no discussion about the rationale.... It never

occurred to these teachers, who by conventional standards were very good, that students should be provided with a rationale, which deserved extended discussion, and that students should have the opportunity to voice opinions. How should we live together and why? ... In these matters it was as if teachers had no respect for the needs and opinions of students. Students were and should be powerless in these matters. Their time would come when they "grew up" (p. 82).

Sarason asks us to consider the following questions: "How do you grow up in or to a role in which you are denied experience or access? When do you start?...When should students begin to experience the nature and dilemmas of power in group living?" (p. 83). The answer he suggests is that teachers "accord students the right *and* the responsibility to participate in forums where the constitution of the classroom is forged. The classroom should be a place where those in it come to feel that they will be governed by rules and values they have had an opportunity to discuss.... The goal is to instill in students an understanding of a commitment to the classroom constitution, a sense of ownership, and an awareness that their opinions will be respected" (pp. 85–86).

    In their case study of a successful participatory learning community of parents, teachers, and students, Barbara Rogoff and her colleagues (2001) write that the foundational step is creating the class constitution. They describe theirs as follows:

- We all value safety, both emotional and physical, in order to foster a classroom where children feel comfortable to be themselves, to ask questions, and to make mistakes and learn from them.

- We all value trust and want to be in a learning environment where children trust parents and teachers and where both parents and teachers trust not only the children but also each other.

- We all value mutual respect, which develops as the community recognizes each person as a unique and worthwhile individual.

- We all value honesty, caring, thoughtfulness, and responsible behavior that fosters learning and friendships (pp. 99–100).

The Tribes Agreements actually operationalize this constitution, providing behavioral norms for living this constitution.

Similarly, Collay and her colleagues write in *Learning Circles* (1998) that, "One of the first critical processes to initiate community is the development of a *covenant*" (p. 20). They state that, "What sets covenant development apart from a single activity is the teacher's belief in the role of the students as members or citizens, rather than consumers of information" (p. 20). They suggest using the following questions as guidelines for developing a learning covenant: "What will build community? What will tear it down? What will support learning? What will get in the way of learning?" (p. 21). This discussion inevitably produces some form of the Tribes Agreements.

Thomas Sergiovanni, the leading scholar of school leadership for community, also speaks to the concept of covenant as well (1994, 1996, 1999, 2000). He writes the following:

> Compacts and shared commitments among principals, parents, teachers, and students, and the moral authority they provide, are key in applying community theory to schools. …Instead of thinking about bureaucratic management and personal leadership as the driving forces that push and pull the school and its members forward, moral voice helps us think of leadership more as the cultivation of a shared followership. Community members are bonded together as they are bound to share commitments in a covenantal relationship (1996, p. 58).

He also differentiates the concept of social covenant from that of social contract, the latter, unfortunately, being the traditional approach to school management, one governed by extrinsic motivators that "offer incentives in exchange for compliance" (1999, p. 10). A social covenant flows from a developmental paradigm that believes in the innate capacity of human beings for good; in contrast, a social contract is grounded in the control paradigm, believing that human beings left to their own devices are basically evil. He quotes Sacks (1997) who argued that "a social contract is maintained by the promise of gain or the threat of external force. A social covenant is maintained by loyalty, fidelity, kinship, sense of identity, obligation, duty, responsibility, and reciprocity" (1999, p. 11). The Tribes Community Agreements, in essence, make behaviorally explicit the covenant or shared mission that binds together a Tribes classroom and school learning community into an environment that can indeed "assure the healthy development of every child so that each has the knowledge, competency and resilience to be successful in a rapidly changing world" (Gibbs, 2001a, p. 18).

Several of the whole school reform models establish community agreements or covenants (American Institutes of Research, 1999). Most notable in this arena are the Child Development Project discussed earlier, Expeditionary Learning Outward Bound, and Accelerated Learning. Child Development Project authors write that, "Helping children establish class norms" is a vital first step in creating "a caring learning environment that fosters and depends on children's intrinsic motivation rather than our external coercion" (Dalton & Watson, 1997). In fact, these shared classroom norms provide the basis for what this scientifically validated approach refers to as "developmental discipline" (Watson, 2003) and what we have here called "restorative justice."

Sharing many components with Tribes, Expeditionary Learning Outward Bound (ELOB) is a comprehensive school design rated as "promising" on research validation by the American Institutes of Research, with studies having found improved student achievement across subjects as well as significant gains in standardized test scores for students (1999, p. 68). ELOB is based on two central ideas: that students learn better by doing than listening and that developing character, high expectations, and a sense of community is as important as developing academic skills and knowledge" (American Institutes of Research, 1999, p. 67). Critical to creating a sense of community is student participation not only in at least daily community meetings but also in creating classroom norms that "reflect and reinforce the school's code of conduct and character" which consist of "courtesy, respect for others, and a commitment to learning" (Expeditionary Learning Outward Bound, 2003, p. 37).

Also sharing many research-based components with Tribes is the Accelerated Schools comprehensive design (now in over 1,000 elementary and middle schools) which seeks to accelerate rather than slow down the learning of children at risk of school failure. Accelerated Schools seek to (1) create a new, supportive school culture that sets high expectations for teachers and students; (2) institute a governance structure characterized by broad staff participation in decision making and by procedures for taking stock of the school's strengths and problems and for generating solutions; and (3) introduce a "powerful learning" approach to curriculum and instruction that is more challenging, interactive, project-based, and relevant for students than traditional approaches. The lead developer, Henry Levin, emphasizes the building of a participatory community based on a shared vision or "community of mind" which is lived through shared and explicit community expectations. He and his colleagues write that, "Teachers who carefully plan the classroom environment with their students at the beginning of the year are often most successful in terms of student learning. Building on strengths and empowerment coupled with responsibility can mean involving the students in setting the routines and boundaries of the classroom and setting up a supportive environment that leads to learning gains for the rest of the year" (Hopfenberg et al., 1993, p. 263). An evaluation conducted by Manpower Demonstration Research Corporation of eight schools nationwide found that this model "improved academic achievement in a group of mostly 'at-risk' students" although the "positive impacts took four to five years to emerge" (Bloom et al., 2001).

Gibbs writes, "The responsibility to honor and to monitor the agreements is systematically transferred from the teacher to the students who work in small permanent-membership cooperative learning groups of 4–5 students called 'tribes' (2003, p. 23). If community agreements are indeed the glue holding a classroom learning community together, cooperative learning or small group learning provides the scaffolding that makes community possible. As we will see in the next section, small groups become the "families" or "tribes," which constitute a healthy learning community.

Cooperative Small Group Learning

■ Quality cooperative learning is democracy and resilience in action—and creates a community of learners

Institutionalizing a culture of caring happens in the Tribes process by the structuring of community in small learning groups—of students, of teachers, of support staff, of administrators, and of parents throughout the school. The Tribes TLC process truly manifests Jerome Bruner's vision of what the ideal learning culture looks like. He writes that schools and preschools can serve "a renewed function within our changing societies" *if* we can do the following:

This entails building school cultures that operate as mutual communities of learners, involved jointly in solving problems with all contributing to the process of educating one another. Such groups provide not only a locus for instruction, but a focus for identity and mutual work. Let these schools be a place for the praxis (rather than the proclamation) of cultural mutuality— which means an increase in the awareness that children have of what they are doing, how they are doing it, and why. The balance between individuality and group effectiveness gets worked out within the culture of the group; so too the balancing of ethnic or racial identities and the sense of the larger community of which they are a part. And since school cultures of mutual learners naturally form a division of labor within them, the balance between cultivating native talent and enabling all to move ahead gets expressed internally in the group in the more humane form of "from each according to his or her ability." In such school cultures... being good at something implies, among other things, helping others get better at that something (1996, pp. 81–82).

This lengthy quote really captures the systemic, transactional nature of cooperative small group learning. Not only does cooperative small group learning impact students; it also further creates a caring culture with school staff, parents, and other school-related groups which, in turn, supports cooperative learning and so on. As Gibbs explains, "The Tribes Learning Community process not only fosters development and learning for [students] but establishes a culture of caring and support, active participation, and high expectations for all groups of the school" (Gibbs, 2003, p. 112). In other words, cooperative leaning through the Tribes TLC process provides all three of the critical protective factors that humans need to support healthy development and learning—caring relationships, positive expectation messages, and opportunities for participation and contribution.

Cooperative learning is commonly defined as "the instructional use of small groups so that students work together to maximize their own and each other's learning" (Johnson et al., 1994b). It is considered a form of collaborative learning that also encompasses a variety of group learning experiences, such as peer tutoring, student-teacher research projects, learning communities, and so on. Because the Tribes

TLC process applies the best practices of *group process,* the research highlighted in this section supports cooperative small group learning, going beyond cooperative learning research to include that on small groups as well.

The research literature on cooperation and competition has a long and rich history. One research brief credits Norman Triplett's research (1897) as the beginning of the study of cooperation (this study is also considered the first in the field of social psychology) (Scheer, 1997). He found that children and adults perform better when involved simultaneously with others rather than on their own. However, once again, John Dewey (1916) is credited as being the educator and philosopher who developed cooperative school communities in highly social interactive settings, which, as discussed earlier, he considered essential for developing students morally and vocationally.

Among the other pioneering researchers was Kurt Lewin who in the 1930s and 1940s studied the effects of social climate (autocratic versus democratic cooperative) on students' interactions. He and his colleagues (1939) found that "after just half an hour [in an autocratic classroom], a group of boys had been transformed from being friendly, cooperative, open, and full of life to being apathetic and lacking initiative" (Scheer, 1997, p. 1). A graduate student of Kurt Lewin, Morton Deutsch (1949) "systematically examined cooperation and competition in group processes, finding that cooperative groups displayed more coordinated efforts, more division of labor, more acceptance of others ideas, and fewer communication difficulties than competitive groups" (Scheer, 1997, p. 1). Overlapping Deutsch's work in the 1960s and 1970s and continuing to this day, David Johnson and Roger Johnson (1989) have been the major researchers of cooperative group processes. Robert Slavin (1990, 1996), Spencer Kagan (1992), Schlomo and Yuael Sharon (1990, 1992), Elliot Aronson (1978, 2000), and Elizabeth Cohen (1994) are other prominent names in the cooperative learning research tradition.

In contrast to most other educational interventions or pedagogies, cooperative learning has amassed an enormous body of research support. Estimates of the number of research studies demonstrating cooperative learning's effectiveness range anywhere from "hundreds of studies" (Slavin, 1996) to over 550 studies (Johnson & Johnson, 1989) to "over a thousand" (International Association for Study of Cooperation in Education). In this section, we will first look broadly at the research rationale for small groups of peers learning cooperatively together, next at the outcomes for students of using a cooperative learning/small group approach, and last at what research has identified as the major components of successful cooperative learning groups.

■ The Case for Small Group Learning

#1: WE ARE WIRED TO COOPERATE

"Call it a clan, call it a network, call it a tribe, call it a family. Whatever you call it, whoever you are, you need one" (Jane Howard, journalist/writer, *Quote of the Week* in PEN NewsBlast, www.PublicEducation.org, date unknown). This quote says so well what scientists have recently documented. According to research published in the July 2002 issue of *Neuron*, cooperation is a pleasurable, biologically-based activity. "Cooperating with others, it appears, activates the brain's reward circuitry and makes us feel good" (*Harvard Women's Health Watch*, 2002, p. 6). In the first study of its kind, scientists at Emory University used functional magnetic resonance imaging (fMRI) to observe the brains of women playing the "Prisoner's Dilemma" game, an exercise long used by social psychologists in the study of cooperation. When the women chose cooperation over competition, according to a *New York Times* article (Angier, July 23, 2002), their brains lit "up with quiet joy." And, "The longer the women engaged in a cooperative strategy, the more strongly flowed the blood to the pathways of pleasure" (Angier, July 23, 2002, p. 1). According to the researchers, "From past results, one can assume that neuro-imaging studies of men playing the game would be similar to [our] new findings with women" (Angier, July 23, 2002, p. 3).

While evolutionary biologists long ago explained the evolution of competitive behavior, they have been confused by the human capacity for altruism, forgoing immediate personal gain for the long-term common good—in spite of a long history even in the biological sciences for the rationale that even animals are cooperative. Although the commonsense answer, and one offered by anthropologists, is that cooperation serves a survival purpose, "It may be that cooperative behavior has genetic and sociocultural roots. Both can influence brain pathways" (*Harvard Women's Health Watch*, November 2002, p. 6). As we will discuss shortly, this conclusion is a long-time-coming as scientists have nearly unifocally studied only the "darker side" of human nature until the last decade or so.

This study is also reinforced by what is considered a landmark UCLA study by stress researchers Shelley Taylor and Laura Klein. They concluded that *tend-and-befriend* is as much a survival response to stress as the two long recognized stress responses, fight-or-flight (Taylor et al., 2000). "Tending involves nurturant activities designed to protect the self and offspring that promote safety and reduce distress; befriending is the creation and maintenance of social networks that may aid in this process" (Taylor et al., 2000, p. 745). Their hypothesis is that this is a biologically-based stress response unique to women. However, given what we have discussed in terms of the power of culture and environment on biology, further study may find this gender difference unsubstantiated. The difficulty in future research of this previously unexplored stress regulatory system in males is that most cultures award the "warrior" role to males.

Cooperation grows from our basic needs for love and belonging, both of which have evolutionary roots. Evolution theorist David Loye writes in his book *Darwin's Lost Theory of Love* (2000) that Darwin himself argued that factors other than random variation and natural selection come into play at the human level of evolution, specifically "the moral sense" and "mutual aid." According to Riane Eisler's discussion of love and evolution in her book *Tomorrow's Children* (2000), "This human yearning for caring connection—the yearning of both young and old for love—is built into our species.... By the grace of evolution, we are provided with chemical rewards of pleasure not only when we are loved but when we love.... It is one of our most basic human drives. It is so basic that the deprivation of empathic love—an early environment where what love we get is linked with insensitivity, neglect, coercion, abuse, and/or violence—has been shown to severely damage, even cripple, our development" (p. 86). She goes on to explain that, "For this reason we humans need a *partnership* rather than a dominator social organization to realize our evolutionary potentials" (2000, pp. 86–87). The partnership model for education she proposes in this book maps well to all the Tribes components.

Thomas Lewis and his colleagues make a similar case for the biological basis for love in *A General Theory of Love* (2000). They assert that humans have the capacity to detect the emotional state of another person and align with it, an attribute often called empathy, bonding, or connection. They refer to this as a process of "limbic resonance," in which one person's limbic brain exchanges information with that of another. We are driven by our biology to make this emotional connection with others—emotional contact is a biological process. In an interview, Dr. Lewis states that, "About the only thing that truly makes people happy is spending time with people they are emotionally close with" (Ellis, 2001, p. 51).

In examining the need for belonging as a driving force for human cooperation, Roy Baumeister and Mark Leary's (1995) research is truly a beacon of light. They bring an empirical research base to earlier hypothesizing by Abraham Maslow (1968) that love and belonging were basic human needs (1968) and to John Bowlby's (1969) attachment theory. They even provide evidence that the need for belonging—which has been far less studied than other needs such as power, achievement, intimacy, and approval—may drive these other needs. "We suggest that belongingness can be almost as compelling a need as food and that human culture is significantly conditioned by the pressure to provide belongingness" (1995, p. 498). Reminiscent of the statement by Thomas Lewis above, they see the need to belong as "something other than a need for mere affiliation; …rather, the need is for regular social contact with those to whom one feels connected" (pp. 500–501). They also state that, "It appears that only bonds marked by positive concern and caring offer satisfaction" for the need to belong (p. 513). According to these researchers, "From an evolutionary perspective, relationships characterized by both of these features would have greater survival and reproductive value than would relationships characterized by only one" (p. 501). So we can add survival and reproductive value to the other benefits of Tribes TLC!

This innate need for belonging is manifested universally in evolution by the presence of the small group. They cite research suggesting that the brain and small group even evolved and adapted together with multiple interrelationships. Barchas (1986) has asserted that "over the course of evolution, the small group became the basic survival strategy developed by the human species" (p. 212). This research, in turn, takes us back to the evolutionary argument for cooperation. Groups cooperate to overcome stress or threat and to gain resources that individuals cannot obtain alone. And, "more generally, helping appears to be increased by the existence of social bonds" (p. 519). In a feed back loop ensuring human survival, belongingness leads to cooperation and cooperation leads to belongingness.

Baumeister and Leary's comprehensive review of "The Need to Belong" provides hundreds of studies linking the need to belong and learning (i.e., "cognitive processes"), emotional patterns, behavioral responses, and health and well-being. They write that, "The desire for interpersonal attachment may well be one of the most far-reaching and integrative constructs currently available to understand human nature" (p. 522). If their conclusion from this review of hundreds of empirical studies is right, offering children and adults in schools the opportunity to belong to a group characterized by positive concern and caring—sounds like a Tribe!—is to enhance not only their academic, social, and emotional learning but is also serving to prevent both behavioral and health problems and to connect them at a moral and spiritual level. In fact, structuring classrooms and schools in small groups could play an even greater part in ensuring the survival not only of humans but of life itself. Ashley Montagu's plea for cooperation, written in 1952 in his book, *Darwin, Competition, and Cooperation,* remains ever relevant today:

> In so far as man is concerned, if competition, in its aggressive combative sense, ever had any adaptive value among men, which is greatly to be doubted, it is quite clear that it has no adaptive value whatever in the modern world.... Perhaps never before in the history of man has there been so high a premium upon the adaptive value of cooperative behavior (p. 72).

While the body of research supporting cooperation, love, and belonging keeps growing, the paradigm of competition has a tenacious stranglehold on our society. This paradigm is based on a skewed view of human nature as basically selfish and aggressive, on the ideas of the "survival of the fittest," a view that we mentioned earlier even Darwin himself criticized. The field of developmental education must be forever grateful for the tireless research of writer Alfie Kohn whose many books summarize comprehensively and beautifully the argument not only against this paradigm but for the developmental paradigm that honors the innate developmental wisdom/intrinsic motivation that guides human behavior towards community, health and well-being. His passionate and well-researched book, *The Case Against Competition* (1986), not only argues against competition but in the process makes a well-articulated case *for* cooperation.

While this eye-opening, paradigm-shifting book was written nearly two decades ago now, the competitive paradigm is alive and flourishing in our schools—perhaps even more so than in the 1980s. He was certainly right when he wrote, competitive individualism "is the common denominator of American life" (p. 1). It is so embedded in our society that we do not even realize its presence. As George Lakoff, University of California cognitive scientist and linguist writes in his new book, *Moral Politics* (2002), this paradigm underlies the "self-interest" values of conservative as opposed to the "common good" or social justice values of progressive politics, applying to our education paradigms as well. It certainly argues against social change that empowers the masses as opposed to the few at the top of the "survival" chain.

Kohn continues his argument in *The Brighter Side of Human Nature: Altruism and Empathy in Everyday Life* (1990), providing us with even more research support for humans being hard-wired for cooperation, altruism, and empathy. He documents how science itself has been dominated by the view of human nature as selfish and aggressively competitive until fairly recently. According to Kohn, "It should not be surprising, in light of this society's widely shared assumptions about human nature, that helping, caring, rescuing, and sharing were not systematically studied until the mid- to late-1960s—and even then were investigated chiefly so that we might understand the reasons for their absence" (p. 63). We could even safely say that the actual questioning of this paradigm itself, which we have earlier referred to as deficit-based, did not occur on a larger scale until almost the 1990s with the growing understanding of resilience research and the positive psychology movement. Tribes practitioners looking for a wealth of information lending research support not only to cooperation but to nearly all of the Tribes research components will be abundantly rewarded in all of Alfie Kohn's prolific works.

#2: ALL LEARNING IS SOCIAL—OR PEERS DO MATTER!

The idea that social interaction is important—and even necessary—for learning is usually credited to Lev Vygotsky (1978), the developmental psychologist often considered the founding father of social constructivism. "Although Piaget acknowledged the role of social experience in intellectual growth, Vygotsky is the developmental psychologist who has placed most emphasis on the essentially social nature of individual thinking processes" (Cowie et al., 1993, p. 44). Vygotsky proposed that children learn through joint interactions with adults and more capable peers. Cultural anthropologist Barbara Rogoff refers to this as an "apprenticeship" approach, stating that, "Cognitive development occurs as new generations collaborate with older generations in varying forms of interpersonal engagement and institutional practices" (Santrock, 2001, p. 112). Tribes fits nicely into this definition as a social constructivist approach, sharing many similarities with Ann Brown's (1997) *Fostering A Community of Learners* program which is considered an exemplar of this approach, having been successful in improving both children's literacy skills and domain subject matter knowledge.

In a recent review of educational "alternatives," Ron Miller (2004), the leading authority on alternative and holistic schooling, explains social constructivism as follows:

> Learning is a *social* endeavor, requiring meaningful interaction between and among persons within an environment that deliberately encourages collaboration, inquiry, and creative problem solving. For educators holding this view, knowledge is neither entirely objective (out in the world) nor entirely subjective (relevant only to the individual's interests); rather, it is dynamically *constructed* through the relationship between and among persons and their social and physical environment (p. 23).

According to Miller, "Social constructivism underlies approaches such as cooperative learning and whole language instruction" as well as project-based learning and even progressive education itself (p. 23). He cites the early childhood Reggio schools in Reggio Emilia, Italy as the premier success story of this approach. "The Reggio schools have inspired thousands of educators around the world with their emphasis on young children's innate creative abilities and the importance of developing a collaborative and supportive learning community. These schools encourage children to engage in extensive projects that reflect their interests, and the teachers help them to work together and find meaning in their activities" (Miller, 2004, p. 23). This last sentence really captures the three protective factors as well as the essence of what a Tribes community does: caring and encouraging relationships between teacher and student and student-to-student, positive expectations for learning based on a child's interests, and active participation through projects that mean something to the child.

The theory goes as follows: On cooperative projects children are exposed to their peers' thinking process; this method not only makes the learning outcome available to all students, but also makes other students' thinking processes available to all. Other researchers (Woolfolk et al., 2002) have found that children can accomplish mental tasks with social support before they can do them alone. Thus cooperative learning provides the social support and scaffolding that students need to move learning forward. Said more poetically by Peter Brock, a leading voice in the field of transformational management, "All learning is social. It is with our peers that we will ultimately find our voice and change our world. It is in community that our lives are transformed. Small groups can change the world" (Sparks, 2004, p. 5).

In essence, this social constructivist, or developmental, perspective argues that peer interaction itself leads to improved academic achievement and other student outcomes. William Damon (1984), one of the leading proponents of peer collaboration proposes the following "conceptual foundation for a peer-based plan of education:"

1. Through mutual feedback and debate, peers motivate one another to abandon misconceptions and search for better solutions.

2. The experience of peer communication can help a child master social processes, such as participation and argumentation, and cognitive processes, such as verification and criticism.

3. Collaboration between peers can provide a forum for discover learning and can encourage creative thinking.

4. Peer interaction can introduce children to the process of generating ideas (p. 335).

Damon and Phelps (1989) even found in their two-year study that, "Gains were made with virtually no instruction from adults other than the initial instructions to work together toward correct solutions.... The children managed their own interactions, invented their own problem-solving procedures, and discovered their own solutions" (1989, p. 151).

The case for learning as a social endeavor is essentially the case for the peer group as a significant influence on learning and development. According to Hartup (1993), "Considerable evidence now shows that peer relations contribute substantially to both social and cognitive development, and to the effectiveness with which we function as adults. Indeed, the best early predictor of adult adaptation is not IQ, or school grades, or classroom behavior but rather the adequacy with which children and adolescents get along with their contemporaries" (p. 3; Parker & Ash, 1987). Peer groups provide young people with the opportunity to fulfill both the task of individual autonomy as well social competence and belonging. "On the one hand, peers provide the young person with the opportunity to see himself or herself as distinct from others. On the other hand, the peer world affords membership in groups, cultures, and ultimately the greater society" (McClellan & Pugh, 1999, p. 2).

Following in the tradition of Erik Erikson's theory on adolescent development (1968), the last fifteen years has seen much new research on the role of peers in adolescent social identity formation (Brown, B., 1990; McClellan et al., 1999; Pugh & Hart, 1999; Youniss & Smollar, 1985; Youniss & Yates, 1997). It is an accepted fact now that, "Peer relations are an essential component of adolescent identity development" and that, "Peer groups are important because identity is constructed within relationships" (Pugh & Hart, 1999, p. 55). Quoting Piaget (1939/1965, p. 393) as succinctly describing this process, Pugh and Hart write that, "In order to discover oneself as a particular individual, what is needed is a continuous comparison, the outcome of opposition, of discussion, and of mutual control." This kind of comparison, according to Piaget's thinking, "can only occur among peers because one can have true discussions and mutual control only among equals such as peers" (Pugh & Hart, 199, p. 56). Furthermore, "Interactions with peers who have similar and divergent values allow for examination of personal values and beliefs, and they provide a forum for individuals of equal status to discuss who they are and who they want to be within a supportive environment" (p. 56). Structuring small groups of peers such as a Tribe, provides this "supportive environment" essential for healthy adolescent identity formation and social development.

The most powerful research-based argument for the power of peer groups in socialization comes from Judith Rich Harris (1995, 1998) who substantiates her theory of "group socialization" with at least 500 studies drawn from behavioral genetics, sociological investigations of intra- and intergroup processes, psychological research showing that learning is highly context-specific, and from evolutionary science. According to Harris, "Intra- and intergroup processes, not dyadic relationships, are responsible for the transmission of culture and for environmental modification of children's personality characteristics. The universality of children's groups explains why development is not derailed by the wide variations in parental behavior found within and between societies" (1995, p. 458). She further explains, "The group is the natural environment of the child.... Think of childhood as the time when young humans turn themselves into accepted and valued members of their group, because that is what they needed to do in ancestral times.... Children identify with a group of others like themselves and take on the norms of the group. They don't identify with their parents because parents are not people like themselves—parents are grownups" (1998, pp. 357–358).

Her research created quite a storm because she challenged a long-held unques-tioned assumption few scientists have dared to challenge: the primacy of the family on human developmental outcomes. While few have linked her research to resilience research, they both provide powerful validation for each other in that both prove "that events taking place outside the family can have a potent effect on children's lives" (Harris, 1995, p. 481) and that "despite vast differences in the way their parents treat them, most children turn out all right" (Harris, 1995, p. 483). Harris' well-doc-umented research-based argument provides Tribes practitioners with yet another powerful body of research to support the basic restructuring of learning into small cooperative peer learning groups. In fact, her closing words in her seminal article might make a good Tribes motto: "There is an African saying, 'It takes a village to raise a child.' In a village, there are always enough children to form a group"(p. 483).

#3: SMALL LEARNING GROUPS PROVIDE OPPORTUNITIES FOR
ALL STUDENTS TO DEVELOP CARING RELATIONSHIPS WITH EACH
OTHER AND TO PARTICIPATE AND CONTRIBUTE AS PEER LEADERS
In Chapter Two we discussed caring relationships and having opportunities for meaningful participation and contribution as two of the three critical protective fac-tors essential in engaging intrinsic motivation for learning and promoting positive

youth development. They are especially essential for promoting the personal characteristics associated with life success: social competence, problem solving, autonomy,
and sense of purpose and future.

Creating classrooms and schools where students are a caring community requires
that schools and classrooms make use of a number of small-group processes. These
approaches, which allow students to practice the values of caring communities,
include cooperative learning, peer tutoring, cross-age tutoring, service learning, conflict mediation, and peer support programs. In such student-to-student relationships,
young people build empathy and experience themselves both as caring and cared for
(Noddings, 1984, 1992). As we will discuss below, these processes have been found
to promote broad positive developmental outcomes as well as increases in academic
success and decreases in health-risk behaviors. Furthermore, peer helping and peer
support programs have been successful in elementary, middle, and high schools in
reconnecting disruptive and alienated students, as well as in building inclusion and a
sense of belonging with new, immigrant, and ESL students and among racially, ethnically, and physically different students (Eggert, et al., 1994).

Moreover, it is through having the opportunities to participate, to be heard in
a physically and psychologically safe and structured environment—to voice one's
opinion, to make choices, to engage in active problem-solving, to express one's
imagination, to work with and help others, to give one's gift back to the community, in essence, to see themselves in leadership roles—that youth develop the
attitudes and competencies characteristic of healthy development and successful
learning: social competence, problem solving, autonomy, and sense of purpose
and future.

Especially critical to developing healthy psychological autonomy, young people
need the opportunity and freedom to grow, make decisions, and safely meet challenges *within* the structure of a safe school community to which they feel connected.
This connection between autonomy and belonging is mutually reinforcing: the
stronger someone's sense of self, the more able he or she is to form healthy connections to other people, with those healthy connections, in turn, further nurturing the
sense of self.

Research has found that students who experience autonomy-supportive school
environments are more likely to be curious, mastery-oriented, problem solvers,

intrinsically motivated, and committed to democratic values, in addition to having a higher sense of self-efficacy (Barber & Olsen, 1997; Chirkov & Ryan, 2001; Deci, 1995; Ryan & Deci, 2000). Participating in decisions about one's life and future and having some power over it is a fundamental human need. Several educational reformers believe that ignoring this need—not only among children but also among families, teachers, and the school staff—makes schools alienating places (Glasser, 1990; Kohn, 1996; Sarason, 1990; Wehlage et al., 1989). If data from California young people is representative, by the time students get to the 11th grade, only 15 percent of them feel that they have opportunities to "help decide things like class activities or rules," "do interesting activities," and "do things that make a difference" at school (http://www.wested.org/hks). Remember Seymour Sarason's classic quote which says it simply: "When one has no stake in the way things are, when one's needs are provided no forum, when one sees oneself as the object of unilateral actions, it takes no particular wisdom to suggest that one would rather be else-where" (1990, p. 83).

Youth who feel a sense of their own autonomy and power in the context of a caring school community also develop self-control. Alfie Kohn's review of the research on student decision-making leads him to conclude that, "It is in class-rooms and families where participation is valued above adult control that students have the chance to learn self-control" (1993a, p. 18). One of the major ways to increase student voice, i.e., autonomy and power, is through infusing group process throughout the curriculum and school day. This means extensive use of cooperative learning, student focus groups, and community circles. It is difficult to imagine a structure that better embodies all three protective factors—caring relationships, high and clear expectations, and opportunities for participation and contribution—than a small group with a common focus. Cooperative learning is an especially salient group process since it can easily be used across the curriculum and at all grades.

Given the powerful research-based argument in support of cooperation and small group learning—research spanning biology, genetics, evolutionary science, sociology, psychology, and education—it should come as no surprise that we do indeed have positive findings of the effects of cooperative small group learning on a wide range of student outcomes.

■   Group membership builds critical resilience skills and attitudes

#4: Positive developmental outcomes for students

Research does not disappoint us in validating the power of group process, i.e., peer-to-peer interaction, especially in the form of cooperative learning. Since research began on this process in the early 1970s, over a thousand studies, according to the International Association for the Study of Cooperation in Education, now corroborate the power of this educational intervention to produce holistic developmental outcomes—cognitive, emotional, social, moral, and spiritual (in terms of meaning and purpose). According to Robert Slavin, "What is remarkable is that each of several quite different methods has been shown to have positive effects on a wide variety of outcomes.... In general, for any desired outcome of schooling, administer a cooperative learning treatment; about two-thirds of the time there will be a significant difference between the experimental and control groups in favor of the experimental group. Rarely, if ever, will differences favor a control group" (1990, p. 53).

Most of this research has focused on four major models of cooperative learning: Student Team Learning (Robert Slavin at Johns Hopkins University), Learning Together (David and Roger Johnson at University of Minnesota), Jigsaw (Elliot Aronson at University of California-Santa Cruz), and Group Investigation (Shlomo and Yael Sharan at Tel Aviv University). Because most of the research on cooperative group learning clearly established its efficacy well over a decade ago, the field has matured enough to have had several handbooks and guides summarizing the research and theory of this approach written by the prominent researchers themselves as well as handbooks summarizing seminal articles (see Brandt, 1992; Cowie et al., 1994; Johnson & Johnson, 1989; Sharan, 1990; Slavin, 1990; Totten et al, 1991). The brief summaries below draw on these handbooks, and Tribes practitioners are referred to these handbooks and guides for in depth coverage of the plethora of confirmatory research studies.

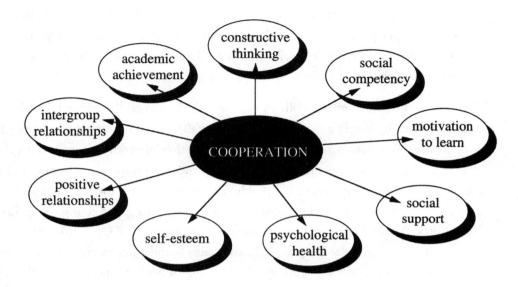

Nearly 30 years of research have found the following benefits of cooperative learning and peer interaction:

- **Academic achievement** This is by far the most studied outcome for cooperative learning experiments. According to Slavin (1996), "Studies of the achievement effects of cooperative learning have taken place in every major subject, at all grade levels, and in all types of schools in many countries" (p. 43). In fact, "Most studies have found equal benefits for high, average, and low achievers in comparison to their counterparts in control groups" (1996, p. 58). While the findings have been consistently positive across all the varieties of cooperative learning compared to individualistic learning over the last three decades, "There is still a great deal of confusion and disagreement about *why* cooperative learning methods affect achievement and, even more importantly, *under what conditions* cooperative learning has these effects" (Slavin, 1996, p. 44). Slavin identifies four theoretical perspectives on why cooperative learning has such positive effects on academic achievement: Motivational theorists emphasize the reward or goal structures; social cohesion theorists emphasize students caring about the group; cognitive theorists emphasize the role of students teaching others in retention of the material; and developmentalists emphasize that interaction among students on learning tasks in itself leads to improved student outcomes (Slavin , 1996). The good news is that each of these perspectives has something to offer and seeing them as complementary and not contradictory is key. Furthermore, Tribes draws on each of these perspectives in its theory of change.

- **Critical/constructive thinking skills** A common finding in all the research handbooks is stated by Roger and David Johnson (1983): "Currently there is no type of task on which cooperative efforts are less effective than are competitive or individualistic efforts, and on most tasks and especially the more important learning tasks (such as concept attainment, verbal problem solving, categorization, spatial problem solving, retention and memory, motor, guessing-judging-predicting) cooperative efforts are more effective in promoting achievement" (1983, p. 146). Damon and Phelps research (1989) mentioned earlier also found gains in creativity, experimentation, problem-solving skills and the learning of deeper concepts (i.e., discovery learning). This category is actually one of the categories of resilience strengths we referred to as "problem-solving" (Benard, 1991; 2004).

- **Social competence** Cooperative learning is above all a social approach, involving teamwork and fun, and thus we would expect to find social outcomes and indeed there are many, some of which are given their own categories below (i.e., intergroup relations). The social outcomes that have been consistently documented include cooperation, altruism, and empathy (Aronson, 2000; Aronson & Patnoe, 1997; Johnson & Johnson, 1989a, 1995; Sharan, 1990; Slavin, 1990; Solomon et al., 1993). Through peer interaction children also learn social skills such as impulse control, communication, and relationship or friendship skills (Berndt & Ladd, 1989; Ladd, 1989). Like problem-solving, these social competence skills are also one of the categories of critical resilience strengths, competencies associated over the human lifespan with success and well-being (Benard, 1991; 2004; Masten & Coatsworth, 1998).

- **Motivation** Sharon (1990) writes in his review of cooperative learning that, "Most authors of professional works and research studies on cooperative learning have asserted that this approach to classroom instruction enhances pupils' [intrinsic] motivation to learn more than the traditional whole-class approach to instruction" (p. 173). His research identified two aspects of cooperative learning that motivates students' academic achievement: positive peer interaction and enhanced decision making. Not surprising, these match two of the critical protective factors, caring relationships and opportunities for participation and contribution that we have discussed. According to Slavin (1990), "One of the most important tenets of motivational theories of cooperative learning is that cooperative goals create peer norms that support high achievement" (p. 46). Much of the early work on norms mentioned in the Community Agreements section provides research support for this hypothesis. Similarly, experimental field research on cooperative learning also supports the concept of peer academic norms (Slavin, 1990).

Slavin also writes, "One behavioral indication of student motivational involvement is the proportion of their class time they spend on-task" which we also call "engaged time" (p. 47). This too is a common finding in his as well as in Johnson and Johnson's and Aronson's research on cooperative learning effects (Aronson & Patnoe, 1997; Johnson & Johnson, 1989a; Slavin, 1990). Robert Slavin summarizes several studies that have also found positive effects on internal locus of control, the belief that through your own efforts you can succeed or fail (1990). Other motivational researchers have found that this belief, which we call achievement motivation in a school setting, is associated with not only school success (Wigfield & Eccles, 2002) but life success as well, including less involvement in substance abuse (Newcomb & Bentler, 1988; Scales & Leffert, 1999; Peng, 1994; Vaillant, 2002). It is a critical component of the category of resilience strengths we called "sense of purpose and future" (Benard, 1991, 2004).

■ **Social support** Perhaps the only social science construct studied more than social support is that of cooperative learning! The study of this concept also began in the 1970s with Cassel's work that found, "People can become physically, mentally, or socially debilitated if they do not receive or perceive signs from significant others that make them feel safe and valued" (in Wasserman & Danforth, 1988, p. 7). Furthermore, Cassel and others, including resiliency researchers, since have contended that the nature and strengths of available *group* supports—especially the mutuality and reciprocity involved—can be protective of health and mental health as well as a buffer for life stress and adversity (Cicchetti et al., 2000; Eccles & Gootman, 2002; Taylor et al., 2002; Werner & Smith, 1992). While most of the early research was on adult support networks, since the late 1980s the study of childhood and adolescent peer relationships and friendships has blossomed. Werner and Smith (1992) found that activities that allowed youth "to be a part of a cooperative enterprise" connected them to a group that could, if needed, serve them as a surrogate family (p. 205).

■ **Psychological health** Lifespan studies of human development have universally found that both social support (caring relationships) and participation—both essential components of cooperation and cooperative learning—are two of the critical lifelong protective factors for psychological *and* physical health (Werner & Smith, 2001; Vaillant, 2002). As discussed earlier in this chapter, researchers have even found "tend and befriend" to be a stress response associated with better health outcomes (Taylor et al, 2000). The slogan for a successful health promotion effort of the California Department of Mental Health in the 1980s said it well: "Friends can be good medicine."

Research linking cooperation, one form of social support that is defined as working with others to achieve our goals, led Alfie Kohn to conclude, "There is also good evidence that cooperation is more conducive to psychological health and to liking one another" than is individualistic competitive approaches (1986, p. 7). Roger and David Johnson have found that, "Cooperativeness is positively related to numerous indexes of psychological health such as emotional maturity, well-adjusted social relations, strong personal identity, and basic trust in and optimism about other people" (1983, p. 140).

■ **Self-esteem** Self-esteem, while a problematic concept to study, is the most studied aspect of cooperation and psychological health. According to Slavin (1990), "Perhaps the most important psychological outcome of cooperative learning methods is their effect on student self-esteem" (p. 44). Cooperative learning research has documented positive effects on the two components of self-esteem: the affective—the feeling of being liked—and the cognitive—feeling successful academically (Aronson & Patnoe, 1997; Johnson & Johnson, 1989; Slavin, 1990). Kohn (1986) offers the proposition that, "We compete to overcome fundamental doubts about our capabilities and, finally, to compensate for low self-esteem" (P. 99). Vorrath and Brendtro write in their now classic work on *Positive Peer Culture* (1985), an approach used successfully for three decades now in creating "therapeutic communities" for troubled youth, that their central position is that young people can develop self-worth, significance, dignity, and responsibility only as they become committed to the positive values of helping and caring for others" (p. xi). This is born out not only in cooperative learning studies but in the evaluations of service-learning (Melchior, 1996, 1998) as well as in anecdotal studies of peer-helping (Tindall, 1995), and lifespan developmental studies (Werner & Smith, 2001; Vaillant, 2002). Self-esteem is a component of that resilience category, autonomy or sense of self (Benard, 1991, 2004; Masten & Coatsworth, 1998).

■ **Positive relationships** If it is true, as Roger and David Johnson write (1995b) that, "Experts on organizations constantly remind us that behavior is 85 percent determined by organizational structure and 15 percent determined by the individual" (p. 31), then cooperative group learning is indeed *the* structural approach for promoting positive classroom relationships. Research does indeed bear this out. Cowie and her colleagues (1993) summarize several studies of cooperative learning interventions that suggest "that cooperation is a trait that can both precipitate friendships and help to maintain them during the childhood [and adolescent] years" (p. 10). This finding has also been universal in the summaries of cooperative learning research (Aronson & Patnoe, 1997; Johnson & Johnson, 1989; Slavin, 1990; Totten, 1991). In a qualitative study of a small cooperative learning community at the college level (most cooperative learning research has been in K–12 classrooms), one of the main reason students valued this experience was for "friendships and a sense of belonging" (Gabelnick et al., 1990, p. 67). The use of small group process was identified by the National Academy of Sciences/Institute of Medicine's study of *Community Programs to Promote Youth Development* (2002) as the primary way to create one of the essential components of effective programs: a sense of belonging. Given that other research on adolescent and adult problem behaviors consistently identifies peer rejection as a risk factor for a broad number of negative outcomes, including bullying and depression (the Columbine High School shootings is a tragic example), this reason alone mitigates for cooperative group learning being the primary structure found in our classrooms and schools.

■ **Intergroup relationships** Perhaps the most exciting universal findings in the cooperative learning and peer-tutoring research literature is their effects on promoting positive intergroup relationships, that is on acceptance and respect for cultural, ethnic, and physical differences. In other words, cooperative learning provides a proven research-based answer to two of the critical issues facing schools: racial/ethnic integration and mainstreaming special needs students.

Specifically, these programs consistently identify significant increases in social interaction, acceptance and liking (as well as in having friends from outside their group) between hetereogenous peers, especially between physically and/or mentally challenged or socially withdrawn children and their peers (Johnson & Johnson, 1989; Mesch et al., 1986; Sainato et al., 1986; Maheady et al., 1988; Slavin, 1990; Strain, 1985) as well as between white and nonwhite peers (Cowie et al., 1994; Johnson & Johnson, 1989; Rooney-Rebeck & Jason, 1986; Slavin, 1990). "Cooperative learning provides daily opportunities for intense interpersonal contact between students of different races. When the teacher assigns students of different ethnic groups to work together, he or she communicates unequivocal support for the idea that interracial or interethnic interaction is officially sanctioned" (Slavin, 1990, p. 35).

What is so compelling about a developmental approach such as cooperative learning is that it achieves positive effects on a problem, in this case, race relations, without ever directly focusing instruction on this issue. "Even though race or race relations per se need not be mentioned (and rarely are) during cooperative learning experiences, it is difficult for a student to believe that the teacher favors racial separation when he or she has assigned the class to multi-ethnic teams" (Slavin, 1990, p. 35). A study done at the University of California-Berkeley by sociologist Troy Duster in the 1990s found that even at the level of higher education students who reported positive inter-racial experiences said these happened when their instructor used small group learning.

The theory underlying why we see these increases in intergroup relationships from cooperative learning and other small group processes is called the "contact hypothesis," which was originally developed after World War II by psychologist Gordon Allport and others. Originally four major variables were hypothesized to account for the positive benefits: cooperative interaction, equal status among participants, individualized contact, and individualized support for the contact" (Stephan & Stephan, 1996). According to the National Research Council/Institute of Medicine (2000), " Since then researchers have added other broader variables— not ones particularly amenable to school-based interventions—that influence whether contact leads to positive results: societal factors, which include the structure of society, the historical and current relations between the groups that are in contact; the cultural background of the groups involved; and personal factors, which include demographic characteristics, personality traits and prejudices, stereotypes, and other beliefs" (p. 7). However, what intergroup researcher Beverly Tatum (author of the popular book, *Why Are All the Black Kids Sitting Together in the Cafeteria,* 2003) found from her data is that, "Young people and adults alike need and benefit from 'safe spaces' to explore personal attitudes and to reflect upon their own and others' racial and ethnic identity" (National Research Council/ Institute of Medicine, 2000, p. 62). Her program used the structure of the small group to create this safe space. She found that, "Creating such opportunities can have a positive impact on interethnic relations in schools" (p. 62).

- **Reduced problem behaviors** Using a developmental approach such as cooperative learning means you are promoting positive development by meeting young people's basic developmental needs such as for safety and belonging, which, in turn, prevents negative or problem behaviors, such as bullying. Unfortunately, most of the hundreds of studies on cooperative learning didn't use pre- and post- data on the problem behaviors policymakers are concerned about, especially alcohol and other drug abuse and violence. Fortunately, we do have research evidence that peer programs are dramatically more effective than all other programs in reducing students' actual use of alcohol, tobacco, and other drugs. The late Nan Tobler conducted a series of meta-analyses over the course of ten years in which she compared the effectiveness of different school-based prevention approaches (Tobler,1986; Tobler & Stratton, 1997; Tobler et al., 2000). Besides finding that "interactive" programs—defined as relying on participatory group process and peer interaction and focusing on interpersonal competence—were far more effective in reducing levels of substance use, she discovered some other findings that support the Tribes TLC approach. She found that program process matters more then program content, that the impact of the school program could be *doubled* if the family and community were involved, and that the programs were more effective in smaller schools (fewer than 500 students). She felt strongly that were she to do meta-analyses of school-based violence prevention programs she would come to the same conclusions (see Benard and Marshall, 2001 for a summary of Tobler's work). Her recommendation for schools, which highly supports the Tribes TLC process, is as follows:

> The paramount question for school boards and administrators is whether they will provide the necessary money, class time, extra personnel, and aggressive teacher training in the use of interactive group process skills. An interactive program must include participation by everyone, preferably in small groups (Tobler & Stratton, 1997, p. 118).

Roger and David Johnson have made violence prevention in terms of conflict resolution one of the foci of their work over the last decade (Johnson & Johnson, 1995b). Results of over twelve experimental research studies examining the effectiveness of their *Teaching Students To Be Peacemakers* program conflict resolution program found program participants significantly more able to handle their conflicts constructively (Johnson & Johnson, 1995c; Johnson, Johnson & Stevahn, 1995). This program, just as we have discussed earlier about Tribes and all other successful programs, begins with the climate and culture. Johnson and Johnson explain that the first step in implementing this program, that is "in teaching students how to manage conflicts, is to create a *cooperative context* where they learn how to define conflicts as mutual problems to be resolved in ways that benefit everyone involved. Once this context is established, [only then can] students can be taught negotiation, mediation, and academic controversy procedures" (1995b, p. 31).

Summarizing the positive findings from cooperative learning approaches, we find not only positive academic outcomes but holistic developmental ones as well. As

Slavin writes (1990), "In summary, cooperative learning has been shown in a wide variety of studies to positively influence a host of important noncognitive variables. Although not every study has found positive effects on every noncognitive outcome, the overall effects of cooperative learning on student self-esteem, peer support for achievement, internal locus of control, time on-task, liking of class and of classmates, cooperativeness, and other variables are positive and robust" (p. 53). Furthermore, he comments, "The breadth of the outcomes affected by cooperative learning strategies is impressive.... The differences in patterns of noncognitive outcomes between methods are not as interesting as their similarities" (p. 53).

Cooperative learning's universally positive effects on academic success as well as on holistic developmental outcomes makes it an exemplar of academic-social-emotional learning and resilience-based practice as well as the essential structure in promoting the "ideal learning culture." However, effective cooperative learning groups don't just happen; rather, like any process, it will be *how* we implement them that will make the difference. It is especially in the arena of implementation that the Tribes TLC process has much to offer the field. Tribes, more than any other cooperative learning approach is built on what we know about effective group process which is the topic of our next section.

Components of effective Cooperative/Small Group Learning

While the research cited above has clearly established the efficacy of cooperative learning versus competitive individualistic learning in experimental control group research, researchers found "important variation in the effectiveness between studies" (Cohen, 1994b, p. 2). This finding has led to more research focused on identifying just what are the essential components of effectiveness. Johnson and Johnson (1989) wrote in *Leading the Cooperative School* that for a lesson to be regarded as cooperative, five basic elements are necessary (elements reminiscent of Allport's original principles of social contact theory). These remain to this day the most often cited criteria for high-quality cooperative learning. They are indeed embedded in the Tribes TLC process.

- **Positive interdependence** Students are linked with each other in a way that one cannot succeed unless all succeed. "Positive interdependence is the heart of cooperative learning. Students must believe that they sink or swim together"

(Johnson & Johnson, 1995a, p. 27). They recommend using several methods to achieve this: a group goal, joint rewards, divided resources (as in jigsaw where each student only has part of the total information required to complete an assignment), and complementary roles, roles whose actions help the group complete the task.

- **Face-to-face promotive interaction** Students orally explain to each other how to solve problems etc. and support each other's efforts to learn. "Accountability to peers, ability to influence each other's reasoning and conclusions, social modeling, social support, and interpersonal rewards increase as face-to-face interaction among group members increases" (Johnson & Johnson, 1995a, p. 28).

- **Individual accountability** The performance of each individual student is assessed and the results given back to the group and the individual so that the group knows who needs more assistance. "Students learn together so that they can subsequently perform better separately" (Johnson & Johnson, 1995a, p. 28). Some ways to structure individual accountability include testing each student individually, randomly selecting one student's product to represent the entire group, and asking students to explain what they have learned to classmates.

- **Social skills** The skills of leadership, trust-building, communication, and conflict management must be taught. Early research studies in cooperative learning led the Johnsons to their conclusion that to be effective students must be directly taught the social skills necessary to be a productive group member. Elizabeth Cohen, whose research has been invaluable in studying effective implementation of cooperative learning, also writes that these studies "suggest a useful generalization: If students are not taught differently, they tend to operate at the most concrete level. If teachers want high-level operation, particularly verbal, the students will require specific development of skills for discourse, either in advance of cooperative learning or through direct assistance when groups are in operation" (1994b, p. 7). The skills identified in the literature are essentially the social collaborative skills emphasized in Tribes TLC and illustrated in the below diagram.

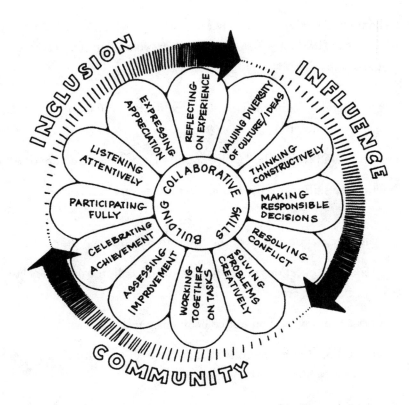

Not unexpectedly, these become the skills and positive developmental outcomes found in cooperative learning evaluations as discussed above and advocated by the leading scholars of group process in the classroom, Richard and Patricia Schmuck (2001). They are also forms of the resilience strengths associated with life success and well-being (Benard, 1991, 2004) and match well to CASEL's essential skills for academic and social-emotional learning (www.CASEL.org).

Tribes TLC uses a process for teaching social skills advocated in most of the literature on social learning and found to be effective by evaluations of social-emotional learning programs (Cohen, 1999, 2001; Elias, 2003; Greenberg et al., 2003; Strayhorn, 1988). Originally developed by Albert Bandura (1969), this process is summarized by Elizabeth Cohen as follows: New behaviors must be labeled and discussed; students must learn to recognize when new behaviors occur; students must be able to use labels and discuss behavior in an objective way; students must have a chance to practice new behaviors; and new behaviors should be reinforced when they occur (1986, p. 42). Gibbs has adapted and amplified these into the following seven steps:

1. Engage students in identifying the need for the skill (using discussion, role-play, story, or situation).

2. Teach the skill (using the Looks/Sounds/Feels-Like structure or other strategy).

3. Practice the skill regularly, and have students give feedback on how well it was used.

4. Transfer the responsibility to the tribes to remind each other to use the skill.

5. Ask reflection questions about the use of the skill in tribes, the class, the playground, at home, etc.

6. Point out times when you notice people using the skill well.

7. Notice and celebrate when the skill is "owned" as a natural behavior in the classroom or school (2001a, p. 124).

This Tribes process, which is closely aligned with that advocated by Johnson, Johnson, and Holubec (1994a,b), has several unique components than the more general social skills literature in that the students do own the skill since they generated the need for it; in teaching the skill multiple ways of learning are employed; and the responsibility for using the skill is transferred to the tribes. It probably goes without saying that the teachers and other adults in the classroom and school should be modeling these skills as well. If most of what we learn is from what is modeled around us, as social constructivists have theorized, then "walking our talk" is critical to successful learning of these life skills. From their observational research in classrooms around the country, Schmuck and Schmuck (2001) created the following list of the attributes that distinguish teachers who are effective "transactional communicators," that is, who are modeling the communication skills we want our students to learn: receptiveness to students' ideas, an egalitarian perspective, openness-candor-honesty, warmth and friendliness, respect for students' feeling/empathy, sensitivity to outcasts, a sense of humor, and a caring attitude (pp. 98–100). These match well to the three protective factors students need for healthy development and successful learning: caring relationships, positive expectation messages, and opportunities for meaningful participation.

■ Group processing/reflection is critical to successful groups/cooperative learning

It is important that groups process how well they are achieving their goals and maintaining effective working relationships. Group processing occurs when members discuss how well they are achieving their goals and maintaining effective working relationships (a process also known as "reflection"). In fact studies have found that group processing or reflection is associated with increased academic learning (Yager et al., 1986) and gaining increased meaning from whatever the activity was (Kolb, 1984). In fact, the Yager, Johnson, and Johnson study just cited found that group processing can *double* the retention of facts and concepts learned in an academic lesson.

The "keys to successful processing are allowing sufficient time for it to take place, making it specific rather than vague, maintaining student involvement, reminding students to use social skills during processing, and ensuring that the purpose of processing has been clearly communicated" (Johnson & Johnson, 1995a, p. 29). According to Elizabeth Cohen, "Available research on the effectiveness of the [cooperative learning strategies outlined above] suggest that investing in such preparation as team-building, skill-building, and time spent on group process can definitely make for more productive groups" (1994b, p. 26). Elsewhere she writes, "Adapting techniques from group dynamics, [many developers of cooperative learning] suggest that groups become aware of their interpersonal and work processes as they work and take time to discuss how they are doing as a group. Available research on the effectiveness of such strategies suggest that investing in such preparation and time spent on group process can definitely make for more productive groups" (1994b, p. 7). Tribes TLC incorporates all three of these recommended strategies: team-building (discussed below in stages of group development), skill-building as discussed above, and group processing.

The purposes of group processing according to Johnson, Johnson, and Holubec (1994) are to continuously improve the quality of the group's taskwork and teamwork; to increase individual accountability by focusing attention on other member's responsible and skillful actions to learn and to help groupmates learn; to streamline the learning process to make it simpler; and to eliminate unskilled and inappropriate actions. It is the teacher's responsibility to structure group processing by setting aside the time and providing procedures for students to use in discussing group effectiveness. The Tribes TLC process provides just these procedures, including forms for students to use.

Johnson, Johnson, and Holubec (1994) describe group processing as consisting of four parts: *feedback* on the effectiveness of taskwork and teamwork; *reflection* in which students analyze and reflect on the feedback they receive; *improvement goals* in which individuals and groups set goals for improving the quality of their work; and *celebration* in which groups celebrate their members' hard work and success. The Tribes TLC process especially emphasizes the reflection and the celebration (appreciation) aspects of group processing.

One of the major contributions of Tribes TLC to cooperative learning implementation literature is the emphasis on reflection (which incorporates "feedback" as defined above) at multiple levels of experience. As Gibbs writes, "The most important part of any Tribes TLC learning experience may be the reflection questions that you ask your students.... Asking good reflection questions within cooperative learning groups can double the rate of retention of knowledge for students" (2001a, p. 171). The Tribes reflection questions asked after a group learning experience reflect the Tribes' core philosophy of human development and learning for each experience is processed on the CASEL, i.e., cognitive, social, and emotional levels. *Content* reflection questions focus on cognitive learning, the academic knowledge gained from the learning experience. *Collaborative* questions reflect social learning, focusing on the interaction and participation of members and the collaborative or social skills they used. *Personal* reflection questions personalize the experience, connecting this learning to prior interests and experiences as well as to personal interests, talents, and skills. As we will see in Chapter Four, this multiple level processing honors how we—as holistic human beings—learn.

Furthermore, "The power of the Tribes process on adolescent development also comes from the practice of giving students opportunities to express appreciation to each other after working together" (2001, p. 127). Since one of the Tribes four

Agreements is "appreciation/no put-downs," it comes as no surprise that appreciation, what the Johnsons call "celebration," is also a focus of group processing.
According to Gibbs, "Statements of appreciation are invited at the conclusion of
every group learning experience, and are modeled by the teacher throughout the day"
(2001, p. 121).

A fairly recent movement, "appreciative inquiry," is actually demonstrating how
not only groups but organizations can transform when the focus shifts from problem-solving (the deficit paradigm) to appreciation (the assets paradigm), that is,
shifting from a focus on what is *not* working to what is working (Anderson et al.,
2001; Cooperrider & Whitney, 1999; Hammond, 1996/1998). It is an exciting
example of a systems-oriented, strengths-based, social constructivist, motivational,
developmental paradigm for change that is grounded in the three protective factors:
caring relationships, positive expectation messages, and opportunities for participa-
tion/contribution. It is essentially the application of the resilience approach to organizational development.

Developed at Case Western Reserve University in the late 1980s by David
Cooperrider and Suresh Srivasta, appreciative inquiry (AI) is an ethnographic
method for examining the life of an organization. It has been used successfully by
major corporations and nonprofits and even governmental agencies such as the
South African government under Nelson Mandela. More recently, it has been used
with schools. Since its inception, the approach, however, has always been applied to
teamwork or groupwork.

Ryan and colleagues (1999) describe how one school was changed through the
application of this process. At the schoolwide level, the AI process basically consists
of training a group of students, teachers, staff, administrators, and family members in
AI who then conduct a series of interviews with all these constituencies using a set
of questions based on what is good about the school. The following are some examples: "What are your memories of your school when it was at its best? In particular,
what teachers, classes, activities, or events surface most vividly in your mind as representing those times when your school was at its best? What is your school doing now
when it is at its best? What is it about this school that makes these experiences possible?" (Ryan et al., 1999, p. 165). As these educational consultants describe the
process, "AI's approach counteracts exclusive preoccupation with problems that all

too often de-energize teachers, staff, and sometimes administrators themselves.... By focusing everyone's attention on what is best about the school, the AI process often blends in with, and nourishes, the sense of possibility embedded in the school's mission. By involving so many of the school's stakeholders, AI also reinforces the likelihood that the school's mission will be embraced by an increasingly broad constituency" (p. 167).

At the group processing level, AI would focus on questions such as, "During the task we just completed, describe a time when you feel the group performed really well. What were the circumstances during that time (such as look-see-feel)?" "Describe a time when you were proud to be a member of the group? Why were you proud?" or "What do you value most about being a member of this group?" (Hammond, 1996/1998). The theory behind AI, just as that of other strengths-based approaches to education or therapeutic interventions such as "motivational interviewing," is that by "Asking appreciative questions, I still get the information I need but the difference is, the organization [or group or person] has the confirmed knowledge, confidence, and inspiration that they did well, and will continue to do well with a heightened awareness of what works. Not only do I have the gift of new eyes, but, hopefully others do too" (Hammond, 1996/1998). Essentially, through appreciation, humans are motivated to change because they feel affirmed and, as a consequence, hopeful—a powerful force of human connection having been made, without which humans do not fair well in this life. As social psychologist Thomas Cottle (2003) discusses in his book *A Sense of Self: The Work of Affirmation*—and a theme of Tribes and this document—we are first and foremost social beings and we come to recognize our selves, that is, forge our identities, through our relationships with others. He concludes by emphasizing what is at stake in the work of affirmation (or appreciation): "Just as the affirming gaze of another nurtures and strengthens one's sense of self, the absence of affirmation—what we might call disaffirmation—can lead to a life of despair, alienation, and even violence" (p. 240).

Expanding from the Johnson's research-based components for effective small group learning, additional components for "productive small groups" comes from the research of Stanford University's Elizabeth Cohen (1986/1994a, 1994b, 2002). Her research findings are also incorporated into the Tribes TLC process, ensuring its effectiveness as a research-based model of cooperative small group learning.

■ **Quality and frequency of interaction** Cohen's research has found that when performing higher order group tasks, just the frequency of students talking and working together in a task-related manner was positively correlated with posttest scores on content-referenced tests. She also summarizes research that has found when groups work on conventional school tasks that could be carried individually, "The most consistent, positive predictor of achievement... is the giving of detailed, elaborate explanations. In other words, the student who does the explaining is the student who benefits" (1994b, p. 9). This finding leads to the next inter-related component for successful groups: the need for authentic group tasks.

■ **Need for authentic group tasks** Cohen's research has found that the simple frequency of interaction of individuals does not predict their achievement. An authentic group task is one that "requires the resources (information, skills, materials) that no single person possesses." Rather, "Success depends on the contribution of many" (1994b, p. 5). An authentic group task also depends on the "mutual or reciprocal interdependence" of the group members. This means that "each student is dependent on the contributions of all others," that helping is not just one way with the stronger students always helping the weaker ones. Creative problem-solving and conceptual learning are especially conducive to cooperative group learning. Cohen calls her model of cooperative learning "complex instruction," which she defines as "a method of small group learning featuring open-ended discovery or conceptual tasks that emphasize higher order thinking skills" (1994b, p. 7). Slavin's review of research on group goals found that, "Seventy-eight percent of studies of methods using group goals and individual accountability found significantly positive effects, and there were no significantly negative effects" (1996, p. 55).

■ **Group evaluation criteria** Cohen's research on group learning (2002) has provided direct empirical evidence of the benefits of students' awareness of evaluation criteria, that is, specific guidelines as to what makes an exemplary group product, or what in Tribes TLC is referred to as learning objectives, which are classified as "content" and "social skills." Cohen writes, "Groups learned particularly well if they knew precisely what criteria would be used to evaluate their product" (p. 1064). She concludes, "Evaluation criteria are a motivational tool helping groups to be more self-critical and increasing their effort to turn out a superior group product"

(p. 1064). She also found that, "Groups without criteria were significantly less task-focused than groups with evaluation criteria" (2002, p. 1059) and engaged in a higher quality of group discussion.

Cohen's research is especially informative in that she has documented empirically that prior academic knowledge had *no* effect on the quality of the group product. "Failure of average pretest score to predict either quality of group product or average essay score suggests that learning arose from the group as a whole." In other words, "Learning was not a matter of relevant academic knowledge that individuals brought to the group but came about through reciprocal exchange of ideas and through a willingness to be self-critical about what the group was creating" (2002, p. 1064).

■ **Peer status issues are addressed** One of Elizabeth Cohen's major contributions to cooperative group learning is her finding that, "Differences in social status such as gender, race, and ethnicity can also affect interaction of schoolchildren" in cooperative learning groups (1994b, p. 23), which in turn affects learning. Her research corroborates findings from several bodies of research on "status characteristic theory" (Berger et al., 1972) as well as research on teacher expectations, more commonly known as the "self-fulfilling prophecy"—and known to researchers as "expectancy communication theory" (Weinstein, 2002)—not to mention the conclusive research on the deleterious effects of tracking/ability grouping on less academically able and low-status children (Oakes, 1985; Molnar, 2002; Wheelock, 1992).

Acccording to Elizabeth Cohen's review of the cooperative learning implementation literature (1994b), "The only result that seems to hold unconditionally is the benefit to the low achiever of being in a *heterogeneous* group as compared to a homogeneously low-achieving group" (p. 11). This conclusion is also found by research on the outcomes for young people who participate in therapeutic or behavior-change groups. For example, Thomas Dishion and his colleagues found that grouping high-risk young people together for a 12-week program designed to reduce problem behavior actually increased their levels of self-reported smoking and delinquency over three years (Dishion et al., 1999).

Cohen and her colleagues specifically found, "The learning gains of low-status children can be inhibited by their failure to have as much access to interaction as high-status children" (Cohen et al., 1990, p. 205). They warn that it is absolutely critical to the success of heterogeneous cooperative learning groups—which is what Tribes and most forms of cooperative learning are and value as a way to create equity in the classroom—that within groups status issues are addressed. They offer several strategies for addressing this issue (1990, 1994b), strategies which are all part of the Tribes TLC process:

◆ **Establishing norms and roles** "The use of training for cooperative behaviors such as listening to each other and giving everyone a chance to talk in combination with the assigning of rotating roles to each members of the group will do much to solve the problem of access of low-status students to interaction" (Cohen et al., 1990, p. 226). Elsewhere she writes, "When students feels that everyone *ought* to have their say and receive a careful hearing, the problems of inequality and dominance can... be solved" (1986, p. 45).

◆ **Curricula for cooperative learning** Cohen and her colleagues discovered that curricular materials "should be rich and not entirely dependent on reading so that different children are able to make different kinds of contributions" (Cohen et a., 1990, p. 227). One of her studies even found that, "The activities themselves presented excellent opportunities for children to display previously unrecognized intellectual abilities... and required aptitudes far beyond what is tested in ordinary achievement tests" (p. 227). The Tribes' activities are especially well-designed to achieve this objective.

◆ **Multiple ability treatment** This is an intervention in which teachers convince students that many different abilities are relevant to the group task, such as reasoning, creativity, and problem solving—emphasizing that skills other than reading and computation are needed—and that each person is has different gifts. "If the teachers are successful in using the multiple ability treatment, students believe that each member of the group will be good at some of these abilities and that no member of the group will be good at all these abilities" (1994b, p. 25). Having Multiple Intelligences as one of the foundational philosophies is particularly conducive in the Tribes model to this treatment.

◆ **Assigning competence to low-status students** This intervention requires the teacher to observe students when they work on multiple ability tasks within groups. "When a low-status student demonstrates competence on an important intellectual ability, the teacher publicly provides an evaluation of that student describing specifically what he or she has done well, what ability he or she is displaying, and why this is an important resource for the group" (1994b, p. 25). Cohen writes, "Teachers who use these two status treatments [multiple ability and assigning competence] more frequently have more equal-status interaction within their cooperative learning groups than teachers who use status treatments less frequently" (Cohen, 1994b, p. 25). These two status treatments are especially salient examples of how teachers communicate that critical protective factor, positive expectation messages.

Stages of Group Development

■ An understanding of group development is essential in creating a learning community and in promoting quality cooperative learning

One of the distinguishing features of Tribes TLC is the emphasis on the stages of group development. Just as teachers and others working with young people should have an understanding of child development, an understanding of group development is essential in creating a learning community in the classroom and in creating effective small group learning. Gibbs writes (2001b), "The success of any group's life together and the individual achievement its members can make depend upon the teacher-facilitator's knowledge and ability to orchestrate activities appropriate to the group's particular stage of development. It strikes us as sad that though all living takes place in groups, we seldom are taught how to make groups work well together" (p. 76). I would venture to assert that it is the lack of understanding of development—both individual and group—on the part of policymakers and practitioners that is the main impediment to school improvement.

The three sequential stages that are at the heart of both the Tribes community circle and cooperative learning groups correspond to our basic human needs discussed in Chapter One. They consist of *inclusion*—the needs for safety and belonging; *influence*—the needs for respect, autonomy, identity, and power; and *community*—the need to be connected to something larger than ourselves that gives our lives meaning and purpose. It is through honoring these needs, which we have earlier called innate resilience or inborn developmental wisdom, that healthy human development and successful learning unfold. I would also venture to say that this attention to these fundamental needs at the individual and group system levels is one of the major reasons Tribes, when implemented by practitioners with this understanding, is perhaps the most comprehensive and effective model of small group learning.

Inclusion, influence, and community as essential stages of group development grew from extensive research on human and group development, both having their roots in humanistic and developmental psychology with Erik Erikson (1963, 1968), Abraham Maslow (1954, 1968), William Schutz (1966), to name a few, as well as the post World War II work of the National Training Laboratory in Group Development of the National Education Association (Bradford et al., 1964). These stages are commonly referred to in the literature, with Schmuck & Schmuck (2001), the leading writers in group processes in the classroom, referring to four similar stages: membership, shared influence, pursuit of academic goals, and self-renewal. Just as individuals pass through stages—not necessarily age-related as you will remember from Chapter One—in their psychological development, "Classroom groups also pass through sequential and successive phases in developing their capacities for effective teaching and learning" (Schmuck & Schmuck, 2001, p. 47). They remind us that these stages are also "cyclical" and will be returned to time and time again. In fact, Gibbs refers to this cyclical process as "the spiral of renewal," writing that "each time the members of a learning community or classroom tribe cone together they need some type of inclusion activity before they begin to focus on task; and influence issues will always need to be addressed" (2001b, p. 84).

Just as the first stage in human development is the development of trust or attachment, and this must be fulfilled before a person can learn, the first stage in group development is developing the capacity for trust and closeness so members feel a sense of inclusion, that is, belonging or membership. Much of the attachment theory research of John Bowlby (1958) and Margaret Ainsworth (1964) and others have supported this developmental stage.

The next stage of influence or the "stage of control" (Schutz, 1966) is the stage when group members feel comfortable enough to want to exert their autonomy and power. At any time, however, that members start feeling a lack of inclusion or belonging, these needs must again be met before the tasks of the influence stage can be achieved. Influence is the stage when leadership begins to transfer to the group and when groups are ready to work on learning tasks together. It is critical that teachers recognize what is happening and support increased student control by providing group learning experiences. Schmuck and Schmuck describe what happens when teachers try to retain all the control:

> Just as young children learn about autonomy and power through the way parents handle their authority, so students in the classroom will learn about influence relationships from the leadership behaviors of the teacher. The teacher who has successfully maintained all power by 'not smiling before Christmas' most likely will produce a well-ordered, formal (possibly even pleasant) classroom in which no student will make any obvious attempt to gain power. Such classes also tend to have students who are alienated from the school and do not consider themselves an integral part of the classroom life; they are classrooms in which there are few public influence struggles, save for two or three isolated bursts of anger and hostility (2001, p. 57).

Also during this stage of influence, group members are trying to exert power and control with each other. It is critical that the teacher-facilitator help students deal with conflict by using the group process techniques described above and especially intervene with "status treatments" recommended by Elizabeth Cohen's research (1990, s1994b).

The last stage of community or self-renewal is reaching a stage of maturity according to Schmuck and Schmuck (2001). "For the healthy student and classroom group, reaching maturity is not an end but rather a state of readiness for continuous development and for the broadening of competence, skill, interest, and self-esteem" (p. 63). They define this as a process of self-renewal (based on John Gardner's 1971 classic book by the same name) and state that, "Self-renewing groups can continue to set up new purposes and procedures out of their own internal resources and wherewithal; and they have the competence to adopt new processes when the old ones are no longer functional.... Members accept the responsibility for the quality of their group life and are continuously striving to improve it" (p. 63). This description fits nicely within the indicators of community that John McKnight and John Kretzmann have described: capacity, collective effort, informality, stories, and celebration (1993). It also takes us back to our earlier descriptions of learning communities—and leads us into our next section, one of the vital components of Tribes and any successful school intervention, the creation of professional learning communities.

Professional Learning Communities

■ Creating a classroom community of learners is dependent on staff having a professional learning community

One of the major theories underlying Tribes TLC is that of systems theory. This perspective, growing out of the fields of biology, psychology, and sociology, focuses on the inter-related nature of a living system and underlies most current thinking in social psychology [see Fritjof Capra's *The Web of Life* (1996) and *The Hidden Connections* (2002) for wonderfully readable overviews of this perspective]. Individuals, families, schools, organizations, and communities are all social systems, made up of yet smaller subsystems. Applying this perspective to a school, schools consist not only of student groups or subsystems but of staff, parents, and other community subsystems. What has become clear is that none of these subsystems operate in isolation and that improving one necessitates improving all the others. The Tribes TLC process recognizes this systemic nature of schools, acknowledging that focusing on human development and learning for students necessitates creating parallel processes for teachers and other school staff as well as for families and the larger community. We must remember that, "Although the individual student is the focus of the learning process,... individual behavior and psychological experiences arise out of a cultural context and are based on interpersonal relations. The systems theory alerts us to the systemic nature of classroom life and turns us away from a narrow individualistic focus" (Schmuck & Schmuck, 2001, p. 33).

Thus the Tribes theory of change focuses on transforming all the subsystems within a school community into learning communities. Especially critical to school transformation is the creation of professional learning communities consisting of teachers and other school staff. In fact, as we will see in this section, research has identified that having a professional learning community is sine qua non the most important factor associated with positive health and learning outcomes for students—and with increased teacher satisfaction and job retention.

The literature is also clear on what constitutes a professional learning community (Darling-Hammond & McLaughlin, 1995; Kruse et al., 1995; Lieberman, 1995; Lieberman & Miller, 1990; McLaughlin & Talbert, 2001; Talbert & McLaughlin, 1994). Summarizing much of what leading school reformers like Linda Darling-Hammond, Milbrey McLaughlin, Ann Lieberman, and Judith Warren Little have advocated, Sergiovanni lists the practices of professional learning communities as doing the following (1996):

- encourage teachers to reflect on their own practice

- acknowledge that teachers develop at different rates, and that at any given time are more ready to learn some things than others

- acknowledge that teachers have different talents and interests

- give high priority to conversation and dialogue among teachers

- provide for collaborative learning among teachers

- emphasize caring relationships and felt interdependencies

- call upon teachers to respond morally to their work, and

- view teachers as supervisors of learning communities (1996, p.142).

If we were to substitute "students" for "teachers" we would have a list to give teachers of just what students need to be successful learners! Both of these lists are what Tribes TLC is all about. As Lieberman (1995) writes, "People learn best through active involvement and through thinking about and becoming articulate about what they have learned. Processes, practices, and policies built on this view of learning are at the heart of a more expanded view of teacher development that encourages teachers to involve themselves as learners—in much the same way as they wish their students would" (p. 592).

Virtually every *research-based* book written on improving schools cited in this document calls for teacher professional community as essential to school change—including those by Michael Fullan, Thomas Sergiovanni, Philip Schectley, Barbara Rogoloff, Seymour Sarason, to name just a few of the scholars. Literally dozens of studies—and even more practitioner books—have been conducted and written on this topic. According to Michael Huberman (1995), "The literature on professional development has become voluminous" (p. 193). We will examine a few of the seminal long-term research endeavors that especially support the importance of teacher professional community: the work of Milbrey McLaughlin and her colleagues at Stanford University's Center for the Context of Secondary School Teaching, of Judith Warren Little at the University of California-Berkeley, of Fred Newmann and Gary Wehlage at the University of Wisconsin' Center on Organization and Restructuring of Schools and their colleagues at the University of Minnesota, Karen Seashore Louis and Sharon Kruse, Valerie Lee and Julia Smith's analysis of the National Educational Longitudinal Study, and Anthony Bryk and his colleagues at the Center for School Improvement and the Consortium on Chicago School Research at the University of Chicago. Interestingly, a sidebar comment in the spirit of collaboration, is the fact that most of these researchers have worked and published collegially with each other over the years.

In a seminal article on school change, McLaughlin revisited a famous Rand study of successful school change efforts (1990). Her analysis identified "teacher collegiality," that is, teachers collaboration and connection with other teachers, as the key to sustaining school improvement. "Reforms or policies that engage the natural networks of teachers can support change efforts in a more sustained fashion… than strategies that adhere solely to a delivery structure outlined by the policy system" (1990, p. 15). In another national study, she and Julie Talbert found that teacher collegiality was the school variable associated with higher levels of student achievement (1993). McLaughlin states: "Teachers within the same school or even within the same department developed different responses to similar students depending on the character of their collegial environment. Which response a teacher chose was a product of his or her conception of task as framed and sup-ported by a particular school or department community" (1990, p. 89).

The data of Talbert and McLaughlin (1994) also found that, "Teachers who par-ticipate in strong professional communities within their subject area departments or other teacher networks, have higher levels of professionalism, as measured in this study, than do teachers in less collegial settings" (pp. 142–143). In other words, local communities of teachers are the vehicles for enhanced professionalism in teaching. Enhancing professionalism according to Talbert and McLaughlin (1994) is be deter-mined locally as colleagues come to share standards for educational practice, that is, to develop shared norms, values, beliefs, and attitudes, including strong commit-ments to students in terms of a mission that includes trusting and caring relation-ships and to their profession. According to Ann Lieberman (1995), one of the scholars of teacher professional communities, "Teachers must have opportunities to discuss, think about, try out, and hone new practices" (p. 593) through structures such as problem-solving groups or decision-making teams—or teacher Tribes—in the context of a culture of "inquiry." In essence, what teachers need in the school is exactly what we have discussed that students need in the classroom—a focus on human development and learning in a culture of caring relationships, positive expec-tation messages, and opportunities for participation (i.e., "inquiry") within the struc-ture of small learning groups. As Fullan and Hargreaves (1991/1996) claim, "Teacher development and student development are reciprocally related" (p. 82).

Judith Warren Little's influential research into teacher professional development (1993) also identified that "subject matter collaboratives" or "teacher networks" or "ongoing local study groups" offer a far more effective approach than the traditional training-and-coaching model of professional development to actually effect the many, forever-changing and complex educational reforms. She writes, "Altogether, the profoundly local character of much reform activity would seem to offer substan-tial opportunity to create and support alternative modes of professional develop-ment—those that enable local educators to do the hard work of reinventing schools and teaching" (p. 146). She, furthermore, identifies the following six often quoted descriptors of what constitutes effective professional development, descriptions that none other than a teacher learning group or teacher Tribe could fulfill:

- Professional development offers meaningful intellectual, social, and emotional engagement with ideas, with materials, and with colleagues both in and out of teaching.

- Professional development takes explicit account of the contexts of teaching and the experience of teachers.

- Professional development offers support for informed dissent.

- Professional development places classroom practice in the larger contexts of school practice and the educational careers of children.

- Professional development prepares teachers (as well as students and their parents) to employ the techniques and perspectives of inquiry…. It acknowledges that our strength may derive less from teachers' willingness to *consume* research knowledge than from their capacity to *generate* knowledge and to *assess* the knowledge claimed by others.

- The governance of professional development ensures bureaucratic restraint and a balance between the interests of individuals and the interests of institutions (pp. 138–139).

Looking at the effects of teacher collegiality on student outcomes, Michael Fullan (1999) refers to the study of school restructuring by Fred Newmann and Gary Wehlage (1995) and their colleagues Karen Seashore Louis and Sharon Kruse (1995) as "providing the most explicit evidence on the relationship between professional community and student performance" (p. 31). Using measures of standardized achievement tests and more 'authentic' performance-based measures of learning, these researchers found that some schools did much better (using student achievement in mathematics, science and social sciences as the indicators). They identified the existence of "high professional community" as the reason for students' better performance. Newmann and Wehlage (1995) claim professional communities work due to the following reasons:

- Teachers pursue a clear purpose for all students' learning.

■ Teachers engage in collaborative activity to achieve the purpose.

■ Teachers take collaborative responsibility for student learning.

■ Schoolwide teacher professional community affected the level of classroom authentic pedagogy, which in turn affected student performance.

■ Schoolwide teacher professional community affected the level of social support for student learning, which in turn affected student performance" (pp. 30, 32).

These assumptions also apply to the underlying Tribes TLC theory of change.

In an influential study supporting teacher collaboration—and one also having import in the small schools movement, Valerie Lee and Julia Smith (1994) studied the effects of restructuring on high-school students using data collected as part of the National Education Longitudinal Study (NELS) in 1988 and 1990. Data on 11,000 students enrolled in 820 high schools nationwide documented that students learn more in schools that are organized "communally" rather than bureaucratically. Specifically, "Increased gains in student engagement and academic performance, as well as in the degree of equity, [were] found in school with communal restructuring practices, compared to schools with traditional [bureaucratic] restructuring practices and schools with no restructuring practices" (p. 4).

The "communal" model of school structure, often referred to now as "the personalized high school" approach, is essentially a developmental model like Tribes TLC in which "contact between people is more sustained and more personal and there is more agreement on organizational mission for which people share responsibility" (Lee & Smith, 1994, p. 2). "In a communally organized school, teachers work collaboratively, often in teams that are formed across subjects. Instead of being governed by top-down directives, teachers have more input into decisions affecting their work. And instead of slotting students into different educational paths, a communal school would group students of diverse talents and interests together for instruction" (Lee & Smith, 1994, p. 16). In essence, a communal school is another way of describing a Tribes school: "In a communal school the educational focus for students and teachers seems clearer to those who experience it, and the increased opportunity for sustained contact in *groups* may heighten the commitment of both teachers and students to succeed. Schools with this form have more meaning for their members" (Lee & Smith, 1994, p. 2).

A follow-up qualitative case study of three "restructuring" schools conducted by Jacqueline Ancess (2000) further validates the power of teacher inquiry groups. Ancess' study, which explored the link between teacher learning, teacher instructional behavior, and student outcomes showed that when teachers engaged in an ongoing learning process, they tended to identify and carry out practices that resulted in increased graduation rates, improved college admission rates, and higher academic achievement for their students. She explains that, "In each case the teachers shared student outcomes and their practice with other faculty in school-wide forums designed for public sharing. Over a period of several years, evidence of improved student outcomes eventually persuaded the entire faculty at each school to adopt these organizational and pedagogical innovations on a school-wide basis" (2000, p. 597). She writes that in each of the schools she studied, "A constellation of nine conditions made the above changes possible: (1) incentives for teacher inquiry, (2) opportunity for teacher inquiry, (3) teacher capacity for leadership in innovation and inquiry, (4) respect for teacher authority, (5) flexible school structure, (6) responsive and supportive administration, (7) sufficient time, (8) sufficient resources, and (9) regulatory flexibility" (2000, pp. 597–598).

Anthony Bryk and his colleagues from the University of Chicago Center for School Improvement and the Consortium on Chicago School Research have done several seminal studies supportive of teacher collegiality and communally organized schools (Bryk & Driscoll, 1988; Bryk, Lee, & Holland, 1993; Bryk & Schneider, 2002). As we discussed in Chapter Two, his latest study with Barbara Schneider (2002), a longitudinal study of 400 Chicago elementary schools, identified that, "Social trust among teachers, parents, and school leaders improves much of the routine work of schools and is a key resource for reform" (Bryk & Schneider, 2003, p. 1). Social or relational trust consists of respect, personal regard, competence in core responsibilities, and personal integrity. "By linking evidence on the schools' changing academic productivity with survey results on school trust over a long period of time, we were able to document the powerful influence that such trust plays as a resource for reform" (p.2). In terms of teacher collegiality, this study found the following effects: (1) "Collective decision making with broad teacher buy-in, a crucial ingredient for reform, occurs more readily in schools with strong relational trust;" and (2) "In schools in which relational trust was improving over time, teachers increasingly characterized their colleagues as committed and loyal to the school and more eager to engage in new practices that might help students learn better;" and (3) "Relational trust is also more likely to arise in schools where at least a modicum of choice exists for both staff and students" (pp. 4, 6).

In another Consortium study with teacher collegiality effects and using the same data base as Bryk et al.'s, Smith, Lee, and Newman (2001) inquired into teacher instructional style, organizational structures, and achievement in Chicago elementary schools. These researchers found the following connection between teacher collegiality and children's higher achievement on standardized tests: Children scored higher on these tests when—contrary to common thought that "skill-and-drill" is more effective for test prep—their teachers used interactive instruction; and teachers who used *interactive* instruction were more likely to be found in schools that supported teachers collegiality, specifically their engagement in reflective discussions about their practice. What we basically find in these last two studies is support for the transformative power of the three protective factors that create a Tribes caring culture for teachers as well as students: caring relationships, positive expectations, and opportunities for participation.

Returning to some of the research we cited earlier in this document, we also find evidence that teacher professional community is a critical component, not only of the whole school reform models examined by the American Institutes of Research (1999) that we discussed earlier such as Comer's model and the Child Development Project of the Developmental Studies Center, but is also found in school effectiveness research and research on high-performing schools. For example, Michael Rutter and his colleagues classic study (1979) of the power of school climate to change holistic student outcomes (discussed elsewhere in this document) also sheds light on the importance of shared staff norms, especially norms around teamwork, cooperation, and shared discipline. This three-year longitudinal study in twelve urban high schools found that: (1) Students achieved more highly in schools where staff members shared expectations to plan the course of study cooperatively. In such schools, the group planning provided opportunities for teachers to encourage and support one another. (2) Students achieved more highly and had fewer behavioral problems in schools where the disciplinary rules for the pupils were set by the teachers as a group (teamwork and cooperation), in contrast to leaving individual teachers to work out the rules of discipline for themselves. (3) Students achieved better in schools where staff norms supported being open and direct with one another. In the less successful schools, faculty members expected one another to be autonomous, private, and aloof.

In examining the common elements of five high-performing, high poverty middle schools, Susan Trimble (2002) found that each of them used teams of teachers and administrators to do the work of the school. "My work with the five high performing schools showed that these schools accomplished their work using a variety of types of teams. In addition to interdisciplinary teams, these other types included administrative teams, grade level teams, school improvement teams, content area teams, student support teams, and special focus teams" (2002, p. 5). She explains their success as follows:

> Teams provide the structure for discussion and problem solving while working with diverse populations of students with complex situations. They also activate the creative thinking processes and group dynamics that generate multiple solutions to problems…. Teams also supply emotional support that can evolve into small groups of communities for learning. In short, teams engage the participants and establish the relationships that Hargreaves and Fullan (1998) deem as "absolutely necessary for successful reform" (p. 5).

Karen Seashore Louis and her colleagues (2003) have conducted research since the 1980s in public schools actively involved in reform, "ranging from projects that chose a diverse national sample of school community environments to those that involved intensive case studies and surveys in two urban districts" (p. 160). They have also focused on high-performing high-poverty schools (2003). Their argument has been and remains that high-quality working environments for teachers, environments that intrinsically motivate them and engage them is the key to systemic reform. Their studies of "teacher engagement" have not only found that sense of community—with each other and with students—is at the heart of creating a professional learning community, they discovered that creating structures to promote teacher decision making and teacher collaboration around curriculum, instruction, and school-wide decisions as well as structures that allowed teachers to interact with students informally and in small groups were critical organizational changes that both reflected and further supported a positive school culture.

One prominent model we have not mentioned that is especially focused on teacher professional community as the catalyst to reform is Ted Sizer's Coalition of Essential Schools (CES) (www.essentialschools.org). It is based on a network model, helping teachers strengthen and use relationships in networks both within and outside their own schools. According to the *Horace* journal published by the Coalition,

> School networks subvert the very function of bureaucracy—to regulate people who are expected to fight with each other—and replace it with looser associations of trust and common purpose. Locally, a network's critical mass and reputation can often protect restructuring schools from reactive political forces. And nationally, networks of like-minded school reformers can wield considerable political clout. At best, networks that create a "system of schools" to counter the convention "school system" hold radical potential for reshaping the way schools work together (Cushman, 1996, p. 2).

The CES model—while an extensive effort involving over 1,000 schools and fifty regional centers and networks, is similar to Tribes in being principle-based and process-oriented and is not a specific model of school reform. Rather, like Tribes, common principles are intended to be used by schools to shape their own reform efforts—including curriculum and instruction—that fit their particular situations. It even has a concentric "circles of support" model similar to "the developmental process of Tribes."

The Coalition of Essential Schools is itself a network, which Theodore Sizer conceived as a "conversation among friends" about his Nine Common Principles (1986/1997). Beginning with small "critical friends" groups focused on creating positive relationships among teachers in which they engage in reflective practice, CES works to create school-to-school networks, regional networks, a national network and now, also participates in a "network of networks." According to one of the regional CES Center directors, "Everyone needs a place to generate ideas, share reflection, get feedback, tackle problems, express frustration. Teaching requires too much energy to be without the regeneration that comes from the

collective intelligence of a strong network" (1996, Cushman, p. 8). Deborah
Meier, the principal of the legendary Central Park East school described earlier,
has this to say about the power of teacher learning groups:

> The basis for all organized learning is to invite in new people who are more
> expert than we are in what we want to do. But this only happens if adults in
> schools have an exciting intellectual life of their own—if we get together the
> way lawyers do, to have good thick conversations in small groups. Without
> this, educating kids is impossible; kids need to experience a responsible,
> thoughtful community of grownups whom they want to be like. We must
> build these structures into the very purpose of schooling, and then hold our-
> selves accountable to providing them (quoted in Cushman, 1996, p. 8).

The 1999 American Institutes of Research study gave a high rating to CES in terms
of an extensive research base on implementation. Their rating of CES' evidence of
success in terms of student achievement was mixed (pp. 38–42). However, since then
a study of 22 low-performing schools in four states using CES as their
Comprehensive School Reform Demonstration model found that, "The percentage
of students in these schools passing state achievement tests increased substantially
from the initial year of testing, and that CES CSRD schools are making significant
progress inclosing the gap between the percentage of their students who are passing
and the state average of students passing the tests. On four tests in two states, CES
CSRD schools not only narrowed the gap but also surpassed the state averages"
(www.essentialschools.org).

One last study we will mention is the evaluation by Linda Darling-Hammond
and her colleagues at Stanford University of San Diego's 5-year school reform effort
(September 2003). These researchers found the schools taking a "collaborative"
approach to professional development were the most successful in raising the
achievement of their students. These were schools who committed to "the provision, development, and nurturing of professional development opportunities and
networks that support continuous reflection and refinement of practice in communal settings (to dislodge norms of private teaching practice)" (Darling-Hammond et
al., 2003, p. 13).

Thomas Sergiovanni makes the argument in all of his books focused on the principalship that creating "reflective, developmental, diverse, conversational, caring, and responsible" communities of learners (1996, p. 139) among students requires the same for teachers. "Few axioms are more fundamental than the one that acknowledges the link between what happens to teachers and what happens to students." For example, "Inquiring classrooms are not likely to flourish in schools where inquiry among teachers is discouraged. A commitment to problem-solving is difficult to instill in students who are taught by teachers for whom problem solving is not allowed. Where there is little discourse among teachers, discourse among students will be harder to promote and maintain" (1996, p. 139).

Sarason documents the systemic nature of this powerlessness in schools in *The Predictable Failure of Educational Reform* (1990). Following his discussion of how teachers consistently deny students the opportunity to have power in decision making (discussed in Chapter Two of this document), he takes the discussion to the next level: how teachers are systematically denied decision-making power in their roles. He writes, "And therein is the irony: teachers regard students the way their superiors regard them—that is, as incapable of dealing responsibly with issues of power, even on the level of discussion" (p. 83). In the cases of both students and teachers, the effect is lethal to interest and motivation and promotes "at best a passionless conformity and at worst a rejection of learning" (p. 83). In what has to be one of the most insightful and wise observations that has not been acknowledged by educational policymakers but is understood by Tribes practitioners and other successful change models, Sarason writes, "When one has no stake in the way things are, when one's needs or opinions are provided no forum, when one sees oneself as the object of unilateral actions, it takes no particular wisdom to suggest that one would rather be elsewhere" (p. 83).

Unfortunately, all too much of the literature, including the research, on the topic of teacher professional community speaks to how rare or uncommon it is. A recent study of teacher community (Grossman et al., 2001) stated, "The simple fact is that the structures for ongoing community do not exist in the American high school.... Despite lip service to lifelong learning, the norms of American schools create a situation in which community for teacher learning is found (if at all) outside the workplace" (p. 947).

And elsewhere is where way too many of our teachers are going, especially our new teachers. The number one reason they cite for leaving is poor working conditions in which they do not feel supported or listened to (Ingersoll, 2001; Johnson et al., 2001). In fact, a report by the Southern Regional Education Board summarizes several studies that found salaries and benefits accounted for only 10% of teachers who left teaching after five years (Bolich, 2001). A chief characteristic of poor working conditions for teachers—as it is for students—is lack of supportive relationships and lack of decision-making involvement. Essentially, "poor working conditions" translates into a nonsupportive school culture, taking us back to Chapter Two of this document, which summarized research validating the importance of school culture to student well-being and success. Culture, however, applies not just to students but is inclusive of all the players at the school.

More recently, teachers have also cited the requirements of NCLB as furthering their stress, resulting in their leaving the profession (Kohn, 2004). Several experts (Neill, November 2003) agree that the virtual disregard of this substantial and conclusive body of research on professional learning community as *the* structure for supporting school reform that supports student learning will ultimately result in the failure of this national policy of one-size-fits-all standards and high-stakes testing to improve schools. Unfortunately, as Alfie Kohn argues in a recent issue of *Kappan* (April 2004), NCLB is opening the gates for the privatization of education in this country.

In the meantime, Bryk and Schneider (2003) remind us of what Tribes practitioners already know: "Good schools depend heavily on cooperative endeavors. Relational trust is the connective tissue that binds individuals together to advance the education and welfare of students. Improving schools requires us to think harder about how best to organize the work of adults and students so that this connective tissue remains healthy and strong" (p. 6). Tribes practitioners can know that Tribes TLC's focus not only on students small cooperative group learning but on teacher learning groups as the structure for both implementing and further creating a caring culture is based on the best of educational research as we work in our spheres of influence to create classrooms and schools that nurture human development and learning.

CHAPTER FOUR

Responsive Education

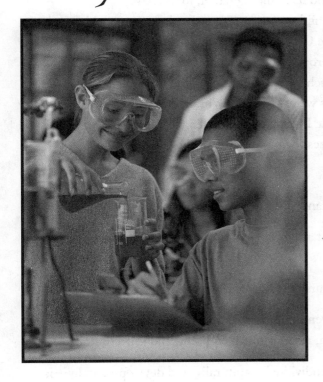

Responsive education is a daily community process lived by teachers, students and the whole school community. It is a caring democratic culture that includes values, and challenges everyone in the school community to participate, to learn and to develop their personal best.

JEANNE GIBBS, 2003A, P. 13

This chapter offers research support to responsive education, the third major Tribes strategy grounded in Tribes core philosophy of human development and learning. It is about the educational practices that operationalize the Tribes goal of promoting human development and learning and that further reinforce the other strategies: a caring culture and the communities of learners structure.

Responsive education is also called student- or learner-centered education. Gibbs defines it as "a synthesis of proven active learning teaching practices that promote academic achievement and social emotional development" (July 15, 2003, p. 24) and elsewhere as "an active learning process that supports the intellectual, social, emotional, physical, and spiritual or inner development of [children and youth]" (2003a, p. 112). This means educational practices are tailored to students' development and ways of learning as well as to their strengths, interests, goals, and dreams. Responsive education, as well as most of the other components of Tribes, is grounded in progressive education and its founding father, John Dewey.

The Northeast Foundation for children (www.responsiveclassroom.org) has published resources on "The Responsive Classroom" for two decades. This organization, like Tribes, provides "a practical approach to teaching and learning that creates safe, challenging, and joyful elementary schools." In principles that echo those of our discussion of the Tribes components as well as the "body/brain compatible elements" of Susan Kovalik's Integrated Thematic Instruction approach (Kovalik & Olsen, 1997, 2001), writer Chip Wood summarizes the basic tenets of the "Responsive Classroom" approach as follows:

- The social curriculum is as important as the academic curriculum.

- How children learn is as important as what they learn: process and content go hand-in-hand.

- The greatest cognitive growth occurs through social interaction.

- There is a set of social skills children need in order to be successful academically and socially: cooperation, assertion, responsibility, empathy, and self-control.

- Knowing the children we teach—individually, culturally, and developmentally—is as important as knowing the content we teach.

- Knowing the families of the children we teach and inviting their participation are essential to children's education.

- How the adults at a school work together is as important as individual competence: lasting change begins with the adult community (1998).

The main strands of responsive education in the Tribes TLC process focus on *student-centered active learning* experiences that are *cooperative, active, reflective, integrated,* and *project-based.* They also are grounded in *authentic* approaches to *assessment.* Because the strands of responsive education are so overlapping, they actually share a research base in terms of basic research, case studies, and whole school reform model comparisons. Thus they are dealt with as strands of active learning (other than *student-centered* which was a focus of Chapter One and *cooperative learning* which was described in detail in Chapter Three), and the research will support this approach as a whole. The following are research-based assumptions guiding the discussion in this Chapter:

- Students learn best when they are actively engaged.

- Students do not all learn alike and need multiple ways of learning.

- Learning is a holistic and need integrated project-based experiences.

- Assessment must also be responsive, i.e., authentic.

Active Learning

In an international study on active learning in eight countries (1997), David Stern from the University of California-Berkeley writes that active learning is *the* educational practice that "develops the capacity for autonomous lifelong learning" which, he claims, is absolutely essential if humans are to adapt to the rapid economic and social changes in the post-industrial world (p. 13). "Preparation for lifelong learning at work necessitates a kind of initial education that fosters curiosity and the capacity to manage one's own learning agenda. Employers say they want workers who can take initiative and solve problems, not only in managerial and professional positions, but also in production and clerical jobs" (p. 13). In other words, according to this researcher, active learning helps students develop the critical resilience strengths of autonomy (includes initiative) and problem-solving. As we will also discover, active learning that involves small group collaboration also develops the other resilient strengths, social competence and sense of purpose.

Active learning like all of progressive education, also has its roots in the constructivist learning theories of Piaget and Vygotsky, which we have discussed earlier in this document. While the constructivist paradigm has come to ascendance in educational research and literature, the political agenda now determining so much of educational policy has virtually ignored this well-supported approach. Stern summarizes active learning as follows:

> Learners construct their conceptions of the world from their own experience, building on previous conceptions. Advances in understanding come about through confrontation with phenomena that existing conceptions cannot explain. In this paradigm, the way teachers enable students to construct new mental models is by presenting problems and providing support for students until they have achieved independent mastery of the new idea. Abstract information acquired in a practical context is more likely to be incorporated into students' repertory of knowledge and skill that can be applied to later problems (p. 15).

The rationale for active learning is in his last sentence: learning in an applied context—what students call "hands on" learning—is learning that lasts.

Active learning is defined along two dimensions according to P.R.J. Simons, one of the researchers in this international study (1997): "Active learning on the one hand has to do with [making] decisions about learning and on the other hand making active use of thinking" (p. 19). He explains that in more active forms of learning, which involve more decision making power, "Learners make their own time plan, they choose learning goals and activities they like, they test their progress, they take care of learning and understanding on their own, and they reflect on errors and successes" (p. 19). He explains the second meaning of active learning (tied to mental activity), as follows:

> It is not so much the number and quality of decisions about learning that count but how much *activity* is asked from the learner. Are students figuring out things on their own? Are they working without teacher supervision? Are they working together in groups? Are they thinking while learning? Are they doing? In this case, the amount of mental activity of learners is the important criterion (p. 21).

The Tribes TLC process of project-based learning (or Discovery Learning) actually qualifies along both of these dimensions of active learning.

Contemporary constructivists like cognitive scientist Lauren Resnick (1987b) recommend learning, both inside and outside of schools, that is *context-bound, tool-oriented, social,* and *problem-specific.* She writes that for the most part, in-school learning is the opposite: decontexualized, symbol-oriented, individual, and general. She advocates a model of "cognitive apprenticeship" in which learning takes place in a real life context with a group of students and a mentor who gradually gives the group more and more responsibilities. In this way, students learn by doing, by observing and imitating the mentor, and by getting feedback from both the mentor and the peer group. Not coincidentally, this apprenticeship approach—which is also advocated by the prominent cultural anthropologist Barbara Rogoff (2001, 2003)—also describes the Tribes TLC process and embodies the three protective factors as well!

Resnick's evaluation (1987a) of apprenticeship programs that helped student acquire school learning skills identified the following characteristics:

- They involve socially shared intellectual work.

- They are organized around mutual accomplishment of tasks so that elements of the skill take on meaning in the context of the whole.

- They make usually hidden processes overt, subject to observation and commentary.

- They allow skill to build up bit by bit, yet permit participation even for the relatively unskilled... *This is often enabled by the social sharing of tasks.*

- The most successful programs are organized around particular bodies of knowledge and interpretation (i.e., subject matter) rather than "general" abilities (pp. 20–21).

She explains this last point as being especially crucial, for in being "project-based" students engage in "processes of meaning construction and interpretation which seem to have the effect of blocking the kind of symbol-detached-from-sense thinking that I have noted as a major problem in school but not in out of school activity. It is just this kind of self-conscious meaning construction and interpretation that is likely to be needed in conditions of breakdown and transition out of school when it is necessary to use one's powers of reflection and analysis to craft sensible responses to new—and as yet ill-understood situations" (p. 21).

In contrast to earlier waves of active learning in the Sixties and Seventies, the current emphasis on active learning not only includes constructivist learning theory and research but also more recent research on specific forms of constructivism such as metacognition (Brown, 1980), on the role of students learning how they learn. "Metacognitive knowledge," according to Simons (1997) refers "to knowing how one is learning, knowing what one knows and what not and knowing when to apply a certain principle and when not" (p. 27). "Metacognitive regulation" is really the monitoring and control of ongoing cognitive processes. "Actions like planning how much time one needs to study a certain part of subject-matter, testing one's progress, monitoring the development of one's understanding and predicting the results one will reach are all examples of these regulation activities" (p. 27). Furthermore, according to an extensive research synthesis on "educational resilience" by Margaret Wang and her colleagues (1993), these metacognitive skills are powerful predictors of success at school. These skills are the Tribes collaborative skills of "thinking constructively," "reflecting on experience," and "assessing improvement" and the resilience strengths of self-awareness (part of autonomy) and problem-solving.

Simons identifies three seminal research studies supportive of teaching students metacognitive knowledge and skills: Palincsar and Brown (1984) on reading comprehension; Schoenfeld (1985) on mathematical reasoning; and Scardamalia, Bereither, and Steinbeck (1984) on writing processes. In each of these studies, which have been extremely influential in their respective fields, "durable, generalizable, and transferable results of training were realized" (1997, p. 26).

He also cites two other forms of active learning theory which are finding positive results. "Anchored instruction" developed by The Cognition and Technology Group at Vanderbilt University (1990) which asserts that constructive learning should always be anchored to authentic experiences, a context resembling the complex world of real problem-solving. The other constructivist approach to active learning is called "cognitive flexibility theory" (Spiro et al., 1991) which posits that, "Knowledge representations become flexible when they are built up in diverse contexts and when they get different kinds of interpretations.... Learning is flexibly crisscrossing through the information on the base of one's own questions, interests and activities. The learner should be revisiting the same material, at different times, in rearranged contexts, for different purposes, and from different perspectives" (Simons, 1997, p. 28). Applying these concepts of "anchored instruction" and "cognitive flexibility" to the Tribes process, we find that Tribes accommodates both in its approach to student-centered active learning.

The group of international researchers conducting the study of active learning in eight countries (Stern & Huber, 1997) used a research protocol based on their consensus as to what constitutes active learning. The core or "primary" characteristics they developed consist of the following:

- **active**—the student must do certain things while processing incoming information in order to learn the material in a meaningful manner

- **constructive**—the new information must be elaborated and related to other information

- **cumulative**—all new learning builds upon and/or uses the learner's prior knowledge

- **goal-directed**—learning is most likely to be successful if the learner is not only aware of the goals but has internalized them, seeing them as important

- **diagnostic**—learners undertake activities like monitoring, self-testing, and checking that help them diagnose and judge whether they are still pursuing the goal they had set, and

- **reflective**—learners are actively aware of their way of learning (Simmons, p. 29–30).

The above serve as guidelines that active learning is taking place although they all won't be found all the time in active learning. Simmons also offers six other "secondary" characteristics that have been proposed but that he cautions should not be used alone or at the exclusion of the above processes:

- **discovery oriented**—a powerful approach, especially in the beginning and final stages of learning

- **contextual**—real-life connections are critical but there should be a balance between contextualization and decontextualization so learning transfers

- **problem oriented**—good for contextualization and motivation

- **case-based**—good for contextualization and motivation

- **social**—important but should also allow for individual learning as well, and

- **intrinsically motivated**—is related to and connecting to desire to learn (p. 31).

A Finnish successor to Vygotsky, Engestrom, studied learning processes in industrial settings and came up with a much shorter list of components that really capture the above descriptors. According to Simons (1997), Engestrom described four characteristics of ideal learning processes and outcomes: they are *complete* (integrated and functional); *holistic* (cognitive, affective); *represented in multiple ways* (i.e., multiple intelligences); and *social* (when one can explain to others what one knows) (p. 33). The Tribes TLC process actually accommodates and advocates not only these last four but most of the above processes as well. Remember, the core characteristics do not have to be present at one time and the secondary ones need to be used selectively and appropriately.

Robert Slavin, a member of this international research team offers a few additional points of clarification about active learning of particular import to Tribes TLC (1997). According to this leading researcher of cooperative learning (1997), "In principal, active learning can exist with students working entirely on their own, but in practice, it almost always incorporates some form of cooperative interaction. To the degree that active learning implies substantial learner freedom to select learning strategies and resources, it is difficult to imagine active learning settings in which students are forbidden to work with others" (p. 159). He points out that of the eleven international case studies in this review, cooperative learning was extensively used in every program evaluated.

Slavin also refers to project-based learning as "true active learning" and says it has not been extensively evaluated in classroom research. However, he makes the case that the substantial body of research on cooperative learning can be used to support the efficacy of project-based learning, given that, "Cooperative learning practice has increasingly shifted toward project-based or active learning in which students work together to produce reports, projects, experiments, and so on" (1996, p. 62).

Summing up our discussion so far in this chapter, we find that constructivist learning theory forms a good background for instruction aimed at active learning. The wonderful cross-cultural team of researchers in this international study have concluded that, "American, European and Russian theories and research show that it is possible to teach students how to learn, that this is effective and leads to performance improvement" (Simons, 1997, p. 39).

What we will now examine are some additional research bases for active learning, beginning with a summary of a whole school reform model based on active, project-based learning and concluding with three of the most powerful evaluations supporting not only active learning but the fundamental core of Tribes itself: the inseparability of human development and learning.

Two recent National Research Council/National Academy of Science reports, *How People Learn* (2003) and *Engaging Schools* (2004) as well as the earlier international report on *Powerful Learning Environments* (De Corte et al., 2003)—along with a whole litany of professional literature—calls for active learning in one form or another as essential to learning, essential to creating schools that engage intrinsic motivation, and essential for powerful learning environments. Similarly, two compendiums of evaluations of youth programs and practices assembled by the American Youth Policy Forum (Halperin & Partee, 1997; James, 1999) find active learning a critical ingredient of programs—including school-based—that produce positive academic and behavioral outcomes in young people. And one more example: According to the Southern Regional Education Board, "In 12 years of data analysis, *High Schools That Work* has found that students learn more when they are [cooperatively] engaged with challenging content through planned learning activities... [that involve them] in solving real-world problems" (Tanner et al., 2001, p. 1). We also find two models of whole school reform models analyzed by the American Institutes of Research (1999) that especially emphasize project-based active learning: Foxfire and Expeditionary Outward Bound schools. While Foxfire has a special place in this writer's heart, the research has not really materialized as of yet. However Expeditionary Learning Outward Bound, mentioned earlier in this document, is rated as having "promising" evidence of positive effects on student achievement. The evidence for this model is also supportive of Tribes TLC as a whole school reform model.

■ Expeditionary Learning Outward Bound

In 1992 Expeditionary Learning Outward Bound (2003), a project-based form of active learning, was created as a whole school reform model that is part of the New American Schools initiative. Four independent recent evaluations of the Expeditionary Learning Outward have found positive results. For example, among ten pilot Expeditionary Learning schools, nine had shown significant improvement on students' standardized test scores. Each year scores continued to rise.

In terms of the environmental protective factors that promote positive youth development and reduce involvement in high-risk behaviors, one study found the following: Compared to students in traditional schools, students in the Expeditionary Learning schools report that their teachers and peers listen to them, that they like and respect their teachers, that the school has a high level of engagement in learning, and that the school has a sense of community. Two-thirds of the sixth grade and high school students said that learning expeditions helped them solve problems, make plans, organize their time, learn how to get needed information, understand how school related to the real world, and learn how to engage with different people [see Box, *Expeditionary Learning Schools in Comparison to Most Other U.S. Schools*].

Moreover, in terms of professional development and teacher empowerment outcomes, teachers said they improved their ability to do the following:

■ Teach students of different ability levels in the same class

■ Be more of a guide on the side instead of a sage on the stage

■ Assess students academically and socially

■ Learn from their colleagues

■ Use parents and outside experts in the classroom

■ Be more confident and rediscover themselves as learners (Academy for Educational Development evaluation, www.outwardbound.org).

EXPEDITIONARY LEARNING SCHOOLS IN COMPARISON TO MOST OTHER U.S. SCHOOLS

Most students in American schools, according to surveys conducted in the U.S. and Canada by Michael Fullan and others, think that:

In contrast, independent evaluations of Expeditionary Learning in ten pilot schools show, among other things:

- Most of their classes are boring

- Teachers seldom ask for their opinions or ideas, and do not understand their point of view

- The vast majority of high school students do not communicate inside or outside of class with the vast majority of other students

- Only a small number of students participate regularly in class discussions

- Students' predominant orientation to curriculum is "to cover course topics and get good grades"

- There are high levels of engagement in learning and sense of attachment to school in all Expeditionary Learning schools

- Most students in these schools report that their teachers and peers listen to what they have to say

- Close bonding between students and teachers is evident in Expeditionary Learning schools; students are more likely to like their teachers

- Most students report their teachers expect a lot of work for them, and encourage students to redo their work until it is as good as it can be

(From Academy for Education Development Evaluation on Outward Bound Website: www.outwardbound.org)

Similarly, another outcome valued by Tribes TLC, parent and community involvement in the schools, increased. In the AED evaluation, one principal commented that, "The school environment is more welcoming to parents, a change that has nearly doubled the number of parent volunteers on the school's roster."

However, the really powerful research support for active learning—and the Tribes TLC process—emanates from three lines of inquiry into active learning: adventure learning, service learning, and arts learning. These studies are also seminal in the growing youth development field, essentially establishing beyond a doubt that human development and learning are two sides of the same coin, that is, the whole child. They also clearly document that the best prevention is youth development.

Adventure Learning

The fields of health promotion, health education, recreation and leisure studies, mental health, juvenile delinquency, and experiential education (usually refers to active learning outside the classroom) recognized that adventure education and outdoor experience programs are a major strategy for accomplishing holistic developmental outcomes in working with young people. Throughout the twentieth century, outdoor experience programs have been used both therapeutically, to provide troubled youth with a healing environment, and educationally (inspired by the work of John Dewey, of course), to allow students to learn through real life experiences in nature and in the community. In either case, youth are involved in doing physical activities away from their normal environments with the goals being personal growth and transformation and life success.

Typically, outdoor education programs have been two to four week-long programs, usually involving small groups of students who are transported to the wilderness with a trained leader in a facilitative role The students are assigned challenging tasks such as mastering a river rapid or hiking to a remote point, tasks that require frequent and intense group problem-solving and decision-making interactions. Outward Bound (www.outwardbound.org), a private, nonprofit group founded in 1941, is the largest of these programs, serving more than 40,000 students worldwide each year. However, since 1971, Project Adventure (www.pa.org) has brought these experiential methods and techniques into the public school and is now in over a thousand schools worldwide.

Unfortunately, as is the case with many developmentally-oriented approaches, experimental, large-scale, and longitudinal studies of adventure learning have been almost nonexistent with most of the research being anecdotal and correlational. In fact, evaluators have been frustrated in that qualitative studies of adventure programs consistently have related positive—even profound—outcomes that they could not express in terms of "statistical significance."

What the prevention and education fields now have, however, is an extensive meta-analysis of adventure programs. Meta-analysis is a procedure that synthesizes findings across many studies, thus avoiding the problems of small samples and diverse outcomes and programs. This statistical procedure can also assess the effects of various moderators and identify the major sources of variability in the program effects. The fundamental unit of analysis is the *effect size*. Effect size basically measures the degree of change.

This meta-analysis, conducted by John Hattie and his colleagues (1997) was based on 1,728 effect sizes drawn from 151 samples in 96 studies of out-of-school adventure programs, primarily in the U.S. and Australia. This study involved 12,057 unique participants of whom 72% were male and 28% female, ranging in age from 11 to 42 years. Two major findings for educators and preventionists were, first, that students made gains on 40 different outcomes, which they categorized into six major categories as follows:

- **Leadership** consisting of conscientiousness, decision making, goal-setting, time management, values, task leadership, teamwork

- **Self-concept** consisting of physical ability, peer relations, general self-esteem, physical; appearance, academic/problem-solving confidence, self-efficacy, family/self, self-understanding, well-being independence/autonomy

- **Academic** consisting of mathematics and reading scores, GPA, problem-solving

- **Personality** consisting of achievement motivation, emotional stability, aggression, locus of control, maturity, neurosis reduction, assertiveness

- **Interpersonal** includes cooperation, interpersonal communication, social competence, relating skills, recidivism [of antisocial behaviors], and

- **Adventuresome** challengeness, flexibility/imaginative, physical fitness, environmental awareness.

Note these categories closely match the positive developmental outcomes for youth in resilience studies as well as are skills, attitudes, and academic outcomes developed by Tribes TLC.

Secondly—and most astounding—the students' gains *increased* over time—sometimes months after participants completed the 20- to 26-day programs. This latter finding contrasts sharply to most educational and prevention interventions in which program effects fade after the program terminates. According to the researchers, "A program effect of .34 and a follow-up of an additional .17, leading to a combined pre-follow-up effect of .51, are unique in the education literature" (p. 70). This also is reminiscent of resilience research findings that document the power of a turn-around person, place, or experience that literally "turn" the course of development onto a positive path (Benard, 2004).

Furthermore, the researchers found no differences relating to ethnic group, socioeconomic status, or prior academic achievement. Nor did they find differences in the effect sizes among non at-risk participants, managers, and "high-risk" youth nor between high school and university students *during* adventure programs. Not unlike other studies, the effect sizes for the "high-risk" youth in the follow-up studies were greater than for the other groups. In terms of gender, they found similar positive effects for both males and females.

A theme underlying the outcomes with the greatest effects related to *self-control* (in the category of self-concept) and included independence, confidence, self-efficacy, self-understanding, assertiveness, internal locus of control, and decision-making. These traits have all been identified in resilience research as protective against involvement in high-risk behaviors and as promoting healthy development. According to the researchers, "Adventure programs appear to be most effective at providing participants with a sense of self-regulation," of being able to actively control oneself in order to respond appropriately to environmental challenges (p. 70). Not to be under-rated, however, is that, "The effects of adventure programs on *self-esteem* exceeds that of other educational programs." They also found their study findings validated those of an earlier and much smaller meta-analysis done solely on adolescent adventure programs (Cason and Gillis, 1994).

Besides these exciting positive developmental outcomes, this study found equally dramatic academic outcomes. Given that most adventure programs do not have goals explicitly focused on academic achievement, "The effects on academic performance [found in this meta-analysis in terms of] both general academic gains such as problem solving and direct effects such as mathematics scores—are most impressive" (p. 68). According to these researchers, the active problem-solving experience, which also involves communication, cooperation, and immediate feedback, generalizes not only to future problem-solving but to educational attainment as well. This corresponds to the resilience literature which identifies problem-solving as one of the most critical individual protective factors in both healthy development and successful learning (Benard, 1991, 2004; Masten and Coatsworth, 1998).

While this meta-analysis included problem (alcohol and drug abuse, teen pregnancy, violence, etc.) as well as positive behavioral measures, the researchers make no specific mention of these outcomes. They include them in the category of *interpersonal* outcomes of which they state, "In our meta-analysis, across *all* interpersonal dimensions, there are marked increases as a consequence of the adventure programs. This is particularly noted with social competence, cooperation, and interpersonal communication" (p. 69). These latter three are also consistently identified in the longitudinal studies of resilience as critical individual protective factors (Benard, 1991, 2004; Masten and Coatsworth, 1998) and by cooperative learning evaluations as three commonly found outcomes. They are also three critical skills developed by the Tribes TLC process.

In the absence of needed *formative* or *process* studies of adventure programs, Hattie and his colleagues make several premises as to why adventure programs have these positive outcomes:

- **Intensity** of the immediate experience which allows the participant full involvement in the activity

- **Challenging and specific goals** that direct attention and effort

- **Amount and quality of feedback** that is vital to the experiential learning process ("Feedback is the most powerful single moderator that improves affective and achievement outcomes")

- **Mutual group support** in which to reflect, dialog, and act as well as to cope with and understand one's world

- **Experiencing a restorative environment** in which students get "out of their typical surroundings; the natural is dominant; there are opportunities for fascination; [and] learning occurs in a set of regularities within the environment that leads to *coherence...*" (p. 76).

Hattie et al. write that creating the context that is conducive to ongoing feedback is critical. "There is more potential to give feedback when the goals are difficult, where class sizes are small, when there is cooperative planning and peer tutoring, and when there is challenging problem-solving" (1997, p. 75). Of most importance is creating this context of *mutual group support* in which youth give each other feedback allows for personal risk-taking, assessment and perspective-taking of one's goals, values, attitudes, and feelings in a safe, respectful social context. Note that all these recommended strategies are part of Tribes TLC and map directly to what resilience research and both prevention and education program evaluation research has found to correlate with successful development and learning: meaningful participation and contribution in a safe and nurturing place, high expectation messages that challenge and motivate, and supportive relationships that connect one to others—all of sufficient intensity to effect positive development and successful learning.

While this study has many implications for school reform, what it confirms for Tribes practitioners is the power of the entire Tribes model of human development and learning, caring culture, small learning communities, and especially active learning. Like other evaluations of *developmental* approaches, this study confirms that it is *how* we do what we do that counts. The context is more important than the content of the intervention; the process is more important than the program per se. "It is clear that adventure programs are not inherently good. There is a great deal of variability in outcomes between different studies, different programs, and different individuals" (Hattie et al., 1997, p. 77). To the extent that the process includes the above attributes—direct experience, challenging and specific goals, ongoing feedback, and mutual group support—that is, the environmental protective factors, that is the degree to which interventions will be successful. It is precisely because these attributes meet human developmental needs for safety, love, belonging, respect, autonomy, challenge and mastery, power, and meaning.

Service-Learning

Service-learning (also called community service-learning) is a form of active learning and project-based learning that integrates students' academic learning with service that meets actual community needs. It provides a "double whammy" effect by drawing together two already effective approaches to education and youth development: experiential learning and community service. Just as young people learn best through their active participation in the learning process, having the opportunity for contribution, to give back their gifts to others, constitutes the most powerful form of participation.

Just as is the case for adventure learning, for many years the positive anecdotes—and they are abundant!—provided the only evidence that this youth participation strategy worked. We now have several evaluations that provide hard evidence to back up these personal stories. This service-learning research summary is based on findings from a rigorous national experimental study of one service-learning approach, the Teen Outreach Program (TOP) (Allen et al., 1997) as well as the interim and final reports of the national evaluation of Learn and Service America (Melchior, 1996; Melchior, 1998), and a statewide evaluation of CalServe, California's service-learning effort (RPP International, 1998).

TEEN OUTREACH PROGRAM

The Teen Outreach Program is a national dropout and teen pregnancy prevention effort for high school age students begun in 1987 by the Association of Junior Leagues International. It is based on the youth development philosophy that successful learning and healthy behaviors can result from programs that focus on providing developmental supports and opportunities. While local coordinators have much flexibility in tailoring the program to local contexts and student needs—and are encouraged to do so—they are expected to adhere to TOP's underlying principles:

- a youth development approach

- strong community-wide partnerships

- learner-centered activities

- connecting learning from service to classroom experiences (James, p. 135).

TOP consists of three highly participatory components: supervised community volunteer service, *classroom reflection* that connects the service experience to students' lives, and classroom discussions and activities around social and developmental issues salient to adolescents—developing self-awareness, dealing with family stress, and friendship and dating issues. All of these discussions take place in *small groups* led by the trained program facilitator/coordinator who has access to a broad array of curriculum support materials from which he or she can choose. Interestingly, given that teen pregnancy prevention is one of the stated goals—but not surprising for a youth development focused intervention—the material on sexuality comprises less than 15% of the written curriculum and often is not used (especially if this information has already been covered in other health classes or if it conflicts with "prevailing community attitudes" (Allen, 1997, p. 732).

The evaluation examined 25 different random assignment sites nationwide from 1991 through 1995. Students were randomly assigned to either Teen Outreach or the control group. The TOP group consisted of 342 students with 86% female, 68% African American, 17% white, 13% Hispanic, and less than 50% in two-parent households. Compared to the comparison group, TOP participants showed a:

- 39% lower rate of course failure

- 42% lower rate of school suspension

- 41% lower rate of teen pregnancy.

The researchers conclude by making the case for youth development: "[These] results are interpreted as suggesting the potential value both of the Teen Outreach Program specifically and also more generally of *interventions that seek to prevent problem behaviors by addressing broad developmental tasks of adolescence* rather than by focusing upon individual problem behaviors or micro-skills" (Allen et al., 1997, p. 729).

THE NATIONAL EVALUATION OF LEARN AND SERVE AMERICA: INTERIM EVALUATION

A three-year interim evaluation study (Melchior, 1996) of more than 1,000 service-learning students (including the comparison group) in high-quality programs in seven middle schools and ten high schools in nine states was conducted by Brandeis University and Abt Associates. Teachers and community agency partners were also surveyed and interviewed in focus groups. This extensive evaluation, part of Learn and Service America (a competitive grants program carried out under the National and Community Service Act of 1993), found positive impacts on not only the students but on cooperating schools, community organizations, and on the larger communities.

Service learning programs showed statistically significant, positive impacts on several measures of student civic and educational development:

- engagement in school

- personal responsibility

- grades

- social responsibility

- core subject GPA

- acceptance of cultural diversity

- educational aspirations

- leadership.

The middle-school service-learning students were also significantly less likely to be arrested and somewhat less likely to get pregnant than students not participating in the program. These impacts held across gender, race, and socioeconomic categories. Besides these positive educational and developmental outcomes, the students actually felt the service-learning experience was valuable and made a difference. An impressive 90% of the student volunteers said they thought others should be encouraged to participate in service-learning; 87% said they learned valuable skills that will be useful in the future; and 75% said they learned more than in a typical class.

This evaluation also surveyed the community agencies, schools, hospitals, and other agencies where students had served. Overall, service-learning fostered positive changes in the community's view of students and their schools as evidenced in the following findings:

- 99% said they would use the students again

- 90% felt the students had helped the agency improve their client and community services

- 75% reported the students had raised the skill levels, engagement, and self-esteem of their clients

- 66% stated that the students had fostered a more attitude toward working with the schools

- 56% indicated that new relationships with the public schools had been produced

- 82% believed the service-learning program had helped to build a more positive attitude towards youth in the community.

As evidenced by these findings, service-learning not only improves individual student educational and social outcomes but fosters positive school-community collaboration and—not to be under-emphasized—improves community life for everyone. A point to remember is that this evaluation included high-quality service-learning programs that met the following criteria: more service hours than most programs, regular use of oral and written reflection, in operation for more than one year, and linked to a formal course curriculum.

This interim evaluation examined the program impacts for students who participated during the 1995-96 academic year. The final report, published in 1998, examined the longer-term, follow-up impacts on student participants. Specifically, the researchers wanted to find if these positive outcomes held over time.

NATIONAL EVALUATION OF LEARN AND SERVE AMERICA SCHOOL AND COMMUNITY-BASED PROGRAMS: FINAL REPORT

In this final report (Melchior, 1998), researchers analyzed seventeen school-based sites across nine states involving 760 students (including comparison students). Forty-five percent of this group had participated in a service-learning class in a prior year. Researchers also conducted teacher and community agency surveys and interviews as well as on-site observation. Overall, the follow-up study found:

- The differences between participants and comparison group members had decreased.

- Significant impacts still held for the outcomes of service leadership, school engagement, and science grades.

- High school participants showed a stronger pattern of impacts than middle school participants.

- Middle school participants were less likely to be arrested than comparison students.

- Impacts were significantly stronger for participants who had continued their involvement in service-learning during the follow-up year.

- Students who had continued their involvement in service-learning showed positive impacts on

    ◆ service leadership

    ◆ service hours

    ◆ school engagement

    ◆ involvement in service

    ◆ college aspirations

    ◆ consumption of alcohol.

In this final report the researchers conducted a cost analysis of the service-learning programs they studied, finding that on the average participants produced services valued at nearly four times the program cost—and this does not even include the benefits from gains in attitudes and academic performance!

AN EVALUATION OF K-12 SERVICE-LEARNING IN CALIFORNIA: PHASE II FINAL REPORT

This study, conducted by RPP International (1998), examined the impacts on students, schools, and teachers in 14 CalServe schools that an earlier study had found were doing quality (well-designed and –implemented) service-learning. Both quantitative findings and qualitative fieldwork found that service-learning benefits students, schools, teachers, community agencies, and community attitudes toward youth and schools.

The CalServe study used the same instrument to collect data on a wide range of student attitudes and behaviors in elementary, middle, and high schools. Significant findings include:

At the middle school level:
- academic achievement

- community service leadership.

At the high school level:
- educational aspirations

- personal and social responsibility

- work orientation.

Besides these positive educational and developmental impacts on students, the evaluation found that, "At schools where service-learning was well-designed and well-implemented, it had substantial benefits for both schools and teachers. The most substantial impacts occurred at schools where service-learning was most widespread—i.e., where more than 20 percent of the school's teachers were using service-learning" (RPP International, 1998, p. v).

Service-learning produced the following effects on and for teachers:

■ **Reinforced and stimulated the use of innovative instructional practices**
Specifically, teachers using service learning were more *student-centered* in their
teaching in terms of using thematic instruction, hands-on activities, project-based
learning, and portfolio assessment. For teachers already using these constructivist
approaches, implementing service-learning was an especially smooth process.

■ **Promoted teacher collegiality** At all but one school in the California evaluation,
"Teachers using service learning reported that their interaction with other teachers
and community partners was a particularly rewarding aspect of service learning"
(1998, p. 91). Not only did they enjoy sharing stories, exchanging ideas, and planning together around service learning, they also extended their interaction to
broader issues of teaching and education.

Teacher collegiality also became the primary means in California for spreading
the concept of service learning, just as it is for spreading Tribes and any other
learning innovation, Sharing their service learning success stories with other teachers, program coordinators, principals, school board members, and even the public
and media helped garner administrative and public support and spread the adoption of more service learning programs. "Some of these success stories, told and
retold, became part of the culture of the service learning programs and, in a sense,
the program's recruitment message" (p. 93).

■ **Evoked enthusiasm for teaching** Most teachers in the California evaluation
expressed enthusiasm for service learning, indicating their intention to continue
using it. They felt more job satisfaction, more energy, and more motivation. They
seldom perceived their extra workload as a serious burden. They enjoyed what they
were doing—including having fun with students!

■ **Began using community resources to support students** Teachers had to work
closely with community partners to help ensure that students would achieve positive academic and developmental outcomes from service activities. Keeping community partners aware of their students' learning objectives was an ongoing task as
community agencies' priorities focused on the delivery of client services.

Teachers who were involved in cultivating their own community resources reported they were beginning to use community partners as guest lecturers in their classes. One teacher commented that, "Students pay attention or consider what they're learning more relevant if a professional, say, a nutritionist, or geriatric specialist, talks to them about the content they're learning in class" (p. 88). Teachers also declared having derived important personal and professional benefits from their efforts to connect with community partners and help their colleagues.

- **School climate** These researchers also found positive effects on school climate. "At some schools that made fairly extensive use of service-learning, teachers and administrators reported a radical change in the school's overall climate…At nearly every school, however, teachers, students, administrators, and others reported that those engaged in service-learning felt more a part of the school community" (p. 71). In fact, at some schools, they found evidence suggesting that service-learning also contributed to reduced teacher turnover. Specifically, this study found the following evidence of school climate improvement:

  - **Students' sense of connectedness to school** Students began to feel a sense of themselves as contributing and respected members of the school community. They began to construct a new idea for themselves—as resources and service providers rather than as problems and recipients of adult services. Administrators and teachers usually noticed this being expressed in the reduced incidents of graffiti and vandalism on the school grounds and increased levels of participation in afterschool extracurricular activities.

  - **Group cohesiveness, mutual respect, and more positive peer interactions among students** Students had the opportunity to work together as members of a team on a meaningful task. As a result they learned to appreciate and respect one another as "doers, knowers, and learners" (p. v).

  - **Improved relationships between students and teachers** Service-learning helped shift the perspective on the part of teachers to the students-as-resources paradigm; i.e., they were able to see students in new ways. Students and teachers were forced to work together in a more collaborative manner.

■ **School-wide goals and restructuring** One last category of school-related impacts of service-learning is in the area of school-wide goals and restructuring. In many of the schools studied, service-learning became seen as a strategic tool for achieving the school's personal, developmental, and educational goals for its students. The CalServe evaluation also found that at some schools service learning provided a strong catalyst for reform, for restructuring school activities from traditional methods to more student-centered approaches. These included moving to block scheduling to provide time for service, creating teacher planning time, and increasing use of interdisciplinary thematic instruction.

Similar to the national Learn and Serve evaluation, the researchers found that service-learning had positive impacts on the community and on community attitudes toward young people and their schools. For example, service learning community effects include the following:

♦ **Fostered positive changes in community views of students and their schools** The impact most often reported by community agencies was their improved perception of students and their schools. They reported students' conduct during service as responsible and helpful. The community views of students from continuation schools—and of continuation schools themselves—especially changed for the positive.

♦ **Positive changes in community perceptions of students and their schools promoted increased community involvement in and support for the schools** Most of the teachers, program coordinators, and community partners surveyed and interviewed reported that as community perceptions of students and schools became more positive as a result of service-learning, increased numbers of community groups and agencies as well as volunteers came forward to get involved. Several administrators mentioned two other benefits: school enrollments increased and more school bond issues were passed as school reputations improved.

♦ **Met real community needs and generated increased community demand for student service** Students often filled the gap between identified needs for services and the availability of community volunteers, met multiple community needs, and often actually identified and met a community need not previously acknowledged. As a result, student work in their communities helped to foster the institutionalization of service-learning by generating a demand for student service. The following moving story, recounted by the evaluation staff, illustrates this point:

> One resident of the [convalescent] home was a younger man with a debilitating disease. Bedridden, overcome with despondency, this man never spoke to or even acknowledged the presence of the home's professional caregivers. A sixth-grade student from a class that was using service-learning—oblivious to adults' pessimistic prognoses—decided to befriend this man. Week after week, the student returned to the man's room to read and talk to him, demanding nothing and assuming nothing. By the end of the semester, the two had become friends. For the first time, the patient acknowledged and responded to another human being—his student friend. An 11-year old had succeeded where professional adults had met only frustration (p. 108).

The above evaluations—along with other studies—have identified the components of effective service-learning programs, programs that produced positive academic and behavioral outcomes. The overall conclusions absolutely support Tribes as a youth development approach grounded in resilience-based supports and opportunities. They document the recurring principle that *it's how you do what you do that counts*—that successful programs are rich in the protective factors of caring relationships, high expectation messages, and opportunities for meaningful participation and contribution. For example, the evaluators of California's service-learning programs concluded that the two most powerful determinants of student learning and growth were the *people* ("the quality of individual teachers") and the *process* ("implementation at the classroom level") (RPP International, 1998, p. 150).

Specifically, effective service-learning approaches comprise the following elements:

- **Staff believe that youth are resources** In a Carnegie funded study (1989), researchers Diane Harrington and Joan Schine and identified the foremost element of successful service-learning to be the staff's youth development philosophy, especially their deep high-expectation belief that youth are resources. According to these researchers, successful service learning in the middle grades is linked to a school's strong *beliefs* that adolescents can make "genuine, lasting, and responsible contributions" to their communities and that they can learn their academic subjects and develop ethics through service learning integrated into the curriculum (1989). Similarly, the evaluation of the National Crime Prevention Council's *Youth As Resources* community service initiative identifies the pivotal role played by staff who do indeed believe youth are resources (Schmidt-Lewis, 1995).

- **Students have leadership roles** The most effective service learning approaches are committed to youth ownership of the learning process (Allen et al., 1997; Harrington and Schine, 1989; Schmidt-Lewis, 1995; KIDS Consortium, 1998). This means that students feel personally and collectively responsible for their service work. This was clearly evident in *The Teen Outreach Program* discussed above as well as that of the *Youth as Resources* initiative; and it is the driving principle of a prominent community service-learning in the Northeast: KIDS As Planners. In fact, the CalServe evaluation found that students' perceived level of responsibility during service is the only characteristic of the service experience that was associated with positive impacts across a wide array of educational and civic outcomes. "Having 'real responsibilities' was positively correlated with engagement in school, homework completion, and work orientation, as well as personal and social responsibility, service leadership, and voluntary service participation" (RPP International, 1998, p. 139).

Both positive academic and youth development outcomes such as cooperation, empathy, problem-solving, autonomy, self-efficacy, responsibility, and sense of purpose result when young people have more freedom and autonomy, "choice and voice," to design, implement, and evaluate a project. In fact, research has found that, "The more intense their involvement in a project, the greater the benefits" (James, 1999, p. 105). This means that students must work in an authentic partnership with adults, making real decisions and solving real problems, and that they are involved in leadership roles in actually planning and implementing the service learning project.

■ **Responsibilities and accountability are clear** Vital to a service-learning program's successful implementation are clearly defined—and documented in writing—roles and responsibilities for schools, districts, parents, students, and community partners. This corresponds also to the finding of the American Youth Policy Forum's analysis that projects that have measurable and discernible results tend to be more successful in retaining youth (Halperin & Partee, 1997; James, 1999, p. 107).

■ **Tasks meet both community and youth needs** The evaluation of the National Crime Prevention Council's Youth As Resources initiative concluded that, "Tasks that met both community needs and youth's needs seemed to yield more success in terms of favorable impact on youth than did those that only stressed one or the other" (in James, 1999, p. 107). This can be explained simply as youth were attracted to projects that met real community needs; however, the projects had to be designed and implemented in such a way that they felt a sense of personal safety, belonging, respect, accomplishment, autonomy, and meaning.

■ **Service is tightly integrated into the curriculum** For academic gains to occur and for young people to feel connected, the service experience must be authentic—truly providing for experiential, hands-on-learning. It cannot be service in name only. The school curriculum enriches service involvement by providing an opportunity for students to apply what they have learned in the classroom to a real world context and vice versa. This principle applies to both after-school as well as in-school service experiences.

■ **The focus is on caring relationships—with teachers and other program facilitators, with peers, and with persons at volunteer sites** Establishing a safe climate in which adolescents can trust is the first task of any youth development program. Foremost in this process are nurturing and committed teachers and program facilitators. The California service-learning evaluation concluded that, "The quality of individual teachers remains the most powerful in-school determinant of student learning and growth" (RPP International, 1998, p. 150). Similarly, the TOPS evaluators had found in an earlier evaluation that, "The most successful program sites were those that aided students in the task of establishing autonomy in the context of positive relationships with peers, with program facilitators, and with persons at volunteer sites… "Feeling safe, listened to, and respected were linked to positive student outcomes" (Allen et al., 1997, p. 739). This quote could also be describing Tribes TLC.

Furthermore, the California evaluation found the more effective service experiences were also those in which the youth also had an opportunity to establish personal relationships with service recipients. This closeness, illustrated in the convalescent home story, promoted empathy, responsibility, acceptance of diversity, and ultimately connectedness with others, with the community, and with life itself.

■ **Time for planning, processing, and reflecting on the part of teachers, students, and community partners is critical** Service-learning occurs through a process of preparation, action, and reflection for all participants. Preparation includes planning as well as becoming familiar with the service site, the recipients, and the work to be done. In the California evaluation, the sites with the most positive outcomes did "service-specific, practical/logistical, affective, and curricular preparation" (RPP International, 1998, p. 148).

Reflection activities include ongoing and regularly scheduled opportunities for students to discuss and write about their service experiences. This process is absolutely essential in producing positive outcomes. It is also a powerful means of promoting critical inquiry and thinking. "Sites where students were required during reflection to suggest probable causes of and solutions for problems that arose during service appeared somewhat more likely to have positive student impacts on measures related to both educational performance and civic responsibility" (RPP International, 1998, p. 149).

Similarly, effective service-learning implementation requires that teachers and community partners also have time for planning, processing, and reflecting on the experience. Essentially, the service-learning experience provided the context for both teacher collegiality and school-community collaboration, two other major strategies for promoting youth development and successful learning. These, in turn, create a supportive school climate conveying the message that teachers are respected and empowered in this school. These are essential attributes of the Tribes TLC.

■ **Teacher control with active principal support, encouragement, and vision is essential** Teacher buy-in and control of the process is crucial to schools adopting service-learning (RPP International, 1998, p. vii). Teachers in the CalServe evaluation did not want service-learning mandated but responded positively to principal support for service-learning training and resources to support implementation. Administrative supports associated with schoolwide adoption of service-learning include providing teachers with opportunities to share their experiences with service-learning, providing on-site mentors and available program coordinators, removing scheduling and logistical barriers to service activities, making adoption of schoolwide service-learning a goal, and creating formal—but flexible and responsive—policies that insure organizational commitment. This finding also has total application to the adoption of Tribes TLC.

■ **High-quality professional development is provided** The CalServe evaluation found that most teachers who were fully implementing service-learning had attended a two- or three-day service-learning institute. However, all trainings were not equal! According to RPP International, the *quality* of the training was more important than its frequency. Specifically, the training needs to include how to integrate the various key components of service-learning (preparation, reflection, student voice, need-based service, collaboration with service partners, and so on). Tribes TLC has a direct focus on high-quality professional development, especially in creating teacher learning communities.

Service-learning, for which Tribes TLC is particularly suited structurally in terms of having the necessary small group learning process, as well as in terms of creating a caring culture focused on human development and learning. The Tribes process applied to service-learning is probably as close as we'll get to an education and prevention lodestone for school engagement and healthy youth development. It is as also as close as we'll get in public schools to fostering spiritual development—that search for meaning that drives a young person's quest to answer life's compelling questions (Muller, 1996): "Who am I? What do I love? How shall I live? What are my gifts to the family of the earth?" And it may be our hope for creating a society that honors and lives an ethic of caring and compassion for other people and for the earth.

PERRY PRESCHOOL PROGRAM

As mentioned earlier in this document, the High/Scope Educational Research Foundation's Perry Preschool Program (PPP) is one of a handful of long-term follow-up evaluations of an actual prevention *intervention*. It is truly one of the most powerful research supports for developmental education, especially at an early age. It began in Ypsilanti, Michigan in 1962 as a longitudinal study of children from poor African-American families who attended a developmental as well as social constructivist preschool program at ages 3 and 4 that focused on their cognitive, language, social-emotional, and behavioral development. The High/Scope model emphasized active child-initiated *active learning,* problem-solving, decision-making, planning, and a high degree of interaction between adults and children and among the children themselves. In addition, teachers conducted weekly home visits and encouraged parents to be involved as volunteers in the classroom.

As reported in *Changed Lives* (Berruta-Clement et al., 1984), children who participated in the program showed the following outcomes at age 19 compared to a control group:

- Increases in cognitive gains

- Improved scholastic achievement during school years

- Decreases in crime/delinquency

- Decreases in teen pregnancy

- Increases in post-secondary enrollment

- Increases in high school graduation rate

- Increases in employment rate

- Benefits exceeded costs sevenfold.

Furthermore, in 1993 the follow-up study of this population was published in *Significant Benefits: The High/Scope Perry Preschool Study through Age 27* (Wiekart & Schweinhart). This study found that project participants have transitioned to adulthood far more successfully than adults from similar backgrounds. They have committed far fewer crimes, have higher earnings, and possess a greater commitment to marriage.

A related High/Scope study (Schweinhart & Weikart, 1986) compared 15-year-olds who participated in the High/Scope model with those from a traditional nursery school approach and a direct instruction, academic-focused approach. The study revealed that students from the High/Scope and nursery school groups reported engaging in:

- one-half as many acts of personal violence

- one-fifth as many acts of property violence

- one-half as many status offenses

- one-half as many acts of drug abuse

- more sports and after-school activities.

In addition, their families reported regarding them more favorably.

A follow-up (Schweinhart & Weikart, 1997) to age 23 of this preschool comparison study found that children in the High/Scope program, which gives children ample decision making over their class activities, or a play-oriented nursery school, committed fewer crimes, had better success on the job, and maintained healthier relationships than those who received direct instruction in which teachers led the activities, workbooks were the only classroom materials, and the acquisition of academic skills was the prime objective. This new research confirms many experts' beliefs that the best preschools offer a *child-directed* active learning curriculum in which teachers let children's interests guide the learning. According to a spokesperson for the National Association for the Education of Young Children, "If we don't work at helping kids learn self-control, it gets difficult later on."

Arts Learning

The growing research support for the role of the arts in human development and learning has been growing exponentially over this last decade, just as has the case for social-emotional learning, physical education, and other forms of active learning. In other words, the research is absolutely validating the role of multiple ways of knowing, i.e., multiple intelligences. This research is indirectly supporting the theory that human learning is an intrinsically motivated process driven by our basic human needs for safety, love, belonging, problem solving, mastery/challenge, autonomy/ identity, and purpose and meaning. That policymakers are far behind the research is evident once again in the almost total neglect to acknowledge and apply the research on multiple intelligences, especially the huge volume on the arts.

In most cultures the arts have been the means for humans to express who we are and what we know about ourselves. Even in the U.S., historically, the arts were woven into the fabric of a child's learning experience. A 1994 report of the Royal Conservatory of Music (Toronto) claims, "The thickly drawn line between arts and non-arts, so evident in our schools today simply did not exist" (quoted in Miller, 2000, p. 75) However, school-based art education barely survived extinction during the 1980s—and now again in the 21st century—with budget cutbacks, the "back-to-basics" movement (which regarded the arts as a peripheral and unnecessary frill and now emphasizes skill-and-drill), and the emphasis on producing workers to compete in the global economy. "That we have relieved the arts of their central role in education is a tragedy. The arts represent a natural and experiential way for children to learn" (report of the Royal Conservatory of Music, quoted in Miller, p. 75).

Like most of the other strategies in this document, the arts—music, dance, theater, creative writing, storytelling, and the visual arts—are forms of active learning or experiential education that produce both positive academic and youth development outcomes. In addition to the program evaluation findings documenting the positive academic, developmental, and behavioral outcomes for youth involved in the arts summarized below, most of the other powerful bodies of research summarized earlier provide an impressive rationale for providing students with ongoing opportunities to experience the many and varied forms of the creative arts. Research from the fields of resilience, multiple intelligences, and brain science are converging to create a compelling case for placing the arts in a central place in today's schools. As we will see in examining the characteristics of successful arts learning, the Tribes TLC process holds the philosophical, cultural, and structural components embedded in arts programs that produce positive whole-child outcomes.

Resilience research documents the critical role that imagination plays in surviving and transcending adversity, trauma, and risk (Higgins, 1994). The arts provide a channel to a positive future to children living in stressful environments. This research clearly shows that anything that can be imagined can become a reality. Through the means of a picture, a story, a poem, a song, a dance, or a drama, young people can tell their stories and thereby create meaning from negative experiences. They can transform suffering into a work of art that brings joy and despair into something of beauty. Resilience research has shown that involvement in the creative arts promotes the positive developmental outcomes of social competence, problem solving, a sense of autonomy, and a sense of purpose and future. Arts participation is a protective factor that not only can prevent depression and suicide but by providing a positive channel for expressing emotions like anger and hatred, confusion and rage, it also serves as effective violence, eating disorder, and alcohol, tobacco, and other drug abuse prevention.

From the field of *multiple intelligences* (Gardner, 1983, 1999) comes the understanding that there are many different ways of knowing as we discussed in Chapter One. According to MI theory, each person possesses at least eight intelligences in varying degrees and is capable of developing each intelligence to an adequate level of competency. Traditionally, however, schools have focused most of their attention on teaching the 20% of the students who learn through only two of the eight intelligences: verbal/linguistic and logical/mathematical methods. National dropout statistics tell us what happens to the other 80% of the students who learn visually/spatially, musically/rhythmically, bodily/kinesthetically, interpersonally, intrapersonally, and naturalistically.

The arts develop and rehearse many, if not all of the intelligences. A pianist simultaneously activates bodily-kinesthetic, musical, and intrapersonal systems; children acting in a drama activate all eight! Ironically, before children enter school they are actively engaged in developing all of these last competencies. Building on these intelligences by providing art experiences honors the different ways students learn and the different strengths and gifts they bring to school. Use of the arts especially provides students who struggle academically to develop their different learning styles and ways of knowing.

A spokesperson for the growing field of *brain science* informs us that, "Evidence from the brain sciences and evolutionary psychology increasingly suggests that the arts play an important role in brain development and maintenance—so it's a serious matter for schools to deny children direct curricular access to the arts"

(Sylwester, 1998, p. 32). The arts appear to lay neural pathways vital to later development. Evidence suggests that music especially facilitates the development of pattern formation and correlates with higher brain functioning in logic, math, and problem solving.

While brain research is really in its infancy and many researchers caution about making applications to education based on a few studies, several findings—with implications for the arts—seem to stand on solid ground. First, brain structures are modified by the environment. In conducive environments, the brain shows incredible plasticity and resilience. Born out by resilience research, this means it is never too late for young people to learn—*if* they experience nurturing environments. Brain researchers define these as environments that are emotionally safe, have appropriate challenges, and provide opportunities for self-constructing meaning (Tomlinson and Kalfleisch, 1998). In essence, we are talking about environments that provide the three protective factors (caring relationships, high expectations, and opportunities for participation and contribution) that meet young peoples' needs for safety, belonging, respect, identity, challenge, and meaning. Coming as no surprise, these are also the same qualities identified in effective arts programs! [see Box: *Compare Characteristics of Effective Arts Programs to Early Childhood Environments*].

Second, brain science tells us that our brains function at multiple levels of skill and understanding. We all learn differently! A "one size fits all" approach to education will clearly not work to create environments conducive to learning. What is comfortable to one student is boring to another and even threatening to yet another. Each brain needs to make its own meaning of ideas and skills—which it does best by "doing" rather than by "absorbing." The arts offer schools ways to reach all students, especially those students not reached in the traditional curriculum. Every youth has the potential to succeed in one or another form of the arts.

Third, brain research documents that emotion is essential in focusing cognitive attention. "The only way to get information into the brain is through our senses" (Wolfe, 1998, p. 61). In other words, in order for the brain to learn cognitively, young people's emotions and needs must be recognized and met. Sylwester writes that, "Emotion drives attention, and attention drives learning, problem-solving, behavior, and just about everything else." Perhaps the power of the arts in producing the positive outcomes discussed below lies in the fact that, "Emotion and attention are central

CHARACTERISTICS OF EFFECTIVE ARTS PROGRAMS

According to the President's Committee on the Arts & Humanities report *Coming Up Taller* (Weitz,1996), effective arts programs:

- Are a delicate balance between flexibility and structure

- Take full advantage of the capacity of the arts and humanities to stimulate ways of knowing and learning

- Use dynamic teaching tactics such as hands-on learning, apprenticeship relationships and modern technology

- Provide children and youth with an opportunity to success. They generate expectations and then provide the means to accomplish defined goals

- Begin small and keep their classes small

- Recognize that positive adult relationships are crucial to success—and recruit accordingly

- Build on what young people already value

- Have clear goals and high expectations

- Provide an accessible safe haven within which to learn

- Are voluntary and shaped by the youth themselves, helping to make the projects "not like schools"

- Provide quality youth workers and quality programming—disadvantaged youth should, like more affluent children, have access to the best society has to offer

- Work in partnerships with parents, but know they offer children something different

- Are committed for the long term—changing lives takes time and children come to count on these projects. It can be cruel to bring them into a positive environment that cannot be sustained

- Are gateways to other services for young people.

CHARACTERISTICS OF HEALTHY CHILDHOOD ENVIRONMENTS

According to Marian Diamond and her learning colleagues at the University of California at Berkeley (1998, *Magic Trees of The Mind*) an enriched environment for children and youth:

- Includes a steady source of positive emotional support

- Provides a nutritious diet with enough protein, vitamins, minerals, and calories

- Stimulates all the senses (but not necessarily all at once!)

- Has an atmosphere free of undue pressure and stress but suffused with a degree of pleasurable intensity

- Presents a series of novel challenges that are neither too easy nor too difficult for the child at his or her stage of development

- Allows social interaction for a significant percentage of activities

- Promotes the development of a broad range of skills and interests that are mental, physical, aesthetic, social , and emotional

- Gives the child an opportunity to choose many of his or her efforts and to modify them

- Provides an enjoyable atmosphere that promotes exploration and the fun of learning

- Allows the child to be an active participant rather than a passive observer.

to all activity in the arts" (Sylwester, 1998, p. 35). The arts engage people young and old at this emotional level, making learning more meaningful and exciting.
It will be obvious to Tribes practitioners that almost all of the characteristics of both effective arts programs *and* early childhood environments are embedded in the developmental process of Tribes.

The following three studies represent, respectively, a compilation to 1995 of representative research and evaluation of arts education documenting positive student outcomes, an analysis of the National Educational Longitudinal Survey focused on arts involvement and student outcomes, and an in-depth examination of how and why community arts programs are changing young peoples' lives.

SCHOOLS, COMMUNITIES, AND THE ARTS: A RESEARCH COMPENDIUM

In 1994 the National Endowment for the Arts commissioned the Morrison Institute for Public Policy at Arizona Sate University to conduct a comprehensive review of current research on the implementation of quality arts programs in schools. The purpose was to make the best information about arts programming available to educational policymakers. The result is *Schools, Communities, and the Arts: A Research Compendium* (SCA), a document designed "as a tool that can help address the kinds of questions local government, business, and community leaders might ask about arts education." Out of approximately 500 applied and academic research studies, the authors identified 49 studies published since 1985 that met their rigorous criteria. These studies ranged from meta-analyses and large-scale qualitative and quantitative evaluations of multifaceted programs to smaller-scale program evaluations. At one end, they looked at discipline-based art education programs that were integrated into the curriculum of the school and at the other, they examined community arts centers that met not only the needs of children and youth but their families as well. While drawing conclusions across these myriad studies is difficult, one recurring theme is that the arts do produce positive outcomes in young people.

Youth development outcomes include increases in:

- planning ability

- belief in value of personal effort

- interest in social studies

- communication skills

- cultural awareness, sensitivity, and appreciation

- alternative ways of seeing

- critical thinking

- self-expression

- resourcefulness

- trust

- achievement motivation

- self-acceptance

- self-esteem

- acceptance of others

- creativity

- self-awareness

- fun/joy

- goal-setting.

This list directly parallels the individual traits that resilience research has found characterize successful overcomers of the odds. It also maps well to the outcomes of cooperative learning groups and to the outcomes we can expect from the Tribes TLC experience. These traits also map well with the competencies identified in the SCANS (Secretary's Commission on Achieving Necessary Skills) report nearly a decade ago as being critical to our nation's healthy workforce. Obviously, then, good arts programs—as a powerful form of active learning—produce the personal attitudes, values, and skills that enable healthy development even in the face of risk *and* that also define a valued and successful worker.

In reviewing this research compilation, it is also clear that good arts programs produce positive academic outcomes as well. One study hypothesized that the open and exploratory nature of art classes allowed students to more actively explore their "regular" core subjects areas.

Academic outcomes include gains in:

- language arts

- math

- reading comprehension

- social studies

- standardized test scores

- English as a Second Language

- higher level thinking skills

  - evaluation and research skills

  - critical thinking

  - problem solving.

While it is clear from the overall positive academic outcomes found in these studies that the arts aid and abet student achievement, several advocates warn against selling the arts *only* for this instrumental value. The arts also effect the wonderful holistic youth developmental outcomes cited above—plus others unexamined such as wonder, awe, and meaning—that reflect young lives learning to understand life in all its possibilities.

While fewer studies examined the effects of participating in arts education on teachers, the few that did found the following *effects on teachers:*

- higher expectations for students

- greater awareness of multicultural issues

- greater willingness to collaborate with colleagues

- greater willingness to take risks.

The one study reviewed (Stinson, 1993) that actually asked students *their* perception of their experiences in arts classes (in this case, dance) shed light on yet another outcome—the positive *school climate effects* that arts classes have. The 36 "at-risk" students interviewed, representing a wide range of school achievement, contrasted their dance class experience sharply with their overall high school experience. They described their other classes as "boring," their teachers as "not caring," and the school rules as "stifling." They described their dance classes, however, in opposite terms. The instructors cared, they nurtured relationships among the students themselves, they emphasized self-expression, and they created a norm of acceptance of others. The students also said they liked learning skills through hard, *active* "work." The review cites one young man as explaining that dance was "a good way to get away from school.... Once you step into the auditorium, everything is kind of shattered.... You can make it what you want. When you first walk in... it's almost like time has stood still outside of those doors."

In sponsoring this research compilation, Jane Alexander, former Chairman of the National Endowment for the Arts, expressed her hopes that this document would help advance the cause of arts in schools:

> This research is about human cognition, about how children and adults learn. Art turns a key in the imagination that unlocks barriers and lets in the light. For parents, community members, educators, researchers, public policy makers, all Americans who are concerned about the life of our children and the future of our nations, I believe that these findings can help illuminate more clearly the unique role the arts play in human understanding (*Foreword*, SCA).

INVOLVEMENT IN THE ARTS AND SUCCESS IN SECONDARY SCHOOL

A substantial case for the importance of the arts in the academic lives of middle and high school youth is made by James Catterall's analysis of data from the National

Educational Longitudinal Survey (NELS) (1997). The NELS survey was begun in 1988 and remains the most important educational survey examining educational conditions and outcomes for over 25,000 students in the U.S. Catterall's analysis of the NELS is the first one examining student participation in the arts—after eight years of available survey data. He claims, "The likely reasons for this [neglect] speak to the lagging place of the arts in the imaginations of most contemporary education leaders, policy makers and researchers…. There is reason to spend more time in our large-scale queries into educational achievement on what we can know about the arts and student development and accomplishment of all sorts. This work is a start on this agenda" (p. 9).

His major findings to date with implications for arts, schools, and young people include:

- Regular involvement in the arts in school seems to decline from 8th grade when about half the students report taking an art or music class at least once per week to 10th grade when only about a third of students pursued art, music, or drama classes.

- Students with *high*-arts involvement (2–3 art classes and/or outside lessons) do better in English, on standardized test scores, and persistence in school than students with *low*-arts involvement (one class or less).

- Students in 10th grade who have high-arts involvement do better on standardized test scores, reading performance, tests of history, citizenship, and geography. They also were more likely to perform community service, believe in the importance of community service, and spend less time watching television.

- Students of higher socioeconomic status are more likely to have high-arts involvement. A student is twice as likely to show low-arts involvement if he/she is form a low income, low educational attainment family. This is probably explained by the fact that higher SES families have the means to pay for outside art classes and transportation to arts activities; they may provide more encouragement for the arts; and their children also attend more affluent school districts that offer more arts.

To find out how arts involvement affects lower SES students, Catterall examined student performance within the lowest SES quartile of all students (6,500 students). Here's what involvement in the arts means for economically disadvantaged 8th and 10th graders:

- About four times as many disadvantaged youth fall into the low-arts group as into the high-arts group. "This data support popular convictions as well as research concluding that access to the arts in inequitably distributed in our society" (p. 9).

- While the overall academic performance levels of the economically disadvantaged group are lower than that of all students, *the positive relationships between arts engagement and academic performance "remain robust and systematic."*

- More importantly, the academic advantages for arts-involved economically disadvantaged students are quite pronounced by grade 10.

- Similarly, dropout rates are 45 percent higher for low-arts, low SES students; for high-arts, low SES students, involvement in community service is greater, and hours spent watching television are lower.

Summing up this study, we can say that the most important longitudinal educational study involving over 25,000 students finds that middle and high school students involved in the arts—*including those from the lowest quartile of family education and income*—do better academically, on standardized test scores, and on a sense of commitment to the community than students with little or no arts involvement. While this quantitative analysis does not attempt to explain why art involvement has this profound effect, the author asks us to consider that in addition to the arguments from brain research and multiple intelligences, involvement in the arts promotes a sense of community as well as a positive peer influence among young people. These two components of youth development programs are not only critical to why Tribes TLC works but are also validated in the following study that not only looked quantitatively at outcomes but *qualitatively* examined the role in young people's lives of community youth programs that center on the arts.

LIVING THE ARTS THROUGH LANGUAGE + LEARNING:
A REPORT ON COMMUNITY-BASED YOUTH ORGANIZATIONS

For over a decade (1987-1998) an interdisciplinary team of researchers, policy analysts, and artists have studied what happens in community youth organizations in low-income neighborhoods in which youth like to spend their time (McLaughlin, Irby, and Langman, 1994). The Carnegie report, *Risks and Opportunities in the Nonschool Hours* (1992) drew public awareness to these organizations and to the fact that students spend only about 26 percent of their time in school; of the remaining time, older children and youth have discretion over about 50% of their time. Shirley Brice Health and her colleagues (1998) were especially curious to find out what these organizations did to engage the very same young people from ages 8 to 20 who had often disengaged from and even dropped out of their local schools. They found, not surprisingly, that most had a youth development perspective and most used active learning, focusing on the arts in one form or another. Drama programs of Boys and Girls Clubs, video arts projects of museums, civic-sponsored choirs, and grassroots visual arts studios are only a few examples of the offerings of these community centers.

The researchers were also curious to discover, "What kind of quality in artistic pursuits can such programs possibly achieve when the young people who participate have had little or no training and few opportunities to attend world-class symphonic and choral concerts, dance and theatre performances, museum and gallery exhibitions or film festivals?" The answers to these research questions provide not only a compelling reason for schools to form partnerships with community-based organizations or CBOs—these very different creatures—but the very ways these organizations engage youth and do art offers schools benchmark youth development practices, benchmark practices that are part of the Tribes TLC process as well.

In order to compare these young people participating in nonschool arts organizations with a national data base of students of a similar age, the research team asked over 100 students to complete a selection of questions used in the National Educational Longitudinal Survey (discussed above). They found that compared to youth in the national sample, youth in nonschool arts-based programs are:

- Attending schools where the potential for violence is more than twice as high

- More than twice as likely to have parents who divorced or lost their jobs in the past two years

- Over five times as likely to live in a family involved with the welfare system in the last two years.

However, they also found that young people working in the arts during their out-of-school hours are:

- Four times more likely to have won school-wide attention for their academic achievement

- Being elected to class office within their schools more than three times as often

- Four times more likely to participate in a math and science fair

- Three times more likely to win an award for school attendance

- Over four times more likely to win an award for writing an essay or poem

- Eight times more likely to receive a community service award

- Participating in youth groups nearly four times more frequently

- Reading for pleasure nearly twice as often.

In examining what *processes* were happening both intrapersonally within the young artists in these programs and interpersonally in the group environment, these anthropologists/researchers report several findings. While the researchers claim that the power of creation is hard-wired in everyone—everyone is an artist!—to hold on to this power during adolescence, replete with self-doubt and struggles with identity, requires youth have "the continuous opportunity to practice, self-discipline, and perform."

They found that the community arts organizations that engaged young people provided the following in order to create this opportunity [see also Box: *Compare Characteristics of Effective Arts Programs to Early Childhood Environments*]:

- Ongoing opportunities to pose problems, assert hypotheses, and practice

- Adult professional artists and older youth members serving as mentors

- Small group work in which youth collaborate to complete a project/performance

- Exposure to local art resources—museums, galleries, theaters, artists.

This environment allowed the young artists to develop a shared language based on critical judgment and systematic reasoning. They noted that the arts provided a level of abstraction rarely achieved in other content areas. They discovered the young artists were actively involved in three pairs of high-level verbal activities:

- **Theory-building and checking out the possible** "Artists and those who critique them over periods of production and performance keep asking things like: 'What do you think will happen if…?' 'Have you thought about trying…?'"

- **Translating and transforming** "Through art, young people transform the world about them by making it their own to create, reshape and carry forward in mental and verbal images."

- **Projecting and reflecting** Through an interactive process of peer critique and dialog, young artists have "extensive practice in getting to know how viewing and listening audiences hear, see, and find meaning in their work." Furthermore, "projections of meaning by others call for reflection on the part of the artist."

This critical judgment—similar to what cooperative learning researchers have found in higher level project learning—formed "habits of the mind" which carried over to other domains of the young people's lives. They could think through outcomes, check ideas with others, and take time to assess options—skills strived hard for in life skills and conflict resolution programs.

Most importantly, these young artists engaged in healthy risk-taking. "Risk is the key element of the arts," these researchers claim. "The essential glue holding effective arts programs together is *risk within a safe space.*" The young artists experiment with something new and challenging in a supportive peer group environment. This leads to a sense of confidence to take on more challenges, solve problems, follow through on plans, and work hard. "Unless organizations keep the stakes high and the demand level bordering on the extraordinary, young people will not sustain involvement and interest.... It is the combination of work and play with risk that carries young people forward in their learning."

In examining the organizational qualities that distinguished these effective organizations, Heath and her colleagues found they shared goals, an ethos, and a management framework. "A single, disarmingly simple goal drives effective arts-based youth programs: excellence in performance or product with community youth support." The ethos, which is also captured in Tribes' two-pronged goal of human development and learning and enables achievement of these goals and determines how adults and youth members work together—is based on the 3 Rs: *Respect* for young people and a deep belief in their capacities; giving *Responsibility* to the young people for keeping the organization *Relevant* to themselves and their communities.

Lastly, the management framework is based on having the young people as part of the organization's governance. They serve as board members, publicists, fundraisers, and staff. The management of these effective arts programs focuses on the 3 Cs: forging links to the *community*, building *connection* to each other and the community, and *commitment* to their craft and to maintaining a nurturing and healthy organizational environment for learning.

What this study clearly elucidates, along with the research on resilience, multiple intelligences, brain science, and the arts themselves is that through the arts young people are engaging their intrinsic motivation to meet their basic developmental needs. Involvement in the arts, as a form of active learning, meets the needs for:

- **belonging**—that powerful drive in adolescence for group identity— in that most art experiences happen in small shared leadership groups

- **respect** because art is taught in an atmosphere of mutual respect and honoring of diversity of learning style

- **mastery and challenge** since art experiences give a majority of students the chance to excel at something

- **identity and autonomy** because making art is about having the freedom to find out and express who we are, what we love, where we want to go, and how we want to live

- **power** since students are manifesting the power of creation and expression burning within them, and

- **meaning** in that making art is an act of creation, of remaking ourselves and our lives and giving meaning to our life experience.

Several of the evaluations discussed above were of community arts centers that served youth and families in poor communities. What became clear was that these centers are transformative for the youth, families, and communities they serve. The following characteristics of what they did become best practice benchmarks for how we do art programs from a youth development perspective. They also mirror most of the components of the Tribes TLC process.

- **Use the power of art to transform and articulate personal and group identities** Through art young people explore the existential questions—Who am I? Why am I here? How should I live?

- **Cultivate strong relationships among teachers, students, parents, staff** They recognize the power of relationships of trust to connect and motivate. These relationships weave the fabric of community that create a safe place in which young people can explore their personal and group identities.

- **Learn and attend to the interests and needs of the communities they serve** They live the youth development perspective in that they understand that meeting young people where they are with whatever issues and needs they bring is part and parcel of effective youth-serving programs.

- **Provide stable safe havens for students and families** Often these organizations are the only safe, respectful, and caring places where residents in poorer communities can go.

- **Attend to their own process of development and transformation** Staff of effective community-based organizations realize they have to "walk the talk" and model the youth development philosophy personally and organizationally.

■ **Believe—and act accordingly—that young people are resources to be engaged and not problems to be fixed** This bottom-line belief in the capacity of youth is at the core of effective arts programs for young people. This contrasts, often sharply, with "Programs that revolve around problems such as delinquency, school failure, drug use, teenage pregnancy, vandalism, and crime [that often] find it difficult to recognize the positive contributions young people can make once they are regarded as resources" (Heath et al., 1998, p. 12).

■ **School-community collaboration** Incorporating the arts into schools exists along a continuum from afterschool arts programs run by community-based art organizations to fully integrated discipline-based arts education curricula. No matter where on the spectrum your arts programming falls, successful arts programs demand working in partnership with community artists, community organizations, and/or community businesses and volunteers. Forming partnerships with youth-serving community-based arts organizations actually enables schools to observe and experience youth development in practice. Some community-based art organizations also are involving family members in family arts programs.

■ **Professional development** Summer teachers' institutes appear to be the sina qua non of effective arts programs. A 5-year study of the National Gallery of Art Teacher Institutes found that teachers who had attended these intensive institutes over the next year had:

  ◆ a new enthusiasm for teaching

  ◆ increased motivation

  ◆ higher morale

  ◆ increased awareness of the arts

  ◆ improved attitudes toward teaching art

  ◆ initiated formal relationships between their school and local museum.

However, as with any system change effort, ongoing opportunities for professional development and collegial support are essential. These opportunities must focus both on instilling and maintaining a youth development perspective and on art-based learning and include the following:

- **Time for collaborative planning** Most successful art programs involve some form of artist-teacher collaboration whether it be with an on-staff art teacher mentor approach or an artist-in-residence apprenticeship model. In these programs, the mentor-teacher and protégé teachers met regularly to discuss program planning and lesson delivery.

- **Interdisciplinary teaching that incorporates the arts into core curriculum areas** Integrating more arts activities into instruction and devoting more time to literacy activities helps engage more students' learning styles and makes all course content more experiential.

- **Instructional practices that actively engage students in the process of learning** In all of the above studies, an explicit positive relationship between teaching practices used and student outcomes exists. Producing or performing art is inherently experiential and hands on. Other practices include interactive classroom discourse, a focus on reflection-dialog-action, more student-initiated topics and discussions, more time engaged in problem-solving activities, student collaboration, and other active learning and experiential practices that engage and connect youth.

- **Enthusiasm of teacher** It goes without saying that the teacher's enthusiasm for whatever art experience is offered is essential. Teachers need to teach their passion.

- **Promote a sense of community in art class/program** Peer group support creates a sense of "family" and "community" and is an essential environmental condition for promoting a love of "art for art's sake" as well as in producing positive youth developmental and academic outcomes.

- **District support for the arts** The longitudinal evaluation of the Getty Center's early attempt to establish a comprehensive discipline-based art education (DBAE) program in 21 school districts in Los Angeles County found that the districts that were successful in this endeavor were distinguished by a high level of district support. This included formal adoption of a DBAE curriculum, adequate allocation of resources for training and instructional materials, school-based program monitoring, and effective communication at all levels within the district (National School Boards Association, 1992).

Overall, bringing the arts and the arts perspective into schools means challenging and changing the culture of the school. The arts challenge the paradigm of schooling—they ask us to embrace the strength, courage, the endurance, the promise, and the uniqueness of every student. As we move into the 21st century and our ever-changing future world, the arts offer not only students but all of us an essential means to communicate and stay connected to our shared human spirit across our increasing diversity. Perhaps more than any other component of the curriculum, the arts can serve as a catalyst for promoting cultural understanding and respect. The late Ernest Boyer of the Carnegie Foundation for the Advancement of Teaching says it well: "Art is humanity's most essential, most universal language.... Now more than ever, all people need to see clearly, hear acutely, and feel sensitively through the arts. These skills are no longer just desirable. They are essential if we are to survive together with civility and joy" (National School Boards Association, 1992).

What all of the above evaluations are validating are all of the research-based components of Tribes—from the philosophical core of human development and learning through the reculturing process to create a caring culture which is expressed in restructuring to small groups of communities of learners that create student-centered learning opportunities that honor multiple ways of learning and are active, cooperative, reflective, integrated, and project-based. One key point that Tribes practitioners must understand in this day and age of standards and high-stakes testing is that most of the evaluations cited above and earlier in this document that have looked for the effects of these research-based components on standardized tests have indeed found them. This is actually astonishing and bears repeating: When classrooms and schools use practices that support holistic development—which does not include didactic teaching to the test!—students actually not only achieve more positive developmental outcomes but improve their standardized test scores!

Let's look at two more examples from research studies that have looked directly at (1) the relationship between students' perceptions of a caring school culture and their standardized test scores and (2) the relationship between interactive teaching methods and standardized test scores. In the first study, Hanson and Austin (2002), using data from the California Healthy Kids Survey's Resilience & Youth Development Module (based on the three protective factors identified by Benard (1991), examined the relationship between students perceptions of the three protective factors at school (caring relationships, high expectation messages, and meaningful participation opportunities) and a school's Academic Performance Indicator (the score on California's high-stakes test). They found that API scores were positively related to the percentage of students who perceived high levels of these protective factors in their school.

In the second study, researchers from the Consortium on Chicago School Research (Smith, Lee, & Newmann, January 2001) found that, "Interactive teaching methods were associated with higher scores on standardized assessments in reading and math" (p. 2). Not only does this study support the use of active learning, they write that their "findings [also] call into serious question the assumption that low-achieving, economically-disadvantaged students are best served by teaching that emphasizes didactic methods and review" (p. 2). This was also a conclusion of the Perry Preschool Program evaluation discussed throughout this document. "Frosting on the cake" for Tribes TLC is also found in this study in that they found one organizational variable correlated with teachers likelihood of using interactive methods of instruction: the presence of a professional community that engaged in reflective dialogue. Reflective dialogue "is the component which more closely aligns with the teacher behaviors that are key to developing interactive methods" (p. 48).

While the above data is critical to justifying developmental approaches to policymakers who want high scores on standardized tests, it is by no means justifying standardized tests as the assessment method for developmental approaches such as Tribes. As we move to our last research-based component, authentic assessment, it bears keeping in mind that standardized testing more or less is a challenge or risk factor we need to live with. Perhaps as we near the conclusion of this lengthy document we might want to keep the following section of an e.e. cummings poem in mind (1923/1959):

While you and i have lips and voices which
are for kissing and to sing with
who cares if some oneeyed son of a bitch
invents an instrument to measure Spring with.

Authentic Assessment

The case against high-stakes testing, an approach that has been called the "standardization of minds" (Sacks, 1999), has been building for almost two decades, concomitantly with the case *for* more authentic forms of assessment. Certainly, since the advent of No Child Left Behind, the literature has grown exponentially! While the list of citations documenting the negative developmental effects of this form of assessment on students as well as the toll it takes on teachers in terms of stress could go and on, the following cites represent just a few of the key authors: Kohn, 2000, 2004; Meier, 2000; Ohanian, 1999; Neill et al, 2004; Popham, 2001; Sacks, 1999; Stiggins, R. 1999; *Voices In Urban Education,* Spring 2003. The adverse effects of high-stakes testing on English learners has been documented by a National Academy of Sciences report (Heubert & Hauser, 1999), and the case is mounting that high-stakes testing decreases students' connectedness to school, the major protective factor in adolescent health-risk behaviors (Blum & McNeely, 2002). According to Richard Stiggins (1999), one of the major detrimental effects is the feeling of hopelessness that is engendered by these tests which often results in students believing they are not capable of learning, in turn, creating a negative self-fulfilling prophecy. Common sense alone tells us what a National Research Council report concludes: "In the absence of effective services for low-performing students, better tests will not lead to better educational outcomes" (Heubert & Hauser, 1999, p. 3).

This entire document consists of research support for just what these "effective services for low-performing students" consist of—and guess what! They need exactly what all young people need: caring relationships, positive expectation messages, and opportunities to participate in actively learning the holistic competencies associated with life success. No study on human resilience has ever even found grades—let alone scores on standardized tests—in school associated with life success! Deborah Meier also reminds us—as do long-term studies of human development and resilience—of what the real criteria for success consists: "The success of Central Park East was not based on test scores but on the remarkable data we collected on who graduated, who went on to college, and, most important, how they fared in real life afterward" (Mathews, 2004, p. 2). In this recent interview, Meier goes on to succinctly summarize how CPE enabled student success:

> We have unusually *high expectations* for ourselves and our kids. Since we want kids who take responsibility for exercising judgment, we surround them with adults who are required to do the same. And we make sure the *relationships* between kids and adults are strong and educative. We invented five habits of mind—basic questions [see our discussion of critical inquiry in Chapter Two]—that we decided were at the heart of the usual academic disciplines, as well as all the disciplines of living. We organized curriculum, pedagogy and assessments so that kids and adults would get *a lot of practice* using their minds in these ways. We wanted a lively *community* in which we learned through the company we kept. Teachers reading scripts was not an answer compatible with our definition of the job. Means and ends need to fit (Mathews, 2004, p. 2).

Even without the added italics, we can see that CPE is a developmental model very similar to Tribes. We can justifiably expect that the same lifelong success rates.

Standardized testing is indeed the proverbial dead horse in terms of the research so we won't go on beating it. As Gibbs (2003a) points out, "The purpose of standardized state tests is political… mainly to motivate schools to increase test scores in order to 'achieve school reform'" (p. 217). As Tribes practitioners and all developmentalists know, threats, bribes, and other fear-driven strategies may be at the forefront of politics but have absolutely no positive effects on human motivation. In fact, research on "authoritarian" family, school, and community practices shows that these practices actually backfire, resulting in poor developmental—including academic and prevention—outcomes (Barber, 2002; Commission on Children At Risk, 2003; Eccles et al., 1993; Steinberg, 2000). Our hope, of course, is that the politicians will come to their developmental senses! A story shared in an action research project report on authentic assessment sheds light on the particularly American obsession with standardized testing: "An American educator who was examining the British educational system once asked a headmaster why so little standardized testing took place in British schools. 'My dear fellow,' came the reply, 'in Britain we are of the belief that when a child is hungry, he should be fed, not weighed'" (quoted in Donovan et al., April 2002, pp. 8-9).

It follows, then, that an approach to assessment for developmental practice must be developmental. In terms of Tribes, this means that assessment must be grounded in a core philosophy of human development and learning, which transfers to having a focus not only on academic outcomes but also on holistic child development ones: social, emotional, cognitive, physical, and spiritual. It follows next that assessment must also examine the culture of the school in terms of the protective factors and the "ideal learning community" components—and the assessment process must incorporate these, that is, be relational, reflect positive expectations, and be participatory. Next, assessment in the Tribes model must examine not only whether small group learning is happening throughout the school environment for all the players but must also examine the qualities of group process, i.e., inclusion, influence, and community, as well as be group-processed based itself. Lastly, developmental assessment must be a student-centered active learning, process itself, being done by, for, and with students as a cooperative, reflective project. In essence, the tools provided in the Tribes books and materials give Tribes practitioners the resources to authentically assess their classrooms and schools.

The above description maps well to what, according to a report by a collaboration of regional educational laboratories (Kusimo et al., 2000) are some of the most widely mentioned criteria for valid, culturally-sensitive classroom assessments, many of them recommended by the National Center for Research on Evaluation, Standards, and Student Testing (CRESST) at UCLA:

- are curriculum-linked

- are flexible (form, administration, interpretation)

- reflect opportunities to learn (fairness issue)

- are cognitively complex

- call on multiple intelligences

- are authentic (make real-world connections)

- are meaningful in themselves

- entail opportunities for self-assessment

- are culturally responsive/allow for variation in language, in cognitive and communicative style, and in beliefs and values

- integrate skills

- are used appropriately and are useful for the purpose for which they are designed (p. 184).

In contrast to high-stakes state tests, authentic (or alternative) assessment is really grounded in the principle of meaningfulness. In fact, a recent Rand Corporation evaluation of statewide standardized tests (2002) concluded, "It is unclear if test score gains reflect *meaningful* improvements in student learning," (Stecher & Hamilton, p. 17). According to one of the many, many "how-to" books on this subject, "Authentic assessment, done in the familiar context of the classroom is at the heart of teaching and learning. Only through knowing children's current knowledge and understandings, their skills, interests, and dispositions, can we develop curriculum that builds on their strengths and provides experiences that support their continued development and learning" (McAfee & Leong, 2002, p. xv). These authors quite simply define authentic or alternative assessment as "ways of finding out about and keeping track of children's development and learning that are an authentic part of ongoing classroom life and typical activities of children" (p. xv).

Unlike standardized, "one size fits all" tests with their narrow focus and demonstrated bias, authentic assessments such as student portfolios, checklists, rubrics, surveys, student-involved assignments, performance tasks, reflections, and student exhibitions, acknowledge and honor students' unique strengths, interests, and accomplishments. They reflect, in essence, the youth development approach to testing and have many potential positive outcomes. Certainly, they can inform instructional planning through assessment activities linked directly to students' learning experiences and to the context of those experiences—including the cultural contexts of a diverse student population (Cooper, 1997; Costa & Kallick, 1995; Estrin, 1993; Herman et al., 1992; Kornhaber & Gardner, 1993; McAfee & Leong, 2002; Rowntree1977/1987).

In other words, authentic assessment is *student-centered*. The end result is students are more intensely connected and engaged in their own learning; student growth and achievement is communicated in a more meaningful way to family and community; and teachers are actively engaged in and motivated to keep their instruction meaning-ful to students. Authentic assessment is integrally tied to authentic instruction, that is, responsive education that is tailored to student development and ways of learning, which as we discussed in Chapter Three involves modes of teaching that foster understanding of rich, integrated content and encourage students' positive engage-ment with the world. Alfie Kohn, always a voice of commonsense, asks us to remem-ber the following: "If students continue arguing about a topic after class, if they read by choice, if they chatter excitedly about something they've figured out—then we're doing something right…. Too much emphasis on *how* they're doing makes that less likely to happen" (quoted in Cooper, 1997, p. 146).

Portfolios are perhaps the most well-known and popular of alternative assess-ments. They are structured collections of student work gathered over time, intended to show a student's development and achievement in one or more subject areas. "They are process tools through which teachers and students evaluate student work together" (Estrin, 1993; Underwood, 1999). Portfolios offer linkages to classroom experiences and students' personal experiences; flexibility to include products in any language or form and to meet student needs and interests; developmental portrayals of student progress, using multiple measures at frequent intervals; self-evaluation/ awareness opportunities for students to learn more deeply what good work looks like and to more clearly understand their own learning processes; parent participation opportunities; opportunities to contextualize student performances; and program coordination support when students have more than one teacher (Estrin, 1993; Kusimo et al., 2000). In essence, portfolios offer one of the best forms of student feedback. According to Neill and his colleagues (2004), "Research has strongly demonstrated that skilled use of feedback to students is among the most powerful means teachers have for improving learning outcomes" (p. 24).

The National Forum on Assessment (*FairTest*, Winter 1995–96) developed a common core set of principles and indicators for student assessment. Principles and Indicators for Student Assessment Systems (1995–96) was signed by 80 national and local education and civil rights organizations dedicated to the following vision:

> Imagine an assessment system in which teachers had a wide repertoire of classroom-based, culturally sensitive assessment practices and tools to use in helping each and every child learn to high standards; in which educators collaboratively used assessment information to continuously improve schools; in which important decisions about a student, such as readiness to graduate from high school, were based on the work done over the years by the student; in which schools in networks held one another accountable for student learning; and in which public evidence of student achievement consisted primarily of samples from students' actual schoolwork rather than just reports of results from one-shot examinations (Neill, 2000, p. 1).

The seven principles endorsed by the Forum are: (1) The primary purpose of assessment is to improve student learning. (2) Assessment for other purposes supports student learning. (3) Assessment systems are fair to all students. (4) Professional collaboration and development support assessment. (5) The broad community participates in assessment development. (6) Communication about assessment is regular and clear. (7) Assessment systems are regularly reviewed and improved.

Essentially, the Forum recommends building "an assessment system from the bottom up, relying on teachers, [using classroom-based approaches], and seeking to improve the quality of curriculum and instruction as well as assessment" (Neill, 2000). Clearly, this is a challenge for youth development advocates in the current "get tough" environment with increases in the use of graduation and even grade-promotion tests— with more testing appearing on the agenda. The Co-Chair of the National Forum on Assessment recommends that youth development advocates and researchers continue to point out the limits of and the harm done by traditional tests to parents and the public; that educators who understand the harm done by the tests should unite against their use; that researchers, foundations, and government agencies shift their emphasis and resources toward classroom-based approaches; that school systems expand and focus professional development on creating schools as communities of learners that integrate curriculum, instruction, and assessment in ways that are helpful to all students; and, finally, that educators implement high-quality classroom authentic assessments and share them with parents and the community. "Widespread use of such assessments can form a base for a renewed effort to curtail traditional standardized tests and to construct assessment systems that support learning" (Neill, 2000, p. 5).

While the above has a poignant feel today after the last few years of No Child Left Behind, these recommendations are even more relevant today—and are actually happening in communities and even some states across the country where families and communities in partnerships with schools are saying no to NCLB—drawing ironically on NCLB's requirement for parent involvement to challenge the worst aspects of the law. FairTest, the leading advocacy organization for authentic assessment, has been collaborating with education, civil rights, parent and community organizations and researchers to develop alternative models of accountability that can be used as a template for overhauling NCLB and restructuring state systems (Neill, 2003; Neil et al., 2004).

They offer the following principles to guide an authentic assessment and accountability system, principles to which the Tribes TLC process also shares a commitment:

1. **Accountable to what ends?** The key purposes are to give feedback to the public for the purposes of school improvement and promoting equity and democracy.

2. **Accountable for what?** Accountability must be based on a shared vision and goals for public education in terms of priorities focused on human development and learning, needed resources provided by the government, meaningful measures of student learning as well as of student well-being, the school environment, and inclusion.

3. **Accountable to whom?** An accountability system must define appropriate expectations for participants in the system with the government being responsible for ensuring adequate provision and fair use of resources for all students, including safeguarding civil and human rights; and local school communities playing the primary role in accountability because they are closest to the classrooms where learning takes place.

4. **Accountable by what means?** The tools used to implement accountability can either support or undermine educational goals and school quality. Use multiple forms of evidence; assess a set of key factors that are know to predict school and system success such as school climate and out-of-school access to health care, housing, and nutrition; use feedback to improve student outcomes; and government should intervene sparingly and with great care (2004, pp. 23–24).

In fact, the Coalition for Authentic Reform in Education (CARE) which is based in FairTest's home state of Massachusetts, has proposed an alternative assessment and accountability plan for Massachusetts to replace the state's reliance on its high-stakes MCAS exams. Monty Neill and his colleagues (2004) offer this plan as a model for revising NCLB. It contains the following elements:

- Local authentic assessments

- Limited standardized testing in literacy and numeracy only and no use of these tests to make decisions about students

- School quality reviews done every 4–5 years

- Annual school reporting of its progress towards its goals and the state's core competencies (pp. 24–25).

Nebraska provides another hopeful example of a model authentic accountability system in its Student-based, Teacher-led Assessment and Reporting System (STARS) which is based on local assessment plans aligned with learning standards. Local assessment portfolios are submitted to the Nebraska Department of Education for review by an independent panel that rates their quality. "Independent reviewers have found that these assessment systems are having a positive effect on teaching and learning in Nebraska" (Neill et al., 2004, p. 26).

The FairTest researchers conclude that ultimately, "The key to the success of this approach will be to persuade policymakers that working with teachers and schools to steadily improve educational quality is preferable to threatening punishments unless they boost scores on narrow tests. It is preferable because it will lead to substantial improvement—provided adequate resources—in ways the test-

and-punish approach cannot" (2004, p. 26). What these researchers are saying is essentially what we have said many times in this document and what Jeanne Gibbs and other developmentalists have argued for for decades: a paradigm shift—or new mental model as Peter Senge would say—based on what we now know about human development and learning, including intrinsic motivation and brain-based learning, not too mention the hundreds of research studies and evaluations put forth in this document. Carole Cooper summarizes these necessary mindshifts about assessment—a list similar to that of Gibbs (2001a, p. 183)—as consisting of the following beliefs, beliefs that are at the heart of the process of Tribes TLC:

- All students can and are learning.

- The overall goal of assessment is *self-assessment.*

- We need to use *multiple forms* of assessment.

- We need to use *multiple assessors* (self, teachers, peers, parents).

- We need to look for success and movement toward desired *outcomes* or learning results.

- Human judgment can be reliable and valid.

- The assessment is based on measurable, precise *criteria.*

- The criteria is *no secret* to the learners.

- We need to assess the *process* as well as the product (meta-cognition and meta-learning).

- Assessment is *on-going* and continuous.

- Assessment is *not finite;* it should not be limiting or set limits on students' learning.

- Assessment results need to *guide instruction.*

- The assessment, itself, is a *learning experience* (1998, p. 13).

It is appropriate that we end this last chapter on the topic of belief in the innate resilience or developmental wisdom, that is, in the capacity, of our students. This loops us back to where we began this document, with a discussion of the foundational core of Tribes that is grounded in the belief in human potential: Every person has the innate capacity for healthy development and learning and that psychological and educational interventions are successful only to the degree that they tap this human potential.

We have also stated that believing in our students necessitates believing in ourselves. This is where all developmental practice begins—in our hearts and minds. Frank Smith (1998) says simply, "There would be no tests if people trusted their own instincts.... Or at least, the tests would be very different. Instead of looking at *how well* learners perform certain tasks, usually arbitrarily selected, the classic [i.e., developmental] approach would be to look at *what* tasks the learners have opportunities to engage in and the degree of their interest and comprehension" (pp. 64–65). In other words, the tests would be authentic, based on the authentic process of human development and learning. He concludes, as we have done in this document, with a plea for commonsense: "There is nothing strange or mysterious about any of this. It is classic common sense—but it can find no place in the indifferent technology of testing" (p. 65).

Conclusion

*I*n this substantial document, I have tried to unpack what is essentially a holistic systemic process in which everything is interconnected. Fritjof Capra writes in *The Web of Life* (1996) that what defines systems thinking is interdependence and that describing this web of relationships requires describing "a corresponding network of concepts and models, none of which is any more fundamental than the others." He goes on to explain that this systems approach to science "immediately raises an important question. If everything is connected to everything else, how can we ever hope to understand anything? Since all natural phenomena are ultimately interconnected, in order to explain any one of them we need to understand all the others, which is obviously impossible" (p. 41). I found myself coming to this conclusion as I wrote about each of the Tribes components. This meant that very often the research cited for one component could also apply to all the others—not an "impossible" task but one in which, like all systems analysts, I had to focus on the specific lens and not the totality. I do think this interdependence of each of the Tribes components speaks to Tribes as an open systems process, as a network of inter-related parts fundamental to all the other parts.

What the open systems process of Tribes offers to educators and others working in human services is a unified conceptual framework for understanding human development and learning. At the core of this model is our deep belief in resilience, in the human capacity for healthy development and meaningful learning. With this belief in our hearts and minds we are able to provide the next layer of the Tribes TLC process: a culture of within our schools and classrooms that grounded in caring relationships, positive expectation messages, and opportunities for everyone to be participate and contribute. We then create the structures that embed and further support a caring culture: small learning communities grounded in group process principles. Given the beliefs, the culture, and the structures, Tribes pedagogy could be none other than responsive education using active learning strategies.

The Tribes research components essentially become what Fritjof Capra in his latest book on systems, *Hidden Connections* (2002), refers to as "design principles…that are consistent with the principles of organization that nature has evolved to sustain the web of life" (p. xix). In examining the nature of social or human systems specifically, he writes that, "A unified view of life, mind and consciousness is inextricably linked to the social world of interpersonal relationships and culture," that is, a "network of communications" through which "meaning (reflective consciousness) is generated and passed on from generation to generation" (p. 74). While these may be fancy words, they describe exactly what Tribes is about and how it operates: beginning with a network (professional learning community) that consciously reflects on the principles of this developmental learning process. It is as simple (not necessarily easy!) as "turning to one another," as another systems person Margaret Wheatley describes in her book (2002) by that name, and having a conversation about what matters. "Human conversation is the most ancient and easiest way to cultivate the conditions for change—personal change, community and organization change, planetary change. If we can sit together and talk about what's important to us, we begin to come alive. We share what we see, what we feel, and we listen to what others see and feel" (p. 3).

This human process, offered to all of us as a gift from the pioneering vision of Jeanne Gibbs, is also what another pioneer of applied open systems, Bill Lofquist (who has worked tirelessly for this approach for about as long as Jeanne!) said constitutes the "scientific process." In a recent interview (Prevention First, 2003) he asks that people be scientists themselves "and make observations about what's going on around them, which is the basis of good science, and make hypotheses about what they think are the things that are contributing to whatever it is they are interested in. Whether it's making a good situation better or overcoming some negative situation and then creating the indicators of change and coming up with strategies to get where they want to go, that's the basis of the scientific method" (p. 24). Furthermore, he asserts, "We need methods that equip local people with ways of being creative and taking responsibility. That's what open-system frameworks do. They don't prescribe anything specific but provide people with the technical knowhow to find their own way. That's what's really valuable" (p. 24).

Tribes TLC is certainly a process that does enable creativity and responsibility. Hopefully, this document will be part of your Tribes "toolchest," which is already filled with wonderful tools to help you engage with your Tribes in this reflective conversation and scientific inquiry. It is the only way change—and even democracy itself—will happen for us, for our children, for our world.

References

Ainsworth, M.D.S. (1964). Patterns of attachment behavior shown by the infant in intereaction with his mother. *Merrill-Palmer Quarterly, 10*, 51–58.

Allen, J., Philliber, S., Herrling, S., & Kuperminc, G. (1997). Preventing teen pregnancy and academic failure: Experimental evaluation of a developmentally based approach. *Child Development, 64*(4), 729–742.

American Association of School Administrators. (1991). *Learning styles: Putting research and common sense into practice.* Arlington, VA: Author.

American Institutes for Research. (1999). *An educators' guide to schoolwide reform.* Arlington, VA: Educational Research Service.

American Psychological Association's Board of Educational Affairs, Learner-Centered Principles Work Group. (1997, November). *Learner-centered psychological principles: A framework for school reform and redesign.* Retrieved March 6, 2004, from http://www.apa.org/ed/lcpnewtext.html

Ancess, J. (2000). The reciprocal influence of teacher learning, teaching practice, school restructuring, and student learning outcomes. *Teachers College Record, 102*(3), 590–619.

Ancess, J., & Darling-Hammond, L. (2003). *Beating the odds: High schools as communities of commitment (The series on school reform).* New York: Teachers College Press.

Angier, N. (2002, July 23). Why we're so nice: We're wired to cooperate. *The New York Times on the Web.* Retrieved March 13, 2004 from http://www.nytimes.com/2002/07/23/health/psychology/23COOP.html

Angell, R.C. (1958). *Free society and moral crisis.* Ann Arbor, MI: University of Michigan Press.

Apple, M.W., & Beane, J.A. (Eds.). (1995). *Democratic schools.* Alexandria, VA: Association for Supervision and Curriculum Development.

Apple, M.W., & Beane, J.A. (1995). Lessons from democratic schools. In M.W. Apple & J.A. Beane (Eds.), *Democratic schools* (pp. 101–105). Alexandria, VA: Association for Supervision and Curriculum Development.

Armstrong, T. (1994). *Multiple intelligences in the classroom.* Alexandria, VA: Association for Supervision and Curriculum Development.

Aronson, E. (2000). *Nobody left to hate: Teaching compassion after Columbine.* New York: Worth Publishers.

Aronson, E., Blaney, N., Stephan, C., Sikes, J., & Snapp, M (1978). *The jigsaw classroom.* Beverly Hills, CA: Sage.

Aronson, E., & Patnoe, S. (1997). *Cooperation in the classroom: The jigsaw method.* New York: Longman.

Ayers, W., Klonsky, M., & Lyon, G.H. (Eds). (2000). *A simple justice: The challenge of small schools.* New York: Teachers College Press.

Ayers, W., & Ford, P. (Eds.) (1996). *City kids city teachers: Reports from the front row.* New York: The New Press.

Baldwin, J. (2001, Spring). Tales of the urban high school. *Carnegie Reporter,* pp. 23–39.

Ball, A.F. (2000). Empowering pedagogies that enhance the learning of multicultural students. *Teachers College Record, 102*(6), 1006–1034.

Bandura, A. (1969). *Principles of Behavior Modification.* New York: Holt, Rinehart & Winston.

Bandura, A. (1997). *Self-efficacy: The exercise of control.* New York: W.H. Freeman.

Banks, J. (1995). Creating multicultural learner-centered schools. In J. Banks, L. Darling-Hammond, & M. Greene (Eds), *Building learner-centered schools: Three perspective* (pp. 1–16). New York: National Center for Restructuring Education, Schools, and Teaching (NCREST) at Teachers College, Columbia University.

Barber, B., & Olsen, J. (1997). Socialization in context: Connection, regulation, and autonomy in the family, school, and neighborhood, and with peers. *Journal of Adolescent Research, 12,* 287–315.

Barchas, P. (1986). A sociophysiological orientation to small groups. In E. Lawler (Ed.), *Advances in group processes* (Vol. 3), pp. 209–246. Greenwich, CT: JAI Press.

Barth, R.S. (1990). *Improving schools from within.* San Francisco: Jossey-Bass.

Battistich, V. (2001, April). *Effects of an elementary school intervention on students' "connectedness" to school and social adjustment during middle school.* Symposium conducted at the annual meeting of the American Educational Research Association, Seattle, WA.

Battistich, V., Solomon, D., & Watson, M. (1998, April). *Sense of community as a mediating factor in promoting children's social and ethical development.* Paper presented at the meeting of the American Educational Research Association, San Diego, CA.

Battistich, V., Schaps, E., Watson, M., & Solomon, D. (1995). Prevention effects of the Child Development Project: Early findings from an ongoing multisite demonstration trial. *Journal of Adolescent Research,* 11, 12–35.

Baumeister, R.F., & Leary, M.R. (1995). The need to belong: Desire for interpersonal attachments as a fundamental human motivation. *Psychological Bulletin,* 117(3), 497–529.

Beane, J.A., & Apple, M.W. (1995). The case for democratic schools. In M.W. Apple & J. A. Beane (Eds.), *Democratic schools* (pp. 1–25). Alexandria, VA: Association for Supervision and Curriculum Development.

Beardslee, W., & Podoresfky, D. (1988). Resilient adolescents whose parents have serious affective and other psychiatric disorders: The importance of self-understanding and relationships. *American Journal of Psychiatry,* 14, 63–69.

Benard, B. (2004). *Resiliency: What we have learned.* San Francisco, CA: WestEd.

Benard, B. (2003). Turnaround teachers and schools. In B. Williams (Ed.), *Closing the achievement gap* (2nd ed., pp. 115–137). Alexandria, VA: Association for Supervision and Curriculum Development.

Benard, B. (1991). *Fostering resiliency in kids: Protective factors in the family, school, and community.* Portland, OR: Northwest Regional Education Laboratory.

Benard, B., & Marshall, K. (1997). A framework for practice: Tapping innate resilience. *Research/Practice: A publication from the Center for Applied Research and Educational Improvement.* (College of Education & Human Development, University of Minnesota), 5(1), 9–15.

Benard, B., & Marshall, K. (2001). Adventure education: Making a lasting difference. *Resilience Research for Prevention Programs.* Minneapolis: National Resilience Resource Center.

Benard, B., & Marshall, K. (2001). Meta-analyses provide decade of evidence: Effective school-based drug prevention programs. *Resilience Research for Prevention Programs.* Minneapolis: National Resilience Resource Center.

Bensman, D. (1994). *Lives of the graduates of Central Park East Elementary School: Where have they gone? What did they really learn?* New York: National Center for Restructuring Education, Schools and Teaching, Teachers College.

Benson, P. (1997). *All kids are our kids: What communities must do to raise caring and responsible children and adolescents.* San Francisco: Jossey-Bass.

Berger, J., Cohen, B., & Zelditch, M., Jr. (1966). Status characteristics and expectation states. In J. Berger & M. Zeldithc, Jr. (Eds.), *Sociological theories in progress* (Vol. 1, pp. 29–46). Boston: Houghton-Mifflin.

Berndt, T., & Ladd, G. (Eds.), (1989). *Peer relationships in child development.* New York: John Wiley and Sons.

Berruta-Clement, J., Schweinhart, L, Barnett, W., Epstein, A., & Weikart, D. (1984). *Changed lives: The effects of the Perry Preschool Program on youth through age 19.* Ypsilanti, MI: High/Scope Press.

Blank, M.J., Melaville, A., & Shah, B.P. (2003, May). *Making the difference: Research and practice in community schools.* Washington, DC: Coalition for Community Schools, Institute for Educational Leadership. Retrieved November 25, 2003, from http://www.communityschools.org/mtdhome-page.html

Bloom, H.S., Ham, S., Melton, L., & O'Brien, J. (2001). *Evaluating the accelerated schools approach: A look at early implementation and impacts on student achievement in eight elementary schools.* New York: Manpower Demonstration Research Corporation.

Blot, R., & Calderwood, P. (1995). *The cultural construction of success in Catholic and public schools: Executive summary.* A project of the Facilitator Center, Pace University, New York.

Blum, R. & McNeely, C. (2002). *Improving the odds: The untapped power of schools to improve the health of teens.* Minneapolis, MN: University of Minnesota, Center for Adolescent Health and Development.

Bolich, A. (2001). *Reduce your losses: help new teachers become veteran teachers.* Atlanta, GA: Southern Regional Education Board.

Borton, W.M., Reston, J., & Bippert, J. (1996). *Validating the Comer Model: The effects of student, teacher, and parent affective variables on reading and mathematics performance outcomes.* Paper presented at the Annual Convention of the American Educational Research Association, New York.

Bowlby, J. (1969). *Attachment and loss: Vol. 1. Attachment.* New York: Basic Books.

Boyer, E. (1995). *The basic school: A community of learners.* Princeton, NJ: Carnegie Foundation for the Advancement of Teaching.

Bradford, L.P., Gibb, J.R., & Benne, K.D. (Eds.). (1964). *T-group theory & laboratory method.* New York: John Wiley & Sons, Inc.

Brandt, R. (1992). Reconsidering our commitments. *Educational Leadership, 50*(2), 5.

Bransford, J., Brown, A., & Cocking, R. (Eds.), (2000). *How people learn: Brain, mind, experience, and school.* Washington, D.C.: Committee on Developments in the Science of Learning, National Academy Press.

Bronfenbrenner, U. (1979). *The ecology of human development: Experiments by nature and design.* Cambridge, MA: Harvard University Press.

Brown, A. (1980). Metacognitive development and reading. In R. Spiro, B. Bruce, & W. Brewer (Eds.). *Theoretical issues in reading comprehension* (pp. 453–479). Hillsdale, NJ: Erlbaum.

Brown, A. (1997). Transforming schools into communities of learners. *American Psychologist, 52,* 399–409.

Brown, B.B. (1990). Peer groups and peer cultures. In S.S. Feldman & G.R. Elliott (Eds.), *At the threshold: The developing adolescent.* Cambridge, MA: Harvard University Press.

Brown, J., & D'Emidio-Caston, M. (1995). On becoming at-risk through drug education: How symbolic policies and their practices affect students. *Evaluation Review, 19*(4), 451–492.

Bruer, J. (1999). *The myth of the first three years.* New York: The Free Press.

Bruner, J.S. (1996). *The culture of education.* Cambridge, MA: Harvard University Press.

Bryk, A.S., & Driscoll, M.E. (1998). *The high school as community: Contextual influences, and consequences for students and teachers.* Madison, WI: University of Wisconsin-Madison, National Center on Effective Secondary Schools.

Bryk, A.S., Lee, V.E., & Holland, P.B. (1993). *Catholic schools and the common good.* Cambridge, MA: Harvard University Press.

Bryk, A.S., & Schneider, B.L. (2002). *Trust in schools: A core resource for improvement.* New York: Russell Sage Foundation.

Bullough, R.V. (2001). *Uncertain lives: Children of promise, teachers of hope.* New York: Teachers College Press.

Caine, R.N., & Caine, G. (1991). *Making connections: Teaching and the human brain.* Alexandria, VA: Association for Supervision and Curriculum Development.

Calderwood, P. (2000). *Learning community: Finding common ground in difference.* New York: Teachers College Press.

Campbell, L., & Campbell, B. (1999). *Multiple intelligences and student achievement: Success stories from six schools.* Alexandria, VA: Association for Supervision and Curriculum Development.

Capra, F. (2002). *Hidden connections: Integrating the biological, cognitive, and social dimensions of life into a science of sustainability.* New York: Doubleday.

Capra, F. (1996). *The web of life.* New York: Doubleday.

Carta, J. (1991). Inner-city children's education. *American Behavioral Scientist, 34*(4), 441–453.

Cason, D., & Gillis, H. (1994). A meta-analysis of outdoor adventure programming with adolescents. *Journal of Experiential Education, 17,* 40–47.

Catalano, R.F., Berglund, M.L., Ryan, J.A.M., Lonczak, H.S., & Hawkins, J.D. (1998, November 13). *Positive youth development in the United States: Research findings on evaluations of positive youth development programs.* Retrieved September 20,

2000, from http://aspe.hhs.gov/hsp/Positive
YouthDev99/index.htm#toc

The catalog of school reform models: Child development project. (1998, November). Retrieved March 6, 2004, from http://www.nwrel.org/scpd/catalog/ModelDetails.asp?ModelID=6

The catalog of school reform models: Different ways of knowing (PreK–8). (2004, January). Retrieved March 6, 2004, from http://www.nwrel.org/scpd/catalog/ModelDetails.asp?ModelID=12

Catterall, J.S. (1995). *Different Ways of Knowing 1991–94 longitudinal study final report: Program effects on students and teachers.* Los Angeles: UCLA.

Catterall, J.S., Dreyfus, J.P., & DeJarnette, K. (1995). *Different Ways of Knowing: 1994–95 evaluation report.* Los Angeles: UCLA.

Chess, S. (1989). Defying the voice of doom. In T. Dugan and R. Coles (Eds.), *The child in our time: Studies in the development of resiliency* (pp. 179–199). New York: Bruner Mazel.

Chirkov, V., & Ryan, R. (2001). Parent and teacher autonomy-support in Russian and U.S. adolescents: Common effects on well-being and academic motivation. *Journal of Cross-Cultural Psychology, 32,* 618–635.

Cicchetti, D., Rappaport, J., Sandler, I., & Weissberg, R. (Eds.). (2000). *The promotion of wellness in children and adolescents.* Washington, D.C.: Child Welfare League of America Press.

Clausen, J. (1993). *American lives: Looking back at the children of the great depression.* New York: Free Press.

Coalition for Community Schools. (2003). *Making the difference: Research and practice in community schools.* Washington, DC: Author.

Coalition of Essential Schools (2002). Students thrive in schools that promote intellectual rigor and personalize learning. Retrived on June 8, 2004 from www.essentialschools.org.

Cognition and Technology Group at Vanderbilt (1990). Anchored instruction and its relation to situated cognition. *Educatonal Researcher, 9*(6), 2–10.

Cohen, E.G. (2002). Can groups learn? *Teachers College Record, 104,* 145–1068.

Cohen, E.G. (1986/1994a). *Designing groupwork: Strategies for the heterogeneous classroom* (2nd ed.). New York: Teachers College Press.

Cohen, E.G. (1994b). Restructuring the classroom: Conditions for productive small groups. *Review of Educational Research, 64*(1), 1–35.

Cohen, E.G., Lotan, R., & Catanzarite, L. (1990). Treating status problems in the cooperative classroom. In S. Sharan (Ed.), *Cooperative learning: Theory and research* (pp. 203–229). New York: Praeger.

Cohen, J. (1999). Social and emotional learning past and present: A psychoeducational dialogue. In J. Cohen (Ed.), *Educating minds and hearts: Social emotional learning and the passage into adolescence* (pp. 3–23). New York: Teachers College Press.

Cohen, J. (2001). Social and emotional education: Core concepts and practices. In J. Cohen (Ed.), *Caring classrooms/ intelligent schools: The social emotional education of young children* (pp. 3–29). New York: Teachers College Press.

Cohen, J. (Ed.). (2001). *Caring classrooms/ intelligent schools: The social emotional education of young children.* New York: Teachers College Press.

Cohen, J. (Ed.). (1999). *Educating minds and hearts: Social emotional learning and the passage into adolescence.* New York: Teachers College Press.

Coleman, J., and Hoffer, T. (1987). *Public and private high schools: The impact of communities.* New York: Basic Books.

Collaborative for Academic, Social, and Emotional Learning. (2003). *Safe and sound: An educational leader's guide to evidence-based social and emotional learning (SEL) programs.* Chicago, IL: Author.

Collay, M., Dunlap, D., Enloe, W., & Gagnon Jr., G.W. (1998). Learning circles: *Creating conditions for professional development.* Thousand Oaks, CA: Corwin Press.

Comer, J.P. (2001, April 23). Schools that develop children. *The American Prospect, 12* (7). Retrieved March 5, 2004, from http://www.prospect.org/print-friendly/print/V12/7/comer-j.html

Comer, J.P. (Ed.), Haynes, N.M., Joyner, E.T., & Ben-Avie, M. (1999). *Child by child: The Comer process for change in education.* New York: Teachers College Press.

Comer, J.P., Haynes, N.M., & Joyner, E.T. (1996). The school development program. In J. Comer, N. Haynes, E. Joyner, & M. Ben-Avie (Eds.), *Rallying the whole village: The Comer process for reforming education* (pp. 1–26). New York: Teachers College Press.

Commission on Children at Risk. (2003). *Hardwired to connect: The new scientific case for authoritative communities.* New York: Institute for American Values.

Cook, T. (1999, Summer). Chicago's Comer schools outperform controls in three major areas. *Institute for Policy Research News, Northwestern University,* 20(2). Retrieved March 5, 2004, from http://www.northwestern.edu/ipr/publications/newsletter/iprn9907/comer.html

Cooper C. (1997). *Learner-centered assessment.* Launceston, Tasmania: Global Learning Communities.

Corbiere, A.O. (2000, May). *Reconciling epistemological orientations: Toward a wholistic Nishnaabe* (Ojibwe/Odawa/Potawatomi) education (Report No. RC-023377). Paper presented at the Annual Meeting of the Canadian Indigenous and Native Studies Association, Edmonton, Canada. (ERIC Document Reproduction Service No. ED467707)

Cottle, T.J. (2003). *A sense of self: The work of affirmation.* Boston, MA: University of Massachusetts Press.

Cotton, K. (2001). School size, school climate, and student performance. Northwest *Regional Educational Laboratory School Improvement Research Series.* Retrieved March 14, 2001, from http://www.nwrel. org/scpd/sirs/10/c020.html

Covington, M.V., & Dray, E. (2002). The developmental course of achievement motivation: A need-based approach. In A. Wigfield & J.S. Eccles (Eds.), *Development of achievement motivation* (pp. 33–56). San Diego, CA: Academic Press.

Cowie, H., Smith, P., Boulton, M., & Laver, R. (1994). *Cooperation in the multi-ethnic classroom: The impact of cooperative group work on social relationships in middle schools.* London: David Fulton Publishers.

Csikszentmihalyi, M. (1990). *Flow: The psychology of optimal experience.* New York: HarperCollins.

Cuban, L. (1973). Ethnic content and "white" instruction. In J. Banks (Ed.), *Teaching ethnic studies: Concepts and strategies* (pp. 102–113). Washington D.C.: National Council for the Social Studies.

Cummings, e.e. (1923/1959). #23. *100 Selected Poems.* New York: Grove Press, p. 29.

Cushman, K. (1996). Networks and essential schools: How trust advances learning. *Horace,* 13(1). Retrieved June 8, 2004, from http://www.essentialschools.org/cs/cespr/view/ces_res/41

Cutler, I, & Edwards, S. (2002). Linking youth and community development: Ideas from the

Community Youth Development Initiative. *CYD Journal,* 3(1), 17–23.

Dalton, J. & Watson, M. (1997). *Among friends: Classrooms where caring and learning prevail.* Oakland, CA: Developmental Studies Center.

Damasio, A. (1994). *Descartes' error: Emotion, reason, and the human brain.* New York: Avon.

Damon, W. (1984). Peer education: The untapped potential. *Journal of Applied Developmental Psychology,* 5, 331–343.

Darling-Hammond, L., & McLaughlin, M.W. (1995). Policies that support professional development in an era of reform. *Phi Delta Kappan,* 76, 597–604.

Day, J. (1994). *Changing lives: Voices from a school that works.* Lanham, MD: University Press of America.

Deal, T., & Peterson, K. (2002). *Shaping school culture: The heart of leadership.* San Francisco: Jossey-Bass.

Deci, E. (1995). *Why we do what we do: Understanding self-motivation.* New York: Penguin Books.

DeCorte, E., Verschaffel, L., Entwistle, N., & van Merrienboer, J. (Eds.). (2003). *Powerful learning environments: Unravelling basic components and dimensions.* San Francisco: Pergamon.

Deiro, J. (2004). *Teachers DO make a difference: the caring teacher's guide to teacher-student relationships.* Thousand Oaks, CA: Corwin Press.

Deiro, J.A. (1996). *Teaching with heart: Making healthy connections with students.* Thousand Oaks, CA: Corwin Press.

Delpit, L. (1996). The politics of teaching literate discourse. In W. Ayers and P. Ford (Eds.), *City kids, city teachers: Reports from the front row.* New York: New Press.

Delpit, L. (1995). *Other people's children: Cultural conflict in the classroom.* New York: The New Press.

Dewey, J. (1916). *Democracy and education.* New York: Free Press.

Diamond, M., & Hopson, J. (1998). *Magic trees of the mind: How to nurture your child's intelligence, creativity, and healthy emotions from birth through adolescence.* New York: Dutton.

Dishion, T.J., McCord, J., & Poulin, F. (1999). When interventions harm: Peer groups and problem behavior. *American Psychologist,* 54(9), 755–764.

Donovan, R., Larson, B., Stechschulte, D., & Taft, M. (2002). *Building quality assessment* (Report No. TM-034-268). Saint Xavie4r University and

Skylight Field-Based Masters Program. (ERIC Document Reproduction Service No. ED466690).

Dryfoos, J. (2003). A community school in action. *Reclaiming Children and Youth: The Journal of Strength-Based Interventions,* 11(4), 203–205.

Dryfoos, J. (1998). *Safe passage: Making it through adolescence in a risky society.* New York: Oxford University Press.

Dryfoos, J., & Maguire, S. (2002). *Inside full-service community schools.* Thousand Oaks, CA: Corwin Press.

Dunn, J., & Plomin, R. (1990). *Separate lives: Why siblings are so different.* New York: Basic Books.

Eccles, J., & Gootman, J. (2002). *Community programs to promote youth development.* Washington, DC: National Academies Press.

Eccles, J., Midgley, C., Buchanan, C., Wigfield, A., Reuman, D., & MacIver, D. (1993). Development during adolescence: The impact of stage-environment fit on young adolescents' experiences in schools and in families. *American Psychologist,* 48(2), 90–101.

Eisler, R. (2000). *Tomorrow's children: A blueprint for partnership education in the 21st century.* Boulder, CO: Westview.

Elias, M.J. (2003). *Academic and social-emotional learning.* Brussels, Belgium: International Academy of Education

Ellis, N. (2001). Tuning in. *Hope,* Summer 2001, pp. 49–51, 61.

Ellison, L. (2001). *The personal intelligences: Promoting social and emotional learning.* Thousand Oaks, CA: Corwin Press, Inc.

Erikson, E. (1963). *Childhood and society.* New York: W.W. Norton.

Erikson, E. (1968). *Identity: Youth and crisis.* New York: Norton.

Eriksson, P. et al. (1998). Neurogenesis in the adult human hippocampus. *Nature Medicine,* Vol. R (11), 1313–1317.

FairTest (1995–1996). Principles and indicators summary. *FairTest Examiner,* 9(4), 22–25.

Felner, R.D. (2000). Educational reform as ecologically-based prevention and promotion: The project on high performance learning communities. In D. Cicchetti, J. Rappaport, I. Sandler, and R.P. Weissberg (Eds.), *The promotion of wellness in children and adolescents* (pp. 271–308). Washington, D.C.: Child Welfare League Association Press.

Felner, R.D., & Adan, A.M. (1988). The school transitional environment project: An ecological intervention and evaluation. In R.H. Price, E.L. Cowen, R.P. Lorion, and J. Ramos-McKay (Eds.), *Fourteen ounces of prevention: A casebook for practitioners* (pp. 111–122). Washington, D.C.: American Psychological Association.

Felner, R.D., Brand, S., Adan, A.M., Mulhall, P.F., Flowers, N., Sartain, B., & DuBois, D.L. (1993). Restructuring the ecology of the school as an approach to prevention during school transitions: Longitudinal follow-ups and extensions of the School Transitional Environment Project (STEP). In L.A. Jason, K.E. Danner, & K.S. Kuralski (Eds.), *Prevention and school transitions* (pp. 103–136). New York: Haworth Press, Inc.

Festinger, T. (1984). *No one ever asked us: A postscript to the foster care system.* New York: Columbia University Press.

Fetler, M. (1989). School dropout rates, academic performance, size and poverty: Correlates of educational reform. *Educational Evaluation and Policy Analysis,* 11(2), 109–116.

Fine, M. (2000). A small price to pay for justice. In W. Ayers, M. Klonsky, & G.H. Lyon, (Eds), *A simple justice: The challenge of small schools* (pp. 168–179). New York: Teachers College Press.

Fine, M. (1994). *Chartering urban school reform: Reflections on public high schools in the midst of change.* New York: Teachers College Press.

Freiberg, H.J. (Ed.). (1999). *School climate: Measuring, improving, and sustaining healthy learning environments.* Philadelphia, PA: Falmer Press.

Freire, P. (1973). *Pedagogy of the oppressed.* New York: Seabury.

Fullan, M. (1999). *Change forces: The sequel.* Philadelphia, PA: The Falmer Press.

Fullan, M. (2001). *Leading in a culture of change.* San Francisco: Jossey-Bass.

Fullan, M. (1994). *Turning systemic thinking on its head,* a paper prepared for the U.S. Department of Education.

Fullan, M. (1993). *Change forces: Probing the depths of educational reform.* Bristol, PA: The Falmer Press.

Fullan, M. (with S. Stiegelbauer). (1991). *The new meaning of educational change.* New York: Teachers College Press.

Fullan, M., & Hargreaves, A. (1996). *What's worth fighting for in your school?* New York: Teachers College Press.

Furstenberg, F., Cook, T., Eccles, J., Elder, G., & Sameroff, A. (1998). *Managing to make it: Urban families and adolescent success.* Chicago: University of Chicago Press.

Gabelnick, F., MacGregor, J., Matthews, R.S., & Smith, B.L. (1990). Learning communities: Creating connections among students, faculty, and disciplines. *New Directions for Teaching and Learning,* 41.

Gambone, M., & Arbreton, A. (1997). *Safe havens: The contributions of youth organizations to healthy adolescent development.* Philadelphia, PA: Public/Private Ventures.

Gardner, H. (2003, September 7). The real head start. *The Boston Globe.* Retrieved September 22, 2003, from http://www. boston.com/news/globe/ideas/articles/2003/09/07/the_real_head_start

Gardner, H. (1999). *The disciplined mind: What all students should understand.* New York: Simon and Schuster.

Gardner, H. (1990). *Art education and human development.* Santa Monica, CA: The Getty Center for Education in the Arts.

Gardner, H. (1983). *Frames of mind: The theory of multiple intelligences.* New York: Basic Books.

Gardner, J. (1971/1981/1995). *Self-renewal: The individual and the innovative society.* New York: W.W. Norton.

Garfield, C., Spring, C., & Cahill, S. (1998). *Wisdom circles: A guide to self-discovery and community building in small groups.* New York: Hyperion.

Gewertz, C. (2002, October 16). 'Trusting' school community linked to student gains. *Education Week,* 22(7). Retrieved October 16, 2002, from http://www.edweek.com/ew/ew_printstory.cfm?slug=07trust.h22

Gibbs, J. (2003). *The research-based components of Tribes learning communities.* Windsor, CA: CenterSource Systems.

Gibbs, J. (2001a). *Discovering gifts in middle school: Learning in a caring culture called tribes.* Windsor, CA: CenterSource Systems.

Gibbs, J. (2001b). *Tribes: A new way of learning and being together.* Windsor, CA: CenterSource Systems.

Ginsberg, M.B., & Wlodkowski, R.J. (2000). *Creating highly motivating classrooms for all students: A schooolwide approach to powerful teaching with diverse learners.* San Francisco, CA: Jossey-Bass.

Glasser, W. (1990). *The quality school: Managing students without coercion.* New York: Harper and Row.

Glickman, C. (1993). *Renewing America's schools: A guide for school-based action.* San Francisco: Jossey-Bass.

Golarz, R.J., & Golarz, M.J. (1995). *The power of participation: Improving schools in a democratic society.* Sebastopol, CA: National Training Associates.

Goleman, D. (2003). *Destructive emotions: How can we overcome them? A scientific dialogue with the Dalai Lama.* New York: Bantam Dell.

Goleman, D. (1995). *Emotional intelligence: Why it can matter more than I.Q.* New York: Bantam Books.

Goleman, D. (2000). Leadership that gets results. *Harvard Business Review* (Reprint no. R00204), March/April, pp. 78–90.

Goodman, J. (1992). *Elementary schooling for critical democracy.* New York: State University of New York Press.

Greenberg, M.T., Weissberg, R.P., O'Brien, M.U., Zins, J.E., Fredericks, L., Resnik, H., et al. (2003). Enhancing school-based prevention and youth development through coordinated social, emotional, and academic learning. *American Psychologist,* 58(6/7), 466–474.

Greene, M. (1998). Introduction: Teaching for social justice. In W. Ayers, J. Hunt, & T. Quinn (Eds.), *Teaching for social justice* (pp. xxvii–xlvi). New York: Teachers College Press.

Grossman, P. Wineburg, S., & Woolworth, S. (2001). Toward a theory of teacher community. *Teachers College Record,* 103, 942–1012.

Haberman, M. (1995). *Star teachers of children in poverty.* West Lafayette, IN: Kappa Delta Pi.

Halperin, S., & Partee, G. (1997). *Some things do make a difference for youth: A compendium of evaluations of youth programs and practices.* Washington, D.C.: American Youth Policy Forum.

Hammond, S.A. (1998). *The thin book of appreciative inquiry* (2nd ed.). Plano, TX: Thin Book Publishing Co.

Hanson, T. & Austin, G. (2002). *Health risks, resilience, and the Academic Performance Index* (California Healthy Kids Survey Factsheet 1). Los Alamitos, CA: WestEd.

Hargreaves, A. & Fullan, M. (1998). *What's Worth Fighting for Out There?* New York: Teacher's College Press.

Harrington, D., & Schine, J. (1989). *Connections: Service learning in the middle grades.* New York: Carnegie Corporation.

Harris, J.R. (1998). *The nurture assumption: Why children turn out the way they do.* New York: Touchstone.

Harris, J.R. (1995). Where is the child's environment? A group socialization theory of development. *Psychological Review, 102*(3), 458–489.

Harrison, R., & Stokes, H. (1992). *Diagnosing organizational culture.* San Diego, CA: Pfeiffer & Company.

Hartup, W.W. (1993). Adolescents and their friends. In B. Laursen (Ed.), *Close friendships in adolescence* (pp. 3–22). San Francisco, CA: Jossey-Bass.

Harvard Women's Health Watch (2002, November). Game-playing women shed light on biology of cooperation, p. 6.

Hattie, J., Marsh, H., Neill, J., and Richards, G. (1997). Adventure education and Outward Bound: Out-of-class experiences that make a lasting difference. *Review of Educational Research, 67,* 43–87.

HeartMath Research Center. (1997). *Research overview: Exploring the role of the heart in human performance.* Boulder Creek, CA: Institute of HeartMath.

Heath, S., Soep, E., & Roach, A. (1998). Living the arts through language and learning: A report on community-based youth organizations. *Americans for the Arts Monographs, 2* (7), November.

Henderson, A.T., & Mapp, K.L. (2002). *A new wave of evidence: The impact of school, family, and community connections on student achievement* (annual synthesis 2002). Austin, TX: Southwest Educational Developmental Laboratory.

Higgins, G. (1994). *Resilient adults: Overcoming a cruel past.* San Francisco, CA: Jossey-Bass.

Hilliard, A. (1991, September). Do we have the will to educate all children? *Educational Leadership, 49*(1), 31–36.

Hillman, J. (1996). *The soul's code: In search of character and calling.* New York: Random House.

Hooks, B. (1994). *Teaching to transgress: Education as the practice of freedom.* New York: Routledge.

Hopfenberg, W.S., Levin, H.M., Chase, C., Christensen, S.G., Moore, M., Soler, P., et.al. (1993). *The accelerated schools resource guide.* San Francisco, CA: Jossey-Bass Publishers.

Hoy, W.K., & Feldman, J.A. (1999). Organizational health profiles for high schools. In H.J. Freiberg (Ed.), *School climate: Measuring, improving, and sustaining healthy learning environments* (pp. 84–102). Philadelphia, PA: Falmer Press.

Huberman, M. (1995). Networks that alter teaching: Conceptualizations, exchanges and experiments. *Teachers and Teaching: Theory & Practice, 1*(2), 173–192.

Huberman, M. (1995). Professional careers and professional development. In T. Guskey & M. Huberman (Eds.), *Professional development in education: New paradigms and practices* (pp. 193–224). New York. NY: Teachers College Press.

Ingersoll, R.M. (2001). *A different approach to solving the teacher shortage problem (Teaching quality policy brief No. 3).* Seattle, WA: University of Washington, Center for the Study of Teaching and Policy.

James, D.W. (1999). *More things that do make a difference for youth: A compendium of evaluations of youth programs and practices, volume II.* Washington, D.C.: American Youth Policy Forum.

James, D.W., Jurich, S., & Estes, S. (2001). *Raising minority academic achievement: A compendium of education programs and practices.* Washington, DC: American Youth Policy Forum.

Jerald, C.D. (2001). *Dispelling the myth revisited: Preliminary findings from a nationwide analysis of "high-flying" schools.* Washington, DC: The Education Trust.

Johnson, D.W., & Johnson, R.T. (1998). *Learning together and alone: Cooperative, competitive, and individualistic learning* (5th ed.). Boston: Allyn & Bacon.

Johnson, D.W., & Johnson, R.T. (1995a). Cooperative learning and non-academic outcomes of schooling. In J. Pedersen & A. Digby (Eds.), *Secondary schools and cooperative learning: Theory, models, and strategies* (p. 83). New York: Garland Publishing.

Johnson, D.W., & Johnson, R.T. (1995b). *Reducing school violence through conflict resolution.* Alexandria, VA: Association for Supervision and Curriculum Development.

Johnson, D.W., & Johnson, R. (1995c). Teaching students to be peacemakers: Results of five years of research. *Journal of Peace Psychology, 1*(4), 417–438.

Johnson, D.W., & Johnson, R.T. (1989a). *Cooperation and competition: Theory and research.* Edina, MN: Interaction Book Co.

Johnson, D.W., & Johnson, R.T. (1989b). *Leading the cooperative school.* Edina, MN: Interaction Book Company.

Johnson, D.W., & Johnson, R.T. (1983). The social-ization and achievement crisis: Are cooperative learning experiences the solution? In L. Bickman (Ed.), *Applied social psychology annual 4*. Beverly Hills, CA: Sage.

Johnson, D.W., Johnson, R.T., & Holubec, E.J. (1994a). *Cooperative learning in the classroom*. Alexandria, VA: Association for Supervision & Curriculum Development.

Johnson, D.W., Johnson, R.T., & Holubec, E.J. (1994b). *The new circles of learning: Cooperation in the classroom and school*. Alexandria, VA: Association for Supervision and Curriculum Development.

Johnson, D.W., Johnson, R.T., & Stevahn, L. (1995). Three new studies on conflict resolution/peer mediation training. Paper presented at the annual meeting of National Association for Mediation Education (NAME), Seattle.

Johnson, S.M., Birkeland, S., Kardos, S.M., Kauffman, D., Liu, E., & Peske, H.G. (2001). Retaining the next generation of teachers: The importance of school-based support. Harvard Education Letter, July/August, pp. 8, 6.

Joyce, B., Wolf, J., & Calhoun, E. (1993). *The self-renewing school*. Alexandria, VA: Association for Supervision & Curriculum Development.

Kagan, J. (1998). *Three seductive ideas*. Cambridge, MA: Harvard University Press.

Kagan, S. (1992). *Cooperative learning* (8th ed.). San Juan Capistrano, CA: Kagan Cooperative Learning.

Kids Consortium. (2001). *Kids as planners: A guide to strengthening students, schools and communities through service-learning*. Lewiston, ME: Author.

Kids Consortium (1998). *Reform, resiliency, and renewal: KIDS in action*. KIDS Consortium: Westbrook, ME.

Kohn, A. (2000). *The case against standardized testing: Raising the scores, ruining the schools*. Portsmouth, NH, Heinemann.

Kohn, A. (1999). *The schools our children deserve: Moving beyond traditional classrooms and "tougher standards."* New York: Houghton Mifflin Company.

Kohn, A. (1997, September 3). Students don't "work"—they learn. *Education Week*, pp. 60, 43.

Kohn, A. (1996). *Beyond discipline: From compliance to community*. Alexandria, VA: Association for Supervision and Curriculum Development.

Kohn, A. (1993a). Choices for children: Why and how to let students decide. *Phi Delta Kappan*, 74(1), 9–20.

Kohn, A. (1993b). *Punished by rewards: The trouble with gold stars, incentive plans, A's, praise, and other bribes*. New York: Houghton Mifflin Company.

Kohn, A. (2004). Test today, privatize tomorrow. *No Child Left, II* (4), 1–11. Originally published in Phi Delta Kappan, April 2004.

Kohn, A. (1990). *The brighter side of human nature: Altruism & empathy in everyday life*. New York: Basic Books.

Kohn, A. (1986). *No contest: The case against competition*. Boston, MA: Houghton Mifflin Company.

Kolb, D.A. (1984). *Experimental learning: Experience as the source of learning and development*. Englewood Cliff, NJ: Prentice Hall.

Kovalik, S.J., & Olsen, K.D. (2001). *Exceeding expectations: A user's guide to implementing brain research in the classroom*. Covington, WA: Susan Kovalik & Associates, Inc.

Kovalik, S. with Olsen, K. (1997). *ITI: The Model*. Kent, WA: Susan Kovalik & Associates.

Kreft, I., & Brown, J. (Eds.), (1998). The zero effects of drug prevention programs: Issues and solutions. *Evaluation Review*. (Special Issue), 22.

Kretzmann, J.,s & McKnight, J. (1993). *Building communities from the inside out*. Evanston, IL: Center for Urban Affairs and Policy Research, Northwestern University.

Kruse, S.D., Louis, K.S., & Bryk, A. (1995). An emerging framework for analyzing school-based professional community. In K.S. Louis & S.D. Kruse (Eds.), *Professionalism and community: Perspectives on reforming urban schools* (pp. 23–42). Thousand Oaks, CA: Corwin.

Kusimo, P., Ritter, M., Busick, K., Ferguson, C., Trumbull, E., & Solano-Flores, G. (2000). *Making assessment work for everyone: How to build on student strengths*. San Francisco: WestEd, Assessment Laboratory Network Project of the Regional Educational Laboratories.

Ladd, G. (1989). Toward a further understanding of peer relationships and their contributions to child development. In T. Berndt & G. Ladd (Eds.), *Peer relationships in child development* (pp. 1–11). New York: John Wiley and Sons.

Lakoff, G. (2002). *Moral politics: How liberals and conservatives think* (2nd ed.). Chicago, IL: University of Chicago Press.

Lambert, L. (1998). *Building leadership capacity in schools.* Alexandria, VA: Association for Supervision and Curriculum Development.

Lazear, D. (1991). *Seven ways of knowing: Teaching for multiple intelligences.* Palatine, IL: Skylight.

Lee, V.E. (2000). School size and the organization of secondary schools. In M.T. Hallan (Ed.), *Handbook of sociology of education* (pp. 327–344). New York: Kluwer Academic/Plenum.

Lee, V.E. & Smith, J. B. (1997). High school size: Which works best and for whom? *Educational and Policy Analysis,* 19(3), 205–227.

Lee, V.E., & Smith, J.B. (1994). High school restructuring and student achievement. *Issues in Restructuring Schools,* 7, 1–8.

Levine, M.D. (2002). *A mind at a time.* New York: Simon & Schuster

Lewis, T., Amini, F., & Lannon, R. (2000). *A general theory of love.* New York: Random House.

Lieberman, A. (1995). *The work of restructuring schools: Building from the ground up.* New York: Teachers College Press.

Lieberman, A. (1994). Afterword: Transforming urban schools: Building knowledge and building community. In M. Fine (Ed.), *Chartering urban school reform: Reflections on public high schools in the midst of change* (pp. 204–270). New York: Teachers College Press.

Lieberman, A. (1992). The meaning of scholarly activity and the building of community. *Educational Researcher,* 21(6), 5–12.

Lieberman, A., & Miller, L. (1990). Restructuring school: What matters and what works. *Phi Delta Kappan,* 71(10), 759–764.

Little, J.W. (1993). Teachers' professional development in a climate of educational reform. *Educational Evaluation and Policy Analysis,* 15(2), 129–152.

Louis, K.S. & Kruse, S. (Eds.) (1995). *Professionalism and community: Perspectives on reforming urban schools.* Thousand Oaks, CA: Corwin Press.

Louis, K.S., & Ingram, D. (2003). Schools that work for teachers and students. In B. Williams (Ed.), *Closing the achievement gap: A vision for changing beliefs and practices* (2nd ed.) (pp. 154–177). Alexandria, VA: Association for Supervision and Curriculum Development.

Loye, D. (2000). *Darwin's Lost Theory of Love.* New York: Writers Club Press.

Luvmour, J. (2003). *Central tenets of natural learning rhythms.* Nevada City, CA: EnCompass Press.

Luvmour, J., & Luvmour, B. (1998). *Tiger by the tail: Essays on the inherent spirituality of natural learning rhythms.* Nevada City, CA: EnCompass Press.

Luvmour, J., & Luvmour, S. (1993). *Natural learning rhythms: Discovering how and when your child learns* (Revised ed.). Berkeley, CA: Celestial Arts.

MacBeath, J., Boyd, B., Rand, J., & Bell, S. (1995). Schools speak for themselves: *Toward a framework for self-evaluation.* London: The National Union of Teachers.

Maheady, L., Harper, G., & Sacca, M. (1988). A class-wide peer tutoring system in a secondary resource room program for the mildly handicapped. *Journal of Research and Development in Education,* 21(3), 76–83.

Maslow, A.H. (1968). *Toward a psychology of being.* New York: Van Nostrand.

Maslow, A.H. (1954). *Motivation and personality.* New York: Harper & Row.

Masten, A. (2001). Ordinary magic: Resilience processes in development. *American Psychologist,* 56, 1–12.

Masten, A., & Coatsworth, D. (1998). The development of competence in favorable and unfavorable environments: Lessons from research on successful children. *American Psychologist,* 53, 205–220.

Masten, A., & Reed, M. (2002). Resilience in development. In C. Snyder & S. Lopez (Eds.), *Handbook of Positive Psychology* (pp. 74–88). New York: Oxford University Press.

Mathews, J. (2004, February 17). Seeking alternatives to standardized testing. *Washington Post* (pp. 1–8). Retrieved on February 21, 2004 from www.washingtonpost.com/ac2/wp-dyn/A47699-2004 Feb17?language=printer

McAfee, O., & Leong, D. (2002). *Assessing and guiding young children's development and learning.* Boston: Allyn and Bacon.

McCombs, B.L., & Pope, J.E. (1994). *Motivating hard to reach students.* Washington, DC: American Psychological Association.

McLaughlin, M. (1990). The Rand Change Agent Study revisited: Macro perspectives and micro realities. *Educational Researcher* 19(9), 11–16.

McLaughlin, M., Irby, M., & Langman, J. (1994). *Urban sanctuaries: Neighborhood organizations in the lives and futures of inner-city youth.* San Francisco: Jossey-Bass.

McLaughlin, M.W., & Talbert, J. (1990). Constructing a personalized school environment. *Phi Delta Kappan,* 72(3), 230–235.

McLaughlin, M. & Talbert, J. (2001). *Professional communities and the work of high school teaching.* Chicago: University of Chicago Press.

McLellan, J.A., & Pugh, M.V. (Eds.). (1999). *The role of peer groups in adolescent social identity: Exploring the importance of stability and change.* San Francisco, CA: Jossey-Bass.

McNeely, C., Nonnemaker, J., & Blum, R. (2002). Promoting school connectedness: Evidence from the National Longitudinal Study of Adolescent Health. *Journal of School Health,* 72(4), 138–146.

McQuillan, P., & Muncie, D. (1994). "Change takes time": A look at the growth and development of the Coalition of Essential Schools. *Journal of Curriculum Studies,* 26(3), 265–279.

Meier, D. (2002). *In schools we trust.* Boston: Beacon Press.

Meier, D. (1995). *The power of their ideas: Lessons for America from a small school in Harlem.* Boston, MA: Beacon Press.

Meier, D. (2000). *Will standards save public education?* Boston, MA: Beacon Press.

Melchoir, A. (1998). *National evaluation of Learn and Serve America school and community-based programs: Final report.* Washington, DC: Corporation for National and Community Service.

Melchoir, A. (1996). *National evaluation of Learn and Serve America school and community-based programs: Interim report: Appendices.* Washington, DC: Corporation for National Community Service.

Mengual, G. (2003). *Best practices for producing community-wide study circles.* Pomfrey, CT: Topsfield Foundation.

Mesch, D., Lew, M., Johnson, D.W., & Johnson, R.T. (1986). Isolated teenagers, cooperative learning, and the training of social skills. *The Journal of Psychology,* 120(4), 323–334.

Mezirow, J. & Associates (2000). *Learning as transformation.* San Francisco: Jossey-Bass.

Miller, A. (1990). *The untouched key: Tracing childhood trauma in creativity.* New York: Anchor Books.

Miller, R. (2004). Educational alternatives—A map of the territory. *Paths of Learning* (20), 20–28.

Molnar, A. (Ed.), (2002). *School reform proposals: The research evidence.* Tempe, AZ: Arizona State University, Education Policy Research Unit. Retrieved on February 5, 2002 from http://www.asu.edu/educ/epsl/Reports/epru/EPRU%202002-101/epru-2002-101.htm

Montagu, A. (1973). *Darwin, competition, and cooperation.* Westport, CT: Greenwood Press.

Moore, D.S. (2002). *The dependent gene: The fallacy of nature versus nurture.* New York: W.H. Freeman & Co.

Morrow, K., & Styles, M. (1995, May). *Building relationships with youth in program settings: A study of Big Brothers/Big Sisters.* Philadelphia, PA: Public/Private Ventures.

Muller, W. (1996). *How, then, shall we live?* New York: Bantum.

Murphy, J., & Louis, K.S. (1994). *Reshaping the principalship: Insights from transformational reform efforts.* Thousand Oaks, CA: Corwin Press.

Myers, C.B., & Simpson, D.J. (1998). *Re-creating schools: Places where everyone learns and likes it.* Thousand Oaks, CA: Corwin.

Nakamura, J., & Csikszentmihalyi, M. (2002). The concept of flow. In C. Snyder & S. Lopez (Eds.), *Handbook of positive psychology* (pp. 89–105). New York: Oxford University Press.

National Research Council and the Institute of Medicine. (2004). *Engaging schools: Fostering high school students' motivation to learn.* Washington D.C.: The National Academies Press.

National Research Council and the Institute of Medicine. (2000). *Improving intergroup relations among youth: Summary of a research workshop.* Washington, D.C.: National Academy Press.

National School Boards Association (1992). *More than pumpkins in October: Visual literacy in the 21st century: A school board member's guide to enhancing student achievement through art education.* Alexandria, VA: National School Boards Association with Getty Center for Education in the Arts.

Neill, M. (2003). Leaving children behind: How "No Child Left Behind" will fail our children. *Phi Delta Kappan,* 85(3), 225–228.

Neill, M. (2000). Transforming student assessment. Cambridge, MA: FairTest. Retrieved on June 20, 2000 from http://www.fairtest.org/MNKappan.html

Neill, M., Guisbond, L., & Schaeffer, B. (2004, May). Failing our children: How "No Child Left Behind" undermines quality and equity in education. Cambridge, MA: FairTest.

Newcomb, M., & Bentler, P. (1988). *Consequences of adolescent drug use: Impact on the lives of young adults.* New York: Books on Demand.

Newmann, F., Rutter, R., & Smith, M. (1989). Organizational factors that affect school sense of efficacy, community, and expectations. *Sociology of Education, 62,* 221–238.

Newmann, F.M., & Wehlage, G.G. (1995). *Successful school restructuring: A report to the public and educators by the Center on Organization and Restructuring of Schools.* Madison, WI: Center on Organization and Restructuring of Schools.

Nicholson-Nelson, K. (1998). *Developing students' multiple intelligences.* New York: Scholastic Professional Books.

Nieto, S. (2003). *What keeps teachers going?* New York: Teachers College Press.

Nieto, S. (1994). Lessons from students on creating a chance to dream. *Harvard Educational Review, 64*(4), 392–426.

Nieto, S. (1992). *Affirming diversity: The sociopolitical context of multicultural education.* White Plains, New York: Longman Publishing Group

Noddings, N. (1992). *The challenge to care in schools: An alternative approach to education.* New York: Teachers College Press.

Noddings, N. (1984). *Caring: A feminine approach to ethics and moral education.* Berkeley, CA: University of California Press.

Noguera, P.A. (2001, February 11). The role and influence of environmental and cultural factors on the academic performance of African American males. *In Motion Magazine.* Retrieved June 9, 2003, from http://www.inmotionmagazine.com/pnaamale1.html#Anchor-The-8545

Oakes, J. (1985). *Keeping track: How schools structure inequality.* New Haven: Yale University Press.

Oakes, J., Quartz, K.H., Ryan, S., & Lipton, M. (2000). *Becoming good American schools: The struggle for civic virtue in education reform.* San Francisco: Jossey-Bass.

Ohanian, S. (1999). *One size fits few: The folly of educational standards.* Heinemann: Portsmouth, NH.

Ornstein, R., & Sobel, D. (1999). *The healing brain: Breakthrough discoveries about how the brain keeps us healthy.* Cambridge, MA: Malor Books.

Ornstein, R., & Swencionis, C. (Eds.). (1990). *The healing brain: A scientific reader.* New York: The Guilford Press.

Outward Bound. (2003). *Expeditionary learning: Core practice benchmarks.* Garrison, NY: Expeditionary Learning Outward Bound.

Palincsar, A., & Brown, A. (1984). Reciprocal teaching of comprehension-fostering and comprehension-monitoring activities. *Cognition and Instruction, 1,* 117–175.

Pan, D., & Mutchler, S. (2000). *Calling the roll: Study circles for better schools.* Austin, TX: Southwest Educational Development Laboratory.

Parker, F. W. (1894/1937/2001). *Talks on pedagogics: An outline of the theory of concentration.* Chicago: Francis W. Parker School.

Parker, J.G., & Asher, S.R. (1987). Peer relations and later personal adjustment: Are low-accepted children at risk? *Psychological Bulletin, 102,* 357–389.

Pearce, J.C. (1992). *Evolution's end: Claiming the potential of our intelligence.* San Francisco: Harper Collins.

Pearce, J.C. (1977). *Magical child.* New York: Plume.

Peng, S. (1994). Understanding resilient students: The use of national longitudinal databases. In M. Wang & E. Gorden (Eds.), *Educational resilience in inner-city America* (pp. 73–84). Hillsdale, NJ: Lawrence Erlbaum.

Perez, A.L.V., Milstein, M.M., Wood, C.J., & Jacquez, D. (1999). *How to turn a school around: What principals can do.* Thousand Oaks, CA: Corwin Press.

Perlstein, D. (1996). Community and democracy in American schools: Arthurdale and the fate of progressive education. *Teachers College Record, 97*(4), 625–650.

Pert, C.B. (1997). *Molecules of emotion: The science behind mind-body medicine.* New York: Touchstone.

Peshkin, A. (1993). The goodness of qualitative research. *Educational Researcher, 22*(2), 23–29.

Peterson, J., Schwager, M., Crepeau, M., & Curry, K. (1998). *The Galef/WestEd evaluation of San Francisco Unified School District's (SFUSD) implementation of Different Ways of Knowing (DwoK) report.* San Francisco: WestEd.

Petrosko, J.M. (1997). *Study A: Implementation of student-centered teaching and learning practices and student assessment results for research demonstration site (RDS) schools participating in Different Ways of*

Knowing. Louisville, KY: Galef Institute-Kentucky Collaborative for Teaching and Learning.

Piaget, J. (1939, 1965). *The moral judgment of the child.* New York: Free Press.

Pianta, R.C., & Walsh, D.J. (1998). Applying the construct of resilience in schools: Cautions from a developmental systems perspective. *School Psychology Review,* 27(3), 407–417.

Pool, C. (1997). Maximizing learning: A conversation with Renate Numella Caine. *Educational Leadership* 54(6), 11–15.

Popham, W. (2001). *The truth about testing: An educator's call to action.* Alexandria, VA: Association for Supervision and Curriculum Development.

Poplin, M., & Weeres, J. (1992). *Voices from the inside: A report on schooling from inside the classroom.* Claremont, CA: School of Educational Studies, Claremont Graduate University.

Prevention First, Inc. (2003). Prevention innovators. *Prevention Forum,* 24(1), 24–25.

Puckett, J.L. (1989). *Foxfire reconsidered: A twenty-year experiment in progressive education.* Chicago, IL: University of Illinois Press.

Pugh, M.V., & Hart, D. (1999). Identity development and peer group participation. In J.A. McLellan & M.V. Pugh (Eds.), *The role of peer groups in adolescent social identity: Exploring the importance of stability and change* (pp. 55–70). San Francisco, CA: Jossey-Bass Publishers.

Putnam, R. (2000). *Bowling alone: The collapse and revival of American community.* New York: Simon and Schuster.

Ragozzino, K., Resnik, H., Utne-O'Brien, & Weissberg, R.P. (2003). Promoting academic achievement through social and emotional learning. *Educational HORIZONS,* Summer 2003.

Remen, R.N. (1996). *Kitchen table wisdom: Stories that heal.* New York: Riverhead Books.

Resnick, L.B. (1987a). *Education and learning to think.* Washington, DC: National Academy Press.

Resnick, L.B. (1987b). Learning in school and out. *Educational Researcher,* 16, 13–20.

Resnick, M., Bearman, P., Blum, R., Bauman, K., Harris, K., Jones, J., et.al. (1997). Protecting adolescents from harm: Findings from the National Longitudinal Study on Adolescent Health. *Journal of the American Medical Association,* 278, 823–832.

Retallick, J. (1999). Transforming schools into learning communities: Beginning the journey. In J.

Retallick, B. Cocklin, & K. Coombe (Eds.), *Learning communities in action: Issues, strategies and contexts* (pp.107–130). New York: Routledge.

Rhodes, W., & Brown, W. (Eds.). (1991). *Why some children succeed despite the odds.* New York: Praeger.

Richardson, G. (2002). The metatheory of resilience and resiliency. *Journal of Clinical Psychology,* 58, 307–321.

Ridley, D.S., & Walther, B. (1995). *Creating responsible learners: The role of a positive classroom environment.* Washington, DC: American Psychological Association.

Roberts, S.M., & Pruitt, E.Z. (2003). *Schools as professional learning communities: Collaborative activities and strategies for professional development.* Thousand Oaks, CA: Corwin Press, Inc.

Rogoff, B. (2003). *The cultural nature of human development.* New York: Oxford University Press.

Rogoff, B., Turkanis, C.G., & Bartlett, L. (Eds.). (2001). *Learning together: Children and adults in a school community.* New York: Oxford University Press.

Rooney-Rebeck, P., & Jason, L. (1986). Prevention of prejudice in elementary school students. *Journal of Primary Prevention,* 7(2), 63–73.

RPP International. (1998). *An evaluation of K–12 service-learning in California.* Sacramento: California Department of Education, CalServe Office.

Rutter, M. (1987). Psychosocial resilience and protective mechanisms. *American Journal of Orthopsychiatry,* 57, 316–331.

Rutter, M., Maughan, B., Mortimore, P., Ouston, J., & Smith, A. (1979). *Fifteen thousand hours: Secondary schools and their effects on children.* Cambridge, MA: Harvard University Press.

Ryan, F.J., Soven, M., Smither, J., Sullivan, W.M., & VanBuskirk, W.R. (1999). Appreciative inquiry: Using personal narratives for initiating school reform. *The Clearing House,* 72(3), 164–176.

Ryan, R., & Deci, E. (2000). Self-determination theory and the facilitation of t\intrinsic motivation, social development, and well-being. *American Psychologist,* 55, 68–78.

Sacks, J. (1997). Rebuilding civil society: A biblical perspective. *The Responsive Community,* 7(1), 11–20.

Sacks, P. (1999). *Standardized minds: The high price of America's testing culture and what we can do to change it.* Cambridge, MA: Perseus Books.

Sainato, D., Maheady, L., & Shook, G. (1986). The effects of a classroom manager role on the social interaction patterns and social status of withdrawn kindergarten students. *Journal of Applied Behavior Analysis, 19*(2), 187–195.

Sale, E. & Springer, F. (2001). Prevention works! The recent National Cross-Site Evaluation of High-Risk Youth Programs reveals the "how" and "why" of prevention. *Prevention Tactics, 4*(3), 1–8.

Sandler, I. (2001). Quality and ecology of adversity as common mechanisms of risk and resilience. *American Journal of Community Psychology, 29,* 19–61.

Santrock, J.W. (2001). *Adolescence* (8th ed.). New York: McGraw-Hill

Sarason, S. (1990). *The predictable failure of educational reform: Can we change course before it's too late?* San Francisco: Jossey-Bass.

Sarason, S.B. (1971). *The culture of the school and the problem of change.* Boston: Allyn and Bacon, Inc.

Scales, P., & Leffert, N. (1999). *Developmental assets: A synthesis of the scientific research on adolescent development.* Minneapolis, MN: Search Institute.

Scardamaglia, M., Bereiter, C., & Steinbeck, R. Teachability of reflective processes in written composition. *Cognitive Science,* 8 173–190.

Schlechty, P.C. (1990). *Schools for the 21st century: Leadership imperatives for educational reform.* San Francisco, CA: Jossey-Bass.

Schmidt-Lewis, P. (1995). *Youth as resources: Special initiative phase II, final evaluation report.* Indianapolis: PSL and Associates.

Schmuck, R.A., & Schmuck, P.A. (2001). *Group processes in the classroom* (8th ed.). New York: McGraw Hill.

Schoenfeld, A. (1985). *Mathematical problem solving.* New York: Academic Press.

Schorr, L. (1988). *Within our reach: Breaking the cycle of disadvantage.* New York: Anchor Books.

Schorr, L. (1997). *Common purpose: Strengthening families and neighborhoods to rebuild America.* New York: Anchor Books.

Schumacher, E.F. (1973). *Small is beautiful: Economics as if people mattered.* New York: Perennial.

Schutz, W. (1966). *The Interpersonal Underworld.* Palo Alto, CA: Science and Behavior Books.

Schweinhart, L., Barnes, H., & Wiekart, D. (1993). *Significant benefits: The High/Scope Perry Preschool Study through age 27.* Ypsilanti, MI: High/Scope Press.

Schweinhart, L., & Weikart, D. (1997). *Lasting differences: The High/Scope preschool curriculum comparison study through age 23.* Ypsilanti, MI: High/Scope Press.

Schweinhart, L., & Weikart, D. (1980). *Young children grow up: The effects of the Perry Preschool Program on youths through age 15.* Ypsilanti, MI: High/Scope Press.

Scribner, A.P., & Scribner, J.D. (2001). *High-performing schools serving Mexican American students: What they can teach us* (Report No. EDO-RC-01-4). Charleston, WV: ERIC Clearinghouse on Rural Education and Small Schools. (ERIC Document Reproduction Service No. ED459048)

Seita, J., Mitchell, M., & Tobin, C. (1996). *In whose best interest: One child's odyssey, a nation's responsibility.* Elizabethtown, PA: Continental Press.

Seligman, M. (1998). *Learned optimism: How to change your mind and your life.* New York: Pocket Books.

Semel, S.F., & Sadovnik, A.R. (Eds). (1998). *Schools of tomorrow, schools of today: What happened to progressive education* (history of schools and schooling, V.8). New York: Peter Lang Publishing.

Senge, P. (1990). *The fifth discipline.* New York: Doubleday.

Senge, P.,, Cambron-McCabe, N., Lucas, T., Smith, B., Dutton, J., & Kleiner, A. (2000). *Schools that learn: A Fifth discipline fieldbook for educators, parents, and everyone who cares about education.* New York: Doubleday.

Sergiovanni, T. (1994). *Building community in schools.* San Francisco: Jossey-Bass.

Sergiovanni, T. (2000). *The lifeworld of leadership: Creating culture, community, and personal meaning in our schools.* San Francisco, CA: Jossey-Bass.

Sergiovanni, T. (1999). The story of community. In J. Retallick, B. Cocklin, & K. Coombe (Eds.), *Learning communities in action: Issues, strategies and contexts* (pp. 9–25). New York: Routledge.

Sergiovanni, T. (1996). *Leadership for the schoolhouse: How is it different? Why is it important?* San Francisco, CA: Jossey Bass.

Sharan, S. (1990). *Cooperative learning: Theory and research.* New York: Praeger Publishers.

Sharan, Y., & Sharan, S. (1992). *Expanding cooperative learning through group investigation.* New York: Teachers College Press.

Simons, P.R.J. (1997). Definitions and theories of active learning. In D. Stern & G.L. Huber (Eds.), *Active learning for students and teachers: Reports from eight countries* (pp. 19–39). Frankfurt am Main: Peter Lang.

Sizer, T. (1984/1997). *Horace's compromise.* New York: Houghton Mifflin.

Slavin, R.E. (1997). Co-operative learning among students. In D. Stern & G.L. Huber (Eds.), *Active learning for students and teachers: Reports from eight countries* (pp. 159–173). Frankfurt am Main: Peter Lang.

Slavin, R.E. (1996). Research on cooperative learning and achievement: What we know, what we need to know. *Contemporary Educational Psychology, 21,* 43–69.

Slavin, R.E. (1990). *Cooperative learning: Theory, research, and practice.* Needham Heights, MA: Allyn and Bacon.

Smith, F. (1998). *The book of learning and forgetting.* New York: Teachers College Press.

Smith, J.B., Lee, V.E., & Newmann, F.M. (January 2001). *Improving Chicago's schools: Instruction and achievement in Chicago elementary schools.* Chicago: Consortium on Chicago School Research,

Smith, J.B., Lee, V.E., & Newmann, F.M. (2001). *Instruction and achievement in Chicago elementary schools.* Chicago, IL: Consortium on Chicago School Research.

Snyder, C., & Lopez, S. (2002). *Handbook of positive psychology.* New York: Oxford University Press.

Solomon, D., Battistich, V., & Watson, M. (1993, March). *A longitudinal investigation of the effects of a school intervention program on children's social development.* Paper presented at the biennial meeting of the Society for Research in Child Development, San Ramon, CA.

Sparks, D. (2003, May). Interview with Peter Block: The answer to 'when?' is 'now'. *Journal of Staff Development, 24*(2). Retrieved May 21, 2004, from http://www. nsdc.org/library/publications/jsd/block242.cfm?printPage=1&

Speck, M. (1999). *The principalship: Building a learning community.* Upper Saddle River, NJ: Prentice Hall.

Spiro, R. J., Feltovich, P. J., Jacobson, M. J., & Coulson, R. L. (1991). Knowledge representation, content specification, and the development of skill in situation-specific knowledge assembly: Some constructivist issues as they relate to cognitive flexibility theory and hypertext. *Educational Technology, 31*(9), 22–25.

Stechler, B. & Hamilton, L. (2002). Putting theory to the test. *Rand Review, 26*(1), 16–23.

Stephan, W.G., & Stephan, W.S. (1996). *Intergroup relations.* Boulder, CO: Westview Press.

Stern, D. (1997a). Genesis of the study. In D. Stern & G.L. Huber (Eds.), *Active learning for students and teachers: Reports from eight countries* (pp. 13–18). Frankfurt am Main: Peter Lang.

Stern, D. (1997b). Study procedures. In D. Stern & G.L. Huber (Eds.), *Active learning for students and teachers: Reports from eight countries* (pp. 40–50). Frankfurt am Main: Peter Lang.

Stern, D., & Huber, G.L. (1997). *Active learning for students and teachers: Reports from eight countries.* Frankfurt am Main: Peter Lang.

Stiggins, R. (1999). Assessment, student confidence, and school success. *Phi Delta Kappan, 81*(3), 191–198.

Stinson, S. (1993). Meaning and value: Reflections on what students say about school. *Journal of Curruculum and Supervision, 8*(3), 216–238.

Stipek, D. (2002). Good instruction is motivating. In A. Wigfield & J.S. Eccles (Eds.), *Development of achievement motivation* (pp. 310–334). San Diego, CA: Academic Press.

Strain, P. (1985). Programmatic research on peers as intervention agents for socially isolated classmates. *The Pointer, 29*(4), 22–29.

Strayhorn, J. (1988). *The competent child: An approach to psychotherapy and preventive mental health.* New York: Guilford.

Sumner, W. (1906). *Folkways.* New York: Dover Publications.

Swadener, B., & Lubeck, S. (1995). *Children and families "at promise": Deconstructing the discourse of risk.* Albany, NY: SUNY Press.

Sylwester, R. (1998). Art for the brain's sake. *Educational Leadership, 56*(3), 31–35.

Sylwester, R. (1995). *A celebration of neurons: An educator's guide to the human brain.* Alexandria, VA: Association for Supervision and Curriculum Development.

Talbert, J., & McLaughlin, M. (1994). Teacher professionalism in local school contexts. *American Journal of Education, 102,* 123–153.

Tanner, B., Bottoms, G., Feagin, C., & Bearman, A. (2001). *Instructional strategies: How teachers teach matters.* Atlanta, GA: Southern Regional Education Board.

Tatum, B.D. (2003). *Why are all the black kids sitting together in the cafeteria?* New York: Bt Bound.

Taylor, E. (1998). *The theory and practice of transformative learning: A critical review.* Columbus, OH: ERIC Clearinghouse on Adult, Career, and vocational Education, Ohio State University.

Taylor, S.E., Dickerson, S.S., & Klein, L.C. (2002). Toward a biology of social support. In C.R. Snyder & S.J. Lopez (Eds.), *Handbook of positive psychology* (pp. 556–572). New York: Oxford University Press.

Taylor, S.E., Klein, L.C., Lewis, B.P., Gruenewald, T.L., Gurung, R.A., & Updegraff, J.A. (2000). Biobehavioral responses to stress in females: Tend-and-befriend, not fight-or-flight. *Psychological Review,* 107(3), 411–429.

Tierny, J., Grossman, J., & Resch, N. (1995). *Making a difference: An impact study of Big Brothers/Big Sisters.* Philadelphia: Public/Private Ventures.

Tindall, J. (1995). *Peer Programs: An in-depth look at peer helping.* Bristol, PA: Accelerated Development.

Tobler, N. (1986). Meta-analysis of 142 adolescent drug prevention programs. *Journal of Drug Issues,* 16, 537–567.

Tobler, N., Roona, M., Ochshorn, P., Marshall, D., Streke, A., & Stackpole, K. (2000). School-based adolescent drug prevention programs: 1998 meta-analysis. *Journal of Primary Prevention,* 20, 275–336.

Tobler, N., & Stratton, H. (1997). Effectiveness of school-based drug prevention programs: A meta-analysis of the research. *Journal of Primary Prevention,* 18(1), 71–128.

Tomlinson, A., & Kalbfleisch, M.L. (1998). Teach me, teach my brain: A call for differentiated classrooms. *Educational Leadership,* 56(3), 52–55.

Totten, S., Sills, T., Digby, A., & Russ, P. (1991). *Cooperative learning: A guide to research.* New York: Garland Publishing, Inc.

Trimble, Susan (2002). Common elements of high performing at risk middle schools. Middle School Journal, 33(4), 7–16. Columbus, OH: National Middle School Association.

Triplett, N. (1897). The dynamogenic factors in pace-making and competition. The *American Journal of Psychology,* 9, 507–553.

Vaillant, G. (2002). *Aging well: Surprising guideposts to a happier life from the landmark Harvard study of adult development.* Boston: Little, Brown, And Company.

Viadero, D. (2003, June 4). Staying power. *Education Week,* 22(39), 24–27. Retrieved June 9, 2003, from http://www.edweek.com/ew/ew_printstory.cfm?slug=39multipleintellience.h22

Vigil, J.D. (1990). Cholos and gangs: Culture change and street youth in Los Angeles. In R. Huff (Ed.), *Gangs in America: Diffusion, diversity, and public policy* (pp. 146–162). Beverly Hills, CA: Sage.

Vorrath, H.H., & Brendtro, L.K. (1985). *Positive peer culture* (2nd ed.) Hawthorne, New York: Aldine de Gruyter.

Vygotsky, L. (1978). *Mind in society: The development of higher psychological processes.* Cambridge, MA: Harvard University Press.

Wang, M.C., Haertel, G.D., & Walberg, H.J. (1997). Learning influences. In H.J. Walberg & G.D. Haertel (Eds.), *Psychology and educational practice* (pp. 199–211). Berkeley, CA: McCatchan.

Wang, M., Haertel, G., & Walberg, H. (1993). Toward a knowledge base for school learning. *Review of Educational Research,* 63(3), 249–294.

Wasley, P., Fine, M., Gladden, M. Holland, N. King, S., Mosak, E., & Powell, L. (2000). *Small schools, great strides: A study of new small schools in Chicago.* New York: Bank Streets College.

Wasserman, H. & Danforth, H. (1988). *The human bond: Support groups and mutual aid.* New York: Springer Publishing.

Waters, T., Marzano, R.J., & McNulty, B. (2003). *Balanced leadership: What 30 years of research tells us about the effect of leadership on student achievement.* Aurora, CO: McREL.

Watson, M., & Ecken, L. (2003). *Learning to trust: Transforming difficult elementary classrooms through developmental discipline.* San Francisco, CA: Jossey-Bass

Watson, M., Battistich, V., & Solomon, D. (1997). Enhancing students' social and ethical development in schools: An intervention program and its effects. *International Journal of Education Research,* 27, 571–586.

Watt, N., Anthony, E., Wynne, L., & Rolf, J. (Eds.), (1984). *Children at risk for schizophrenia: A longitudinal perspective.* New York: Cambridge University Press.

Wiekart, D., & Schweinhart, L. (1993). *Significant benefits: The High/Scope Perry Preschool Study through age 27.* Ypsilanti, MI: High/Scope Press.

Weinstein, R.S. (2002). *Reaching higher: The power of expectations in schooling.* Cambridge, MA: Harvard University Press.

Weitz, J. (1996). *Coming up taller: Arts and humanities programs for children and youth at risk.* Washington, D.C.: President's Committee on the Arts and the Humanities.

Werner, E. (1986). Resilient offspring of alcoholics: A longitudinal study from birth to age 18. *Journal of Studies on Alcohol,* 14, 34–40.

Werner, E. (in press 2004). What can we learn about resilience from large-scale longitudinal studies? In S. Goldstein & R. Brooks (Eds.), *Handbook of resilience in children.* New York: Kluwer Press.

Werner, E., & Smith, R. (2001). *Journeys from childhood to the midlife: Risk, resilience, and recovery.* New York: Cornell University Press.

Werner, E., & Smith, R. (1992). *Overcoming the odds: High risk children from birth to adulthood.* New York: Cornell University Press.

Werner, E., & Smith, R. (1982). *Vulnerable but invincible: A longitudinal study of resilient children and youth.* New York: McGraw Hill.

Wheatley, M. (2002). *Turning to one another: Simple conversations to restore hope to the future.* San Francisco: Berrett-Koehler Publishers.

Wheelock, A. (1992). *Crossing the tracks: How "untracking" can save America's schools.* New York: The New Press.

Whiting, B., & Whiting, J. (1975). *Children of six cultures: a psycho-cultural analysis.* Cambridge, MA: Harvard University Press.

Whyte, W.F. (1943). *Street corner society.* Chicago, IL: University of Chicago Press.

Wigfield, A., & Eccles, J.S. (Eds.). (2002). *Development of achievement motivation.* San Diego, CA: Academic Press.

Wilkes, G. (2002). Abused child to nonabusive parent: Resilience and conceptual change. *Journal of Clinical Psychology,* 58, 261–278.

Williams, B. (Ed.). (2003). *Closing the achievement gap: A vision for changing beliefs and practices* (2nd ed.). Alexandria, VA: Association for Supervision and Curriculum Development.

Williams, B. (Ed.). (1996). *Closing the achievement gap: A vision for changing beliefs and practices.* Alexandria, VA: Association for Supervision and Curriculum Development.

Wilson, B., & Corbett, H. (2001). *Listening to urban kids: School reform and the teachers they want.* New York: SUNY Press.

Wilson, D., Gottfredson, D., & Najaka, S. (2001). School-based prevention of problem behaviors: A meta-analysis. *Journal of Quantitative Criminology,* 13(3), 247–272.

Wimberly, G.L. (2002). *School relationships foster success for African American students* (ACT Policy Report). Iowa City, IA: ACT.

Wolin, S., & Wolin, S. (1993). *The resilient self: How survivors of troubled families rise above adversity.* New York: Villard Books.

Wolfe, P. (1998). Revisiting effective teaching. *Educational Leadership,* 56(3), 61–64.

Wood, C. (2003). *Yardsticks: Children in the classroom ages 4–14* (Expanded ed.). Greenfield, MA: Northeast Foundation for Children.

Woolfolk, A.H., Demerath, P., & Pape, S. (2002). Teaching adolescents: Engaging developing selves. In T. Urdan & F. Pajares (Eds.), *Adolescence and education* (pp. 119–169). Volume I. Greenwich, CT: Information Age Publishing.

Yager, S., Johnson, D., Johnson, R., & Snider, B. (1986). The impact of group processing on academic achievement in cooperative learning groups. *The Journal of Social Psychology,* 126, 389–397.

Youniss, J., & Smollar, J. (1985). *Adolescent relations with mothers, fathers, and friends.* Chicago, IL: University of Chicago Press.

Youniss, J., & Yates, M. (1997). *Community service and social responsibility in youth.* Chicago, IL: University of Chicago Press.

Zigler, E., & Hall, N. (1989). Physical child abuse in America: Past, present, and future. In D. Cichetti & V. Carlson (Eds.), *Child maltreatment: Theory and research on the causes and consequences of child abuse and neglect,* pp. 56–XX.

Zins, J.E., Weissberg, R.P., Wang, M.C., & Walberg, H.J. (Eds.). (in press). *Building school success through social and emotional learning.* New York: Teachers College Press.

Zull, J. (2002). *The art of changing the brain: Enriching teaching by exploring the biology of learning.* Stylus Publishing.

Bring your school to life with Tribes Learning Communities®

"What Tribes can bring to a class is dynamite—what it can bring to a total staff is spectacular!"

Tribes is a community building process—a culture and active learning pedagogy best learned by experiencing it. You can make the process come alive for your district or school by scheduling training for your teachers, administration and support staff.

Schedule an overview presentation or classroom demonstration at your school where the key concepts of Tribes are explained and demonstrated through typical training strategies and our videos. Give your administration, school board and staff the information they need to consider whole school training with the following staff development opportunities:

■ Tribes TLC®—Building Community for Learning (Basic Training)

The purpose of this 24-hour training is to prepare teachers, administrators and support staff personnel to develop a caring school and classroom environment, and to reach and teach students through an active learning approach that promotes student development, motivation and academic achievement.

Educators will learn how to:

- Develop a positive learning environment in the classroom and whole school community
- Teach students specific collaborative skills to work well together
- Transfer responsibility to students to help each other learn academic material and to maintain the positive Tribes agreements and environment
- Use the process for problem-solving and conflict resolution
- Design cooperative learning lesson plans
- Initiate faculty groups for planning, co-coaching and support.

■ Discovering Gifts in Middle School with TRIBES TLC®

The purpose of this training is to provide a research-based approach for middle level school educators to focus their schools on the critical developmental learning needs of young adolescents. The training illuminates how to transform the cultures of middle schools into caring learning communities that support the full range of students' growth and development as well as establishing academic excellence.

Middle school educators will:

- Recognize the critical importance for the middle level school to make, as its focus, all aspects of the development of its young adolescent students
- Learn how collaborative groups of learners (students, teachers, administrators and parents) can create and sustain a caring school culture
- Understand why and how group learning supports adolescent development
- Learn how teachers can move through sequential stages toward excellence and into responsive education and discovery learning
- Design active group learning experiences that develop student-centered classrooms
- Realize the need for fairness, equity and social justice in middle schools
- Learn why democratic leadership is needed in a middle school that is focused on students' development and learning
- Understand the need for and power of reflective practice throughout all groups in the school community
- Learn how authentic assessment promotes learning and student development
- Realize what a responsive middle level school is—the gifts students discover and the meaningful learning that is achieved!

■ Tribes TLC®—University Course

The purpose of the university course is to teach the theory, basic research, active learning process and cooperative group learning approach to pre-service and in-service teachers, graduate interns, administrators and other professionals who are committed to school improvement and education that is responsive to the developmental growth and learning needs of today's students.

■ The Artistry for Learning

The purpose of this 24-hour experiential training is to increase the capacity of teachers and administrators within Tribes Learning Community Schools to intensify quality implementation of the research-based developmental process of Tribes—thereby to assure that all students, no matter their diversity and ability, achieve higher social, emotional and academic learning.

   Participants will:

- Reflect upon their professional learning and progress in using the process of Tribes TLC
- Discover the sound framework that underlies the Artistry for Learning
- Understand how social emotional learning leads to greater academic achievement and success in school and life
- Learn how the process of Tribes contributes to the development of resilience
- Become familiar with the palette of seven research-based components that catalyze student learning
- Begin to deepen their understanding of the research-based components of Tribes Responsive Education by working with the "colors" of the palette
- Assess their own preferred ways of learning and plan how to differentiate curriculum to reach students of multiple intelligences
- Learn a variety of ways to assess student-learning experiences
- Select a current curriculum theme or unit and design a cooperative learning experience that integrates several components of the palette
- Discuss specific ways that cooperative or discovery (constructivist) pedagogy can be utilized to make the content meaningful and lasting for students
- Recognize the importance of teachers having designated time in on-going collegial groups to confer, plan and assess student achievement.

■ Multi-Year TRIBES TLC® Training Plans

CenterSource Systems can help you design a multi-year training program to meet the needs of your school by implementing several of the professional development opportunities mentioned above. When integrated into the whole school community, Tribes can effect system-wide change by creating a caring culture and cooperative learning community, which fosters student growth and achievement, strengthens staff relationships and collegiality, and effectively redesigns the learning community.

■ Training-of-District Trainers

CenterSource Systems has designed a *capacity building model* for professional development so that your district or school can have your own certified Tribes TLC® trainers to provide on-going training, coaching and support to teachers, administrators, resource personnel and parent community groups. The CenterSource Training-of-District Trainers provides in-depth skills, knowledge, experience and quality training materials for your own qualified personnel.

Follow-up coaching and support at your school site is available throughout the year so that your staff can fully implement the process of Tribes and intensify its use throughout the whole school community.

Tribes TLC® was chosen as a "SELect Program" by the Collaborative for Academic, Social and Emotional Learning, www.casel.org.

For additional
information call

CENTERSOURCE SYSTEMS

800-810-1701

or visit www.tribes.com

About the Founder

JEANNE GIBBS has spent her professional career studying, writing and implementing systemic processes and programs to support children's development and prevent youth problems. Her perspective on human development is a systems approach that encourages schools, families and communities to create healthy environments in which children can grow and learn. The developmental culture and educational process now known as "Tribes Learning Communities" evolved out of years of studies Jeanne has pursued to synthesize a wealth of literature pertaining to the ecology of human development and learning. She is convinced that well being and success for students is not a result of curriculum, instruction and assessment—nor of intelligence—but the result of a school finally focusing on the growth and whole human development of its students in all aspects of their individual uniqueness and brilliance. The vision takes on reality whenever a school system focuses first on creating and sustaining a caring culture in which children truly are able to discover themselves and succeed.

Jeanne supervised implementations of the community learning process throughout hundreds of schools and youth-serving agencies for more than ten years while managing a non-profit corporation, which she established in 1972. Though serving as the executive director, she continued to research, refine and author publications—until her first formal retirement. Since then, Jeanne has retired many times—none of which last long due to her passionate purpose. Ever-growing requests from schools throughout the United States, Canada and other countries for professional development and quality materials led her to establish CenterSource Systems in 1995 as "the home of Tribes."

Her primary interest now centers on the potential of school reform being achieved through reflective Learning Communities that are responsive to the developmental and learning needs of their students. It is no surprise that people across the country know Jeanne for her warm and generous spirit… and ability to build community wherever she goes.